PARKS
FOR
PROFIT

PARKS
FOR
PROFIT

▬

SELLING
NATURE
IN THE
CITY

KEVIN LOUGHRAN

Columbia University Press   *New York*

Columbia University Press
Publishers Since 1893
New York   Chichester, West Sussex
cup.columbia.edu

Library of Congress Cataloging-in-Publication Data
Names: Loughran, Kevin, author.
Title: Parks for profit : selling nature in the city / Kevin Loughran.
Description: New York : Columbia University Press, 2021. |
Includes index.
Identifiers: LCCN 2021017227 (print) | LCCN 2021017228 (ebook) |
ISBN 9780231194044 (hardback) | ISBN 9780231194051 (trade
paperback) | ISBN 9780231550628 (ebook)
Subjects: LCSH: Gentrification—United States—
Case studies. | Social stratification—United States—Case studies. |
United States—Economic conditions—20th century. |
Parks—United States—Case studies.
Classification: LCC HT175 .L68 2021 (print) | LCC HT175 (ebook) |
DDC 307.3/4160973—dc23
LC record available at https://lccn.loc.gov/2021017227
LC ebook record available at https://lccn.loc.gov/2021017228

Cover design: Lisa Hamm

For Caroline, of course

CONTENTS

ACKNOWLEDGMENTS

F IRST, I want to thank Eric Schwartz, editorial director of Columbia University Press, for believing in my vision for this book. From our first meeting in 2017, Eric has shown great enthusiasm and a judicious editorial eye—true gifts to a first-time author. Columbia is the perfect home for this book, and I could not imagine a better person to guide it from start to finish. All authors should be fortunate enough to have someone like Eric in their corner. Many thanks as well to the kind, organized, and highly professional Lowell Frye, associate editor at Columbia University Press, who offered great support for this book and has been an absolute pleasure to work with.

This book literally would not exist without Jim Elliott, who graciously invited me to join the Department of Sociology at Rice University as a postdoctoral fellow in 2017. From there, Jim provided a stream of resources and goodwill that enabled me to investigate Houston's Buffalo Bayou Park and become immersed in the city's history and culture. My three years spent in Houston were a time of considerable creative and intellectual ferment, thanks in large part to my collaboration with Jim. Thanks, Jim, for giving me the opportunity to write this book, and for everything else, too.

My friends and colleagues at Rice provided a constant source of encouragement and camaraderie, especially my fellow 2017 arrivals—Max Besbris, Cayce Hughes, and Anna Rhodes—fellow urbanists whose collective bonds formed quickly as we rode out Hurricane Harvey just a few weeks into our time in Houston. I'm grateful to the members of the appropriately named SPACE Co. working group—led by Jim Elliott and Liz Roberto—who graciously included me in their collective and who kindly read a draft of chapter 8. Thanks to Jim and Liz, along with Asia Bento, Leah Binkovitz, Phylicia Lee Brown, Jaleh Jalili, Alex Priest, and Katie Turner, for offering smart, tough, and helpful feedback.

My thinking on parks and all things sociological was profoundly shaped by the Department of Sociology at Northwestern University, arguably the best place to become a sociologist of culture, race, and cities. My gratitude for Mary Pattillo is immeasurable—my incomparable adviser, life coach, and all-around genius who helped me get this project off the ground and has always had my back. Thank you, Mary, for shaping this book and my career. I owe you a debt that can only be paid forward. I'm supremely grateful to Gary Alan Fine, who has been a fantastic supporter, coauthor, and intellectual foil over the almost-decade that I have known him. Gary has always made my work better, and the memory of his famous brick—the one inscribed "Write It Down, Mothafucka"—remains an indelible source of motivation while grinding out these pages many years later. In writing this book, I benefited greatly from the advice of my other supporters at Northwestern, who saw promise in an embryonic vision. Wendy Griswold's brilliance pushed me to take my ideas further; Wendy is an intellectual force whose towering abilities as a writer, teacher, and mentor I remain in awe of and can only hope to emulate. Many thanks are due to Aldon Morris, who took me on a Du Boisian journey that changed the trajectory of my writing and thinking, and who has inspired me through his ongoing engagement in the politics of sociological knowledge. Tony Chen and Kevin Boyle generously lent their wisdom and collective eye for empirical rigor to my studies. I also thank Al Hunter, Michael Rodríguez-Muñiz, and Celeste Watkins-Hayes for their warm support and generosity of spirit. Thank you as well to Northwestern alumni Japonica Brown-Saracino, Marcus Hunter, Judith Levine, and Carla Shedd, kind fellow travelers who helped me in ways they could not have perceived at various points in my academic journey.

I also want to acknowledge the faculty at Columbia University who nurtured my exploration of the High Line while I was a very green master's student: Cassie Fennell, who got me thinking about social space in 2010 and I haven't stopped since; Shamus Khan, who was nice to me when he had no reason to be; the late, great Manning Marable, who showed me what it really meant to write a book; and Herb Gans, whose Field Methods course was an ethnographic baptism by fire and a proving ground for my earliest observations and theories of the High Line. My work in New York is also indebted to Columbia alum Greg Smithsimon, who happily shepherded my research from his perch at Brooklyn College and whose analysis of urban public space remains the standard.

I'm grateful for the support of my friends and fellow graduate students from Northwestern and Columbia. I was fortunate to share my time at both universities with many like-minded scholars, especially Robin Bartram, Juliette Galonnier, Heba Gowayed, Ryan Hagen, and John Robinson. Two people deserve special mention: Nobody encouraged me more, pushed me harder, or kept me saner than Jordan Conwell, a brilliant scholar who sees the big picture—in sociology and in life—better than most, and whose high character continues to serve as a moral compass for me. Nicholas Occhiuto is a treasure. He cut a striking figure when we first met, and we've been attached at the hip ever since, from our long walks to the East Side (sorry I never invited you in for dinner) to a million hours rapt on the phone together. Nick, thanks for being a constant beam of light in my life all these years later. And thank God for Heba.

I also benefited from a network of urbanists whose work has informed my own thinking, and whose conversations about matters of urban sociology and beyond I have always enjoyed. My sincere thanks to Hillary Angelo, Neil Brenner, Ryan Centner, Prentiss Dantzler, Junia Howell, Brad Hunt, Eric Klinenberg, Liz Koslov, Jeffrey Parker, Forrest Stuart, David Wachsmuth, Fred Wherry, all those named above, and many others. I thank audiences who offered feedback on parts of this project over the years at annual meetings of the American Sociological Association, the Association of American Geographers, the Urban History Association, the Social Science History Association, the Society for the Study of Social Problems, the Chicago Ethnography Conference, the Midwest Sociological Society, and the Eastern Sociological Society. I'm appreciative of the Black Metropolis Research Consortium, which provided critical financial support and opened doors to a fantastic community of archivists and historical researchers in Chicago. Thanks are also due to Allison Yelvington for providing expert research assistance at a key point in the development of this book.

I'm grateful to the archivists, librarians, and those who gave their time to be interviewed for the different parts of this project. Special and profound thanks are due to Frances Whitehead, who generously shared her experiences, documents, and brilliance with me; my understanding of the Bloomingdale Trail/606 would have been seriously impoverished without her insights. I'm also grateful to the anonymous reviewers of this manuscript, whose critiques helped me make needed clarifications and improvements.

The analytical journey of this book is also clearly autobiographical, as my observations of urban public space moved with me from New York to Chicago to Houston. In an unbelievable stroke of good fortune, I write these acknowledgments from my hometown of Philadelphia, where I am very happy to be a new member of the Department of Sociology at Temple University. I thank all of my new colleagues for providing such a warm welcome during a rather unusual year.

Finally, there are my family members who hold this all together. My writing abilities were developed and encouraged at a very young age by my wonderful parents, Joe and Eileen, and this book certainly would not have been possible without their support. Likewise, I'm grateful to my brothers Chris, Michael, Patrick, and Mike, who have always indulged my creative pursuits, no matter how strange. Brendan Devine was there in Chicago and Houston (and briefly in New York, too); thank you for supporting all of my endeavors. The extended Loughran and Dougherty clans have long kept the wind at my back; I'm grateful to be part of such a motley, loving crew. I've also been fortunate to marry into another motley and loving group of people, the Miller, Graham, Roome, and Daly-Pavlis families. Special thanks to my in-laws, Melanie, Sanford, Stephen, Ann, Anaïs, Jill, Margaret, Charlie, Lil, Emily, and Justin, whose genuine interest in my work over the years has meant a lot.

Whatever I could say about Caroline Graham would be a woefully insufficient tribute compared to all that she has given me over the past thirteen years. Her love, empathy, grace, and support have propped up and propelled my life. The journeys contained in this book, from New York to Chicago to Houston to Philadelphia, are hers too. However large or small the achievement of writing this book, I quite simply could not have done it without her. A better achievement than this book is the loving family we have built together. Lou and Teddy, being your dad is the greatest joy of my life; hanging out with you two and your mom is a lot more fun than writing a book. Let's go get a muffin.

PARKS
FOR
PROFIT

I

INTRODUCTION

1

SOMETIME IN 2009

IT was my first year in New York and I'd started hearing about this High Line thing. I was twenty-three and not exactly the most clued in to the cultural scene, unless it involved finding the best arepa in the five boroughs. My social circle at the time consisted largely of my girlfriend's friends: classmates from a small liberal arts college who'd grown up in LA and Manhattan. They were much cooler than I was, of course, and I spent a lot of my time in their company quickly becoming acculturated to the norms of bourgeois young adulthood in New York City.

Chief among the culturally inclined New Yorker's habitus is a certain skeptical disposition: discerning the "cool" from the "uncool" is no mere aesthetic judgment—it requires taking the temperature in the room of the other cultural consumers.[1] Popularity, even limited popularity among the cognoscenti (mainstream popularity is just gauche, of course), can prove a death knell to the latest and greatest scene. (The retreat of the cool kids being the ultimate loss for any aspiring restaurateur or musical act.)

Imagine my surprise, then, at the resoundingly warm reception for the High Line when it opened in 2009. This new park-in-the-sky was constantly packed, teeming with tourists. But architectural critics and the cool kids loved it regardless: the High Line was somehow hewing the line between haute and popular.

Unlike some of the High Line's saviors, who have wistfully documented their first trips atop the viaduct, I can't say that I recall my first visit to the park.[2] What I do remember is the energy around it: it became a singular cultural phenomenon in a city full of the new and the exceptional.

• • •

Without question, the High Line's aesthetics drive much of its cultural and economic appeal. Many parks before it had been gussied up, rebranded, and had gourmet food carts parachuted down to lure that beloved "creative class."[3] Bryant Park and Union Square, both just a few avenues over from the High Line, were recent examples.[4] In an age of entrepreneurial urbanism, parks— like public transit and schools—had to be "competitive."[5] City and federal governments were giving less money to parks while at the same time the recolonization of downtowns by White professionals and tourists was spurring demand for high-end civic spaces.[6]

Beginning in the 1990s, the transformation of public spaces in New York and other cities was aided and abetted by aggressive police tactics that cleared the homeless, the mentally ill, and poor people of color. Critics decried "the end of public space" as private interests, heavy securitization, and architectural blandness reigned supreme: the suburban shopping mall transported to the city.[7] Prominent public spaces were also commercializing at this time, and their surrounding streetscapes were becoming sterile and corporate, with the much-decried "Disneyfication" of Times Square being a famous example.[8]

By 2000, public spaces in gentrified areas had newfound cultural and aesthetic potential. New or redeveloped public spaces could lure visitors with a constellation of amenities, and by 2010, a certain familiar public space recipe had taken hold.[9] Nearly every city now has a "cool" park where artisanal food, expensive coffee, and art vendors congregate. Many such parks have packed events schedules—summer movies, live music, guest lectures—and relaxed rules about alcohol.

The High Line did all this and a lot more. No mere reproduction of a New Urbanist public square, the High Line transported visitors to a new kind of urban flora and a new perspective on the urban landscape.[10] Even for jaded New Yorkers, there was something undeniably cool about standing outside, in a public space, four stories above ground. In a city where waterfronts historically served economic and not aesthetic logics, there were few public places as hospitable to taking in the Hudson River south of Seventy-Ninth Street. And no sidewalk could offer such imposing views of the Chrysler and Empire State buildings, let alone the charming side streets of Chelsea and the Meatpacking District.

• • •

The High Line was cool because it was different. The High Line's location amid both vernacular and spectacular built environments, coupled with the fact that the park itself sits atop a piece of industrial infrastructure, creates a unique tension when juxtaposed with wild-looking plants that appear to sprout haphazardly at the park's edges and between the paved walkways.[11] Almost as soon as the park opened, city leaders across the globe were clamoring to build their own "High Lines." Two of the first to be completed were the Bloomingdale Trail/606 in Chicago and Buffalo Bayou Park in Houston. Like the High Line, these parks are redeveloped linear spaces offering distinct immersion in both "the city" and "nature," and have become economic engines.

How did this model of public park become so powerful, so quickly? In New York, there are a few answers to this question. The first and most celebrated answer involves the dedicated politicking and fundraising of the Friends of the High Line and its two cofounders, Joshua David and Robert Hammond. This group formed in 1999 to oppose Mayor Rudolph Giuliani and an assemblage of real estate companies that collectively sought to tear down the High Line—then a rusting heirloom of Chelsea's industrial past. The resulting triumph of the private park group and its city government allies has long since been mythologized by the principals and their admirers.[12] A more critical reading of these events views the rise of the Friends of the High Line as emblematic of troubling trends in urban governance, including the flow of public money toward private interests and the elevation of select prominent parks at the expense of parks equity across the city.[13]

The High Line's political appeal rests on its appearance as the ultimate "green" intervention: it was environmentally responsible, economically appealing, and incredibly popular. Postindustrial parks like the High Line therefore seem like win-win propositions. Are they?

2

VARIETIES OF URBAN CRISIS

New York, Chicago, Houston

THE High Line—the park—sits atop the historical High Line, an elevated rail viaduct that transported train traffic in and out of the Meatpacking District and the manufacturing facilities of Chelsea between 1934 and 1980. The park's distinctive landscape is in fact a reproduction of what existed in the space between 1980 and the park's development after 1999. Described by Friends of the High Line cofounder Robert Hammond as "another world, right in the middle of Manhattan," the High Line's original imbricated space was a rusting, rotting urban railway teeming with wild grasses and flowers.[1] Human hands had not made this first flowering High Line—it was the absence of human activity that allowed nature's forces to take over the once-industrial space.

The High Line's original convergence of city and nature is distinctly postindustrial, requiring the joint legacies of industrialization and subsequent abandonment. While the entire current wave of postmodern, commercialized public parks is embedded in the rise, fall, and return of American cities in the twentieth century, postindustrial parks are literally rooted in the spaces where those transformations have taken place, as railways and other industrial and infrastructural sites have gone from working landscapes to imbricated ruins to celebrated public spaces. For the High Line and other postindustrial parks built in its image, those site histories matter because they provide the social and visual materials that park architects, boosters, and visitors tap into for cultural and economic purposes.

Site histories are nested within broader spatial histories—of neighborhoods, cities, and urban regions—that open and limit possibilities for transformation. To understand postindustrial parks, we have to understand the industrialization and deindustrialization of both the sites and the settings. For New York's High Line, Chicago's Bloomingdale Trail/606, and Houston's Buffalo Bayou Park—the three parks that are the focus of this book—those histories and trajectories informed how planners, politicians, and park developers could bend different disused infrastructures to the same end goal.

NEW YORK

Surrounding the High Line in its first decades was Chelsea's manufacturing economy—a nexus of meatpackers, food processers, and garment factories—which thrived from the late nineteenth century up until the 1930s.[2] Its eventual decline, brought about as companies moved to the suburbs, the Sunbelt, or overseas in search of cheaper labor and overhead costs, left the area with a disused trove of industrial built environments: warehouses, factories, and lofts, along with the corresponding rail infrastructure that allowed for the movement of raw materials and consumer goods.

New York in general and Chelsea in particular were hard hit by the urban exodus that defined the older cities of the Northeast and Midwest in the post–World War II decades. For New York's business owners, the outmoded buildings and infrastructure of Chelsea held little appeal in the second half of the twentieth century. Manufacturing companies could build new, horizontal facilities in the suburbs, where land was cheaper and taxes more favorable. Corporate firms found that White Plains and Stamford were just as accommodating as midtown Manhattan—and a more pleasant commute from executives' homes in Greenwich and Bronxville.[3]

Labor joined capital in this flight from the city proper. Forged by federal home mortgage policies that created racially segregated suburbs, the national phenomenon of "White flight" fostered a new racial-spatial order in the New York metro area.[4] This interclass phenomenon drew White workers to Levittown, White elites to Westport, and the White middle class to everywhere in between.[5] Between 1940 and 1980, Manhattan lost 24 percent of its population, declining from nearly 1.9 million to less than 1.5 million, while the city's immediate suburbs—the low-density Westchester, Rockland, Bergen, Fairfield, Suffolk, and Nassau counties—grew by 159 percent, from 2.1 million to 5.4 million.[6]

The long arc of post–World War II upheaval reached its nadir in 1975, when thirty years of federally subsidized suburbanization finally crippled the city's tax base and left its balance sheet on the verge of insolvency. The problem coursed over several months, with Mayor Abraham Beame and Governor Hugh Carey pursuing $6.8 billion in loans and other relief between 1975 and June 1978 (approximately $32 billion in 2018 dollars).[7] In October 1975, President Gerald Ford famously rebuffed the city government's initial request for a bailout—resulting in the *Daily News*'s "FORD TO CITY: DROP DEAD" headline—partly on the advice of close advisers Donald Rumsfeld and Alan Greenspan.[8] It was only the purchasing of $2.5 billion worth of city bonds by the city's public sector unions that in the end compelled the federal government to loan $2.3 billion to New York City—with the condition that the city government impose sweeping austerity measures.[9]

Other events in the mid-1970s further suggested to city residents, as well as to outside observers, that New York's crisis was as much social as it was economic. These included the "Son of Sam" murders in July 1977 (an exemplar of the city's rising violent crime rates) and the days of the Bronx's infamous "burning" in the mid-to-late 1970s.[10] Though the South Bronx became especially identified with the sharp rise in the city's building fires—often arsons of tenement buildings committed by property owners seeking insurance payouts, which had become a more lucrative income stream than rent—other neighborhoods that had been devastated by governmental disinvestment and White flight, including Bushwick, East New York, and the West Bronx, were similarly ablaze as the city pursued a racist policy of "planned shrinkage," closing firehouses, subway stations, and public services in poor communities to focus resources elsewhere.[11]

The social consequences of New York's "urban crisis," no secret decades later, were clearly visible as they were initially unfolding. This crisis affected not just New York but cities across the country that encountered the pernicious mix of declining tax bases, rising crime and unemployment rates, and political upheaval, all of which were intertwined with racial segregation in housing and labor markets, global economic stagflation, and welfare-state retrenchment.[12]

The urban crisis had another dimension that especially affected New York: it was not only a fiscal crisis and a social crisis; it was also an "image crisis."[13] As the nation's largest city, its trials and tribulations were fodder for global schadenfreude; much as Detroit would occupy a similar singularity in later decades as an icon for a failed brand of urbanism, boosters in other American cities, especially in the Sunbelt, celebrated the decline and apparent death of the Keynesian-Fordist city.[14] Images of New York in despair were ubiquitous in mass media and popular culture: photos of vacant lots and graffiti gracing the pages of national magazines, burning buildings on display during game 2 of the 1977 World Series, and films like *Taxi Driver, Death Wish,* and *The Panic in Needle Park* placing dramatized visions of the city's underclass (or "scum," as Robert De Niro's Travis Bickle preferred to put it) on big screens across the country.[15] That such portrayals were fictional—and that the social problems they dramatized could be found in every American city, Sunbelt included—was irrelevant: "crime and urban violence [had become] uniquely associated in the public's mind with New York."[16] A city wrecked by national and global political and economic forces that were far beyond the control of its mayor or city council, experiencing pressures that were by no means unique to its borders, New York nevertheless became a powerful symbol of liberalism run amok, urban depravity, and "the last days of American civilization."[17]

• • •

It was in the midst of New York's crisis that the High Line was closed down. The two-mile spur had little utility as Chelsea's manufacturing facilities closed. (The final voyage of goods was a shipment of frozen turkeys in April 1980.)[18] The High Line, completed in 1934 as the city faced the Great Depression, had just a few decades of regular use as a railway. It was built, as Mayor Fiorello La Guardia toasted at the viaduct's unveiling, to bring "death to Death Avenue"—the moniker given to Eleventh Avenue, where a surface railway had historically crossed several dozen city streets at grade level.[19] The High Line was built as a part of the West Side Improvement—a massive, $200 million public-works project (roughly $3 billion in 2018 dollars) funded by the city, state, and federal governments along with the New York Central Railroad—which included the development or improvement of rails, highways, parks, bridges, and buildings.[20] For New York's infamous master planner, Robert Moses, the West Side Improvement was a means of upgrading the transportation connections across Manhattan's entire western edge and up into the Bronx—"its scope all but unprecedented in urban America."[21]

How much utility the High Line had, even in its heyday, is unclear. Built at the peak of the Depression as industrial out-migration was already under way, by the suburban boom of the 1950s its tracks had become outmoded with the advent of interstate highways and containerized shipping.[22] Even the companies that remained in Chelsea and the Meatpacking District no longer relied on trains to conduct business. It is safe to say that by 1980 the rail viaduct had become an afterthought as a piece of transportation infrastructure. In its final decade-plus of rail use, other transportation projects—such as the proposed Westway highway project, which was to replace the West Side Highway (partly via Hudson River landfill), and deteriorating bridges and roads across the city—commanded the attention of policy makers and the city's public.[23] The local newspapers carried no mention of the High Line's closure; a celebrated piece of infrastructure when it opened in the 1930s, it went out with a whimper.

CHICAGO

New York was not the only American city to undergo major demographic and economic changes after World War II. The trajectory described above—of an older urban core slowly bleeding out its tax base, jobs, and White population—was national in scope. Its effects were devastating in other areas of the Northeast and Midwest, where industrial urban economies had few of New York's buffers—finance, real estate, and tourism—but many of its problems.[24] Though New York's image crisis and centrality in mass media and popular culture suggested otherwise, Detroit, St. Louis, Cleveland, Buffalo, Philadelphia, and other cities could just as easily have served as icons of urban decay.

Of the cities of the Rust Belt, none has been as persistently influenced by New York as Chicago. While firmly embedded in the social and economic flows of the Midwest, from Chicago's settler-colonial founding in 1833 generations of city leaders have tended to look past Detroit, Cleveland, and other regional rivals—to New York.[25] Famously maligned as America's "second city," Chicago's rapid rise in the nineteenth century—from an outpost of two hundred settlers in 1833 to a metropolis of 1.7 million by 1900—made it the second-largest city in the country and a legitimate economic and cultural peer to New York.[26]

Chicago had likewise built its economic power on a mix of finance and industry: it was both "hog butcher for the world" and investment capital of the "Great West."[27] In its first century, city leaders leveraged Chicago's central place in the nation's rail system and the vast commodities of the North American plains to dominate other would-be Midwestern powers.[28]

That Chicago grew outward to its present-day limits during the golden age of rail transit endowed the city with a system of transportation infrastructure largely distinct to the Midwest: a vast network of railways that serve a variety of social and economic needs. With the exception of a few downtown blocks, city subways and regional commuter lines run above ground here. Miles of heavy rails and open railyards mark the land that had been transformed for industrial use.[29]

Rails are omnipresent in Chicago: more than just a means of movement, they form a persistent backdrop to street life. They shape community boundaries and impart a gritty aesthetic to the city. Rails in Chicago are not confined to a few industrial districts at the city's periphery; though denser in some areas, they are everywhere, their monumental proportions belying the strange intimacy they can produce. With the rise of a postindustrial economy in recent decades, some railways have seen diminishing traffic and have fallen into disrepair. Like the High Line, they tend to deteriorate in situ, but continue to exert social influence—forming neighborhood exoskeletons and producing a local nuisance, or a local redevelopment opportunity, depending on the beholder.

With rails everywhere, and with the city's domestic rival, New York, building an iconic rail park for the twenty-first century, it is unsurprising that park developers in Chicago quickly followed New York's lead in building the Bloomingdale Trail, also known as the 606. To understand the Bloomingdale Trail/606, first understand that this particular railway is part of the vernacular landscape of the city: there is nothing strange or remarkable about it.

• • •

In 1975, as the Bronx was burning and New York's image crisis was shown for all the world to see, Chicago was reeling from its own transformation. The city's century of racial-spatial stasis was in collapse: the boundaries of the Black Belt, long the five-square-mile container for Black residents, now extended the length of the South Side as the Civil Rights Movement and the 1948 *Shelley v. Kraemer* Supreme Court decision (which struck down restrictive covenants) opened new housing opportunities for Black Chicagoans. Meanwhile, other forms of segregation were taking new and more concrete forms: project towers, which were built atop much of the Black Belt's historical footprint along with other areas of Black settlement on the West and Near North sides, effectively resegregated the city.[30] Chicago's Black population, which numbered thirty thousand in 1900, grew to 1.1 million by 1970 as the two waves of the Great Migration radically remade the city's demographics.[31] These new arrivals moved initially to the edges of the Black Belt—neighborhoods like Woodlawn, Kenwood, and Oakland—and later into areas of the Far South, Southwest, and West sides that were vacated as federally subsidized suburbanization and fears of racial integration sent many Whites beyond city limits.[32]

Meanwhile, in-migration from Puerto Rico and Mexico accelerated, with ethnic enclaves flourishing in Pilsen, Little Village (*La Villita*), and two neighborhoods that straddled the Bloomingdale elevated rail line, West Town and Humboldt Park.[33] Chicago's Hispanic population, numbering 16,000 in 1940, reached 250,000 by 1970 and 420,000 by 1980.[34] By that time, a new, tripartite racial-spatial structure had emerged, with the city's Whites, Blacks, and Latinos contending for political power—each with a distinct geographic base: the White North Side, the Black South and West Sides, and the Latino Northwest and Southwest Sides.[35]

As in New York, these post–World War II economic, racial, and spatial changes pushed the limits of Chicago's particular mode of urban governance.

• • •

For much of the twentieth century, Chicago politics were controlled by the Cook County Democratic Party. This entity was itself the de facto property of the city's Irish Catholics, whose base of power up to the 1960s resided largely in South Side neighborhoods like Bridgeport, Canaryville, and Armour Square.[36] As the Chicago city government grew significantly under the rule of the Democratic machine (with much expansion occurring as the federal government rolled out New Deal programs in the 1930s), the spoils flowed to Irish Catholic wards, with the Chicago Police Department, the Chicago Park District, and other agencies providing wells of employment for loyal Democratic operatives.[37]

Chicago's patronage politics were solidified in the post–World War II decades by Richard J. Daley, whose tenure as mayor lasted from 1955 to his death in 1976. Daley was a scion of the Cook County Democratic Party and, in his youth, the South Side's Irish Catholic "athletic clubs" (which functioned in part as anti-Black street gangs).[38] Daley rose through the ranks of the Democratic machine as a loyal political soldier in the 1930s and '40s and became the third consecutive Irishman to hold Chicago's mayoralty in 1955.[39] During his two-plus decades as mayor, Daley ruled over the modernization of the city, using federal urban renewal funds to build highways and university campuses and advance an office-tower boom in the Loop, among other putative accomplishments.[40] Daley also attempted to harden the segregated status quo by targeting Black neighborhoods for public housing development and taking a repressive approach to civil-rights complaints.[41]

Between 1945 and 1970, a range of institutional spaces would replace or segregate Black neighborhoods, and some emerging Latino areas as well, evincing how urban planning could be used to control social space. At the north end of the Black Belt, the Prairie Shores and Lake Meadows housing complexes were to offer a buffer for the Loop.[42] At the Black Belt's western edge, eight thousand units of public housing were built—neatly lined up in a north-south row—along with the Mies van der Rohe–designed campus of the Illinois Institute of Technology.[43] These spaces, which included the well-known Robert Taylor Homes, were placed next to the fourteen-lane Dan Ryan Expressway (another postwar creation), which turned Wentworth Avenue (the historical boundary between the Black and White South Sides) into a forbidding barrier.[44]

Though public housing towers were visually austere, becoming the sites of a thousand sociological studies, the resegregation of Chicago after World War II also took hold in tenements and two-flats, where unenforced building codes and other forms of neglect left the city's growing Black and Latino populations with decayed, sometimes uninhabitable housing—circumstances that led to civil-rights organizing by groups like the Chicago Urban League, the Black Stone Rangers, the Nation of Islam, the Black Panthers, and the Young Lords.[45]

Such activism meant little to Daley and the White power structure, which expected that Black and Latino grievances could be adjudicated with token gestures rather than meaningful social and political reforms.[46] As racial tensions increased throughout the 1960s, Daley matched historical oppression with police repression, relishing a violent approach to controlling public order that would have been right at home in Montgomery or Selma.[47]

In the late 1960s, after more than a decade of stonewalling by Mayor Daley and the city government, the cauldron of segregation, inequality, and raw anger finally burst open, spilling into the streets of the West Side. In June 1966, after Chicago police shot and killed a young Puerto Rican man, residents of West Town and Humboldt Park (by then the center of the city's Puerto Rican community) rioted on Division Street.[48] That July, uprisings broke out in West Garfield Park (which had become a predominantly Black area in the postwar decades), leading to two civilian deaths, several hundred arrests, and use of the National Guard.[49] Two years later, following the murder of Martin Luther King in Memphis on April 4, 1968, the West Side's Black ghetto fully erupted along Madison Street. In the span of two days, eleven people were killed, hundreds were injured, and 2,150 were arrested, as arsonists burned down the length of the commercial hub and some surrounding residential areas.[50] In August of the same year, police attacked mostly White antiwar protesters outside the Democratic National Convention, held in the Loop, suggesting that Daley had become determined to suppress dissent at all costs.[51]

Righteous discontent, in the end, perversely served the segregating mission of a Chicago growth coalition seeking to buttress the economic stability of the Loop and the North Side amid population loss and deindustrialization.[52] The two miles of Madison Street that burned in the aftermath of King's assassination would remain largely vacant for decades. With postwar institutional spaces like the University of Illinois at Chicago and the Illinois Medical District, along with the Kennedy and Eisenhower expressways, providing spatial buffers for the Loop, for the city's White power brokers, the ruins of the Black West Side were effectively out of sight and out of mind. Successfully partitioned from White Chicago, the burned-out blocks seemed to justify a cycle of public and private disinvestment in Black neighborhoods.[53]

The Chicago found at the beginnings of the nation's so-called "urban crisis" was already in crisis. While New Yorkers lived on the anxious edge of "Fear City," Chicago's worst racial fears had already been realized. The city and its suburbs were emblematic of the socio-spatial upheaval that had been wrought all over the United States in the post–World War II decades. What unfolded between the 1940s and the 1970s was a series of intertwined events: the rupture in Chicago's redlined racial boundaries, incredible in-migration of all kinds, suburbanization and White exodus, and ultimately, the resegregation of the city along White, Black, and Latino lines—all happening under the watch of one of the nation's most authoritarian mayoral regimes, with both a militarized police force and billions in federal urban-renewal dollars at its disposal. It happened, too, despite the determined protest of national civil-rights leaders and local grassroots organizers, who had hoped that the redevelopment of the city might proceed along more equitable lines.

• • •

HOUSTON

The struggles faced by New York, Chicago, and other cities of the Northeast and Midwest were to the benefit of Houston, Phoenix, Las Vegas, and Los Angeles. These places were home to cheap land, cheap labor, and, most crucially, the arrival of federal wartime spending for aerospace, petroleum, scientific research, and other industries that proved foundational to Sunbelt economies in the 1940s and '50s.[54] The influx of private manufacturing firms and public infrastructural investment allowed these longtime boondocks to be transformed into massive metropoles in a matter of decades—much as Chicago had been during an earlier era of urbanization.

The Sunbelt cities that blossomed in the post–World War II period were not the historical economic and cultural capitals of the South and West. The paths of San Francisco, New Orleans, Richmond, and their ilk more closely mirrored the Rust Belt—cities that had reached their apex in an earlier epoch and experienced significant postwar retrenchment and population loss.[55] Instead, it was the yet-untapped places that presented opportunities for socio-spatial arbitrage.

Houston fit fully into the social and economic shifts that were reshaping the nation's regional power structure. A city of just forty-five thousand in 1900—then the eighty-fifth-largest in the United States—Houston was already on a growth trajectory by the time the Sunbelt began taking off after 1945. Houston had been founded in August 1836 by two New York real estate speculators, the Allen brothers, just four months after the Republic of Texas won its independence from Mexico (Texas was ultimately annexed by the United States in 1845).[56] The Allen brothers' priority was profit, not developing a sustainable city, and they claimed to prospective buyers back East that their southern swamp was an oasis, containing "an abundance of excellent spring water, . . . the sea breeze in all its freshness."[57]

In its first decades, Houston was a small trading post fully implicated in the South's cotton economy and system of chattel slavery. With a population of fewer than five thousand people (including more than a thousand slaves) at the beginning of the Civil War in 1860, Houston paled in comparison to Southern cities like New Orleans (168,675—then the sixth-largest in the United States and to be the largest in the Confederacy), Louisville (68,033), and Charleston (40,522).[58] Houston's economic function was rooted, like that of early Chicago, in its rail infrastructure, as it was a junction for Gulf Coast rail routes.[59]

Three events sharply changed the developmental course of the city. First, the destruction by hurricane of Houston's regional rival, Galveston, in 1900 propelled Houston to local dominance. The staggering loss of property and life—upwards of twelve thousand people were killed—drove outside investment and migration patterns to Houston, fifty miles to the northwest. Second, the discovery

of oil in southeast Texas in 1901 led to a massive boom as spec-
ulators were soon finding petroleum reserves all over the region;
Houston quickly settled in as the economic hub of this activity.[60]
Third, the creation of the Houston Ship Channel in 1914—a joint
venture of Harris County and the federal government that opened
Houston to the water traffic promised nearly a century prior by the
Allen brothers—allowed Houston, located forty miles inland from
the Gulf of Mexico, to become a viable port city.[61]

By the time the Sunbelt was booming during and after World
War II, Houston was at the center of the world's largest oil-
producing region. Oil and its subsidiary products defined the
city's economy for most of the twentieth century: much of the
wealth that subsequently filtered into real estate, banking, health
care, aerospace, and the arts originated in dark primordial pools.
Building and maintaining this fossil-fuel economy was a group
of private elites, often described as an "old boys' club," of White
Houstonians who used their extreme wealth to shape the city's
politics in their own image. The tenets were simple: keep the oil
and the profits flowing; the resulting social inequalities and environmental degradation were merely externalities.[62]

Typical of the Sunbelt configurations that gave rise to nationally prominent conservatives like Barry Goldwater, postwar
Houston was a fertile field for the marriage of free-market capitalism and social conservatism that would later define the national
Republican Party.[63] In the decades before the post–civil rights
party realignment, Houston was, like the rest of Texas and the
"Solid South," under Democratic control. This partisan affiliation
had a different complexion than in New York, Chicago, and other
Northern cities where Democratic principles centered on strong
governmental involvement in housing, employment, and social
safety nets. In Houston, where ties to the federal government and
the national party were less extensive and strong labor unions and

a political machine were absent, the meaning of Democratic affiliation was more malleable in a one-party town, where questions of local power, especially economic and racial power, were more pressing than specific political platforms.[64] Nevertheless, tensions had emerged between Houstonians and the national party beginning with Roosevelt's New Deal and eventually led to some support for the "Dixiecrats" after 1948 and the full-on retreat of White conservatives from the Democratic Party after 1968.[65]

In a city where terms were just two years, six different mayors served between 1945 and 1970. Although the rotating cast—which included millionaire businessman Oscar Holcombe, who served eleven nonconsecutive mayoral terms between 1921 and 1958, and developer/judge Roy Hofheinz—held important decision-making power, more powerful than any of them was the informal organization known as the "8F crowd," named for the suite in the Lamar Hotel where the city's White power brokers regularly convened.[66] While Houston was by no means unique in having a power elite, in a city with disenfranchised voters of color and a weak local government there were few venues for contesting this concentration of influence.[67] The central figures included Jesse H. Jones, owner of the Lamar Hotel and a well-connected developer who dominated the city's political-economic affairs from the 1910s onward and remained 8F's "godfather" until his death in 1956; developer brothers Herman and George R. Brown; oilmen Bob Smith and James Abercrombie; William Hobby, former Texas governor and publisher of the Houston *Post*, along with his wife, Oveta Culp Hobby, who served as secretary of the U.S. Department of Health, Education and Welfare under Eisenhower; and Gus Wortham, insurance magnate and president of the chamber of commerce.[68]

Although the group would see its influence gradually erode by the 1970s as women and people of color gained political power, the legacy of their pro-growth agenda has persisted.[69] The ol' boys were staunchly pro-business and, in the tenor of the postwar period, staunchly anticommunist. With the editorial pages of the *Post* and the *Chronicle* leading the charge, the 8F crowd not only backed the authoritarian tactics of Senator Joseph McCarthy but also supported Houston's own "red scare" inquisition in the late 1940s and early 1950s.[70] Many of the federal government's social programs were shunned: notably, the city's school board rejected the federal free lunch program for two decades over concerns about communist influence.[71]

But not all federal funds met the ire of Houston's ruling class. Indeed, despite the self-styled Texan mythos of a bootstraps-libertarian-cowboy civic ideal, the reality is that contemporary Houston was fully shaped by federal funds and federal policies in the twentieth century. Centrally, these included Federal Housing Administration policies that encouraged sprawling, suburban-style residential development; interstate highways that set an expansive template for the city's growth; Army Corps of Engineers projects and National Flood Insurance policies that subsidized development in flood-prone areas; and construction of the National Aeronautics and Space Administration's mission control center.[72] The federal policies that encouraged cities across the country to decentralize in the post–World War II decades, creating car-centric regions, generated high demand for oil and therefore great wealth for the oil-producing regions of the Southwest in general, and Houston in particular.[73] Indeed, it is a fitting irony that in this purported monument to the free market, Houston's City Hall was built with New Deal funds in the 1930s. Though rooted in fiction, the myth of a modern city built by the market nevertheless serves an important ideological purpose. Beyond suiting the sensibilities of local elites, this long-standing antigovernment streak among Houston's governing class enabled ascendant economic sectors—especially real estate—to progress unencumbered by regulation, to the point that the city's "no zoning" mandate has long been its most sacred political cow.[74]

Along with this commitment to oil-driven urban growth, Houston's foremost twentieth-century social issue was upholding racial segregation. With a population of nearly six hundred thousand by 1950, Houston had become the nation's largest Jim Crow city.[75] Strict racial segregation in schools, housing, and public accommodations was the rule for the city's entire history up until Supreme Court decisions and federal legislation overturned the South's racial caste system in the 1950s and '60s. Unlike boosters in other Southern cities, notably Atlanta and Charlotte, who would attempt to offer a civic brand of racial moderation as cities "too busy to hate," Houston's White leaders were more than content with the racist status quo.[76] Houston would not see a liberally minded mayor until the election of Fred Hofheinz in 1974, and he was ousted after one term.[77]

Houston's racial amalgam did not fit neatly into a Black-White binary despite Jim Crow's insistence. The assumptions of biological racial difference that underpinned this system denied the reality that racial groups were an ongoing social production—not to mention the centuries of mixing that White Southerners would rather deny—and Houston's postwar demography included groups that had themselves been created by miscegenation: Creoles, who maintained a culturally distinct community in Frenchtown, and ethnic Mexicans (Tejanos), who formed a growing presence on the North and East sides.[78] Despite fluidity at the margins, Houston's residential geography reflected the rigidity of top-down racial boundaries. In 1950, the city's 125,000 Black residents were not confined to a single Black Belt, as in Chicago, but limited to a set of neighborhoods in the Third, Fourth, and Fifth wards, where they formed more than 98 percent of the local population.[79] The Black population grew quickly in subsequent decades (to 317,000 by 1970), but the White population grew at about the same rate, as migration to Houston accelerated with the postwar boom. Houston therefore remained a proportionally rather White city compared to New York and Chicago, with Whites forming more than 70 percent of the population through 1970.[80]

The same Black neighborhoods ghettoized under Jim Crow were summarily destroyed or further segmented by the vast expansion of Houston's highway system in the 1960s. With White Houstonians able to move outward into new tract housing, Black residents remained concentrated in the Third, Fourth, and Fifth wards, located, respectively, just to the south, west, and northeast of downtown. In the late 1940s, 85 percent of new residential development was happening outside of Houston's municipal boundaries. Owing to liberal annexation laws, however, this flight was largely contained within (growing) city limits: just seventy-three square miles in 1940 (about a third the size of Chicago), Houston would encompass 350 square miles by 1960.[81]

Given this decentralization of the city's White population, the areas around downtown were becoming heavily Black and Latino. Like Chicago's leaders, Houston's power brokers created imposing spatial barriers between downtown and these communities of color. In particular, the construction of a massive interchange of Interstate 10 and U.S. 59 at the southwestern edge of the Black Fifth Ward destroyed Lyons Avenue, the commercial and cultural heart of the neighborhood; in similar fashion, Interstate 45 cut off the Third Ward's Dowling Street (since renamed Emancipation Avenue) and also sliced through the Black Fourth Ward, severing it from downtown.[82] Other communities of color fared slightly better during this period of "slum clearance," as the major highway project to target Mexican Americans came after the destruction of the Black wards, and that knowledge, coupled with rising Chicano activism generally, led activists to defeat the proposed Harrisburg Freeway in the late 1960s.[83]

Highways were the preferred mode of federal urban-renewal spending in Houston; city leaders pursued very little public housing construction. Sprawling urbanization also required the expansion of city services and infrastructure over a vast territory. In addition to the demand for police, fire, and emergency services, this growth required new sewage systems and the draining and channeling of the region's fragmented waterways.[84] These efforts included concretizing many of Houston's bayous, which enabled new development to unfold in local floodplains. Denaturing the region's drainage system moved water downstream, solving flooding in one area by sending the water elsewhere. This piecemeal environmental planning, deployed in the service of real estate development, created, on a metro level, as many problems as it solved.[85]

. . .

The sum portrait of Houston's developmental history is that of a city constantly on the make. From its origins, as a site sold to speculators like snake oil, through its meteoric rise after the discovery of actual crude oil, Houston's path was one of growth, both economic and geographic. Houston's environmental resources, which enabled much of its early prosperity, have over time proved to be hazards: flood risks, along with air, land, and water pollution associated with oil production—a dialectic exacerbated in a fragile ecological region by unchecked urbanization.

With the city's massive wealth built on degrading the environment, and with little in the way of centralized environmental planning, it is unsurprising that Houstonians have had little use for the city's parks master plan, which dates to 1913.[86] Parks, like cultural achievements more generally, have been a consistent afterthought in a city where economic gain is paramount. Houston is therefore an unlikely place for people to install parks or the environment at the forefront of civic consciousness. The fact that, in the twenty-first century, Houston is one of the first cities to become home to a new park in the mold of the High Line reveals what the High Line, the Bloomingdale Trail/606, and Buffalo Bayou Park are actually about.

II

GROWTH MACHINES IN THE GARDEN

3

"THE YUPPIE EXPRESS"

WHILE the High Line received no official elegy, the first mention of its afterlife came in the early 1980s, when Peter Obletz, a Chelsea resident, arts administrator, activist, amateur preservationist, and rail enthusiast who owned several antique train cars, initiated a campaign to save the structure.[1] Though the High Line's impending demolition would later catalyze a preservation movement in 1999, Obletz—a self-proclaimed transportation expert who would go on to chair Community Board 4 and consult with the Metropolitan Transportation Authority—was initially concerned about the wasted right-of-way and hoped to reinvigorate rail traffic on the High Line.[2] Dreaming of a nonprofit light-rail that would connect the West Village with points north—all the way to the Bronx—he founded the West Side Rail Development Foundation, Inc. in 1984.[3]

Obletz became an important and somewhat mythic figure in the ultimate redevelopment of the High Line. Though he passed away three years before the Friends of the High Line formed in 1999, he was the rare figure in the 1980s and '90s who, in opposition to real estate developers, local residents, and the city government, saw the structure as a resource—rather than an impediment to new development in Chelsea and the Meatpacking District. With Conrail—the company that owned the High Line at the time of its closure—eager to remove the structure and its presumed liability (from falling debris, etc.) from its ledger, Obletz was able to purchase the High Line for a mere $10 in 1988— though this sale would be overturned in court.[4]

In a neighborhood that, despite its decline, was seeing the seeds of regeneration as gentrifiers and art gallery owners moved into the brownstones and old industrial lofts, Obletz's 1984 proposal for the railway's reinvention won him few friends among these new residents and the city's developer class.[5] One pair of new homeowners, whose "front windows look out on the southern end of those tracks," were concerned enough to write to the *Times* decrying Obletz's plan and requesting that other new residents "join us in vigorously opposing any plan to invade our quiet corner of Manhattan with an elevated railroad."[6] Soon Obletz was not the only person or institution eyeing a revival of rail traffic on the High Line. In 1986, the Koch administration initiated a $1.5 million federally funded study to consider a light-rail option for the High Line.[7] This plan was also criticized—including by Obletz—for privileging big-money interests. A local state senator disparaged it as "the Yuppie Express," and West Side transit advocates—including those who had defeated the proposed Westway highway project in the late 1970s—believed that the plan was a "thinly disguised boondoggle designed to hasten the same development projects that were contemplated as part of the highway plan."[8]

With redevelopment a contentious topic, the other initial reaction to the disused railway was to remove it. Beginning in the early 1980s, most local politicians and developers saw the hulking, decaying structure as a serious impediment to the neighborhood's renewal. A number of the city's political leaders and real estate developers went on the record in favor of tearing it down.[9]

But if reviving traffic on the High Line seemed logistically and politically complicated, so too was demolition: owing to federal regulations, the Surface Transportation Board, which governs all railways in the United States, had mandated that transportation infrastructure could be dismantled only if it could be considered fully abandoned.

The role of the federal government in the High Line's future would therefore be significant; so too would be local political coalitions. In New York, land use is tightly regulated by American standards—far more so than in Sunbelt cities like Houston, which famously has no zoning. While New York does not have a comprehensive land-use plan, development proposals that require altering zoning rules are heavily scrutinized and subject to significant public input. Particularly at the neighborhood level, the city's fifty-nine community boards have a legal voice in such proposed projects via New York's Uniform Land Use Review Process.[10] With developers salivating that a demolished High Line would open up the Far West Side (much of which was zoned for manufacturing and industrial use) to new high-rise housing, Manhattan Community Boards 2 and 4 (the two that included the High Line within their borders) would nevertheless have a say in what would happen with the High Line and on any new development in the surrounding area.

Part of what made the High Line a highly visible and contentious piece of transportation infrastructure was its location and function within the changing social geography of Chelsea. For much of the twentieth century, the brownstone blocks to the east of Tenth Avenue were occupied mostly by middle-class Whites. The High Line, running just west of Tenth Avenue, was a spatial and symbolic boundary, dividing the brownstones and apartment buildings from the light-manufacturing district that ran west to the piers along the Hudson River.

By 1980, the year the High Line closed, this local demography was changing (though the High Line still formed a barrier). The area west of the railway was one of the least populated places in Manhattan, with just 626 people living in the forty-block area. Demographically the area was 36 percent White, 37 percent Hispanic, and 25 percent Black; the median household income was just over $9,000 (in 1979 dollars—almost $33,000 in 2018 dollars). In the area east of the High Line, the population in 1980 was nearly two-thirds White, with incomes more than 50 percent higher than in the area west of the High Line.[11] The difference was most pronounced in the heart of Chelsea's brownstone district, where the median household income was more than $16,000 ($58,000 in 2018 dollars) and the population was more than 70 percent White.[12]

Population movement to Chelsea had two major streams in the early 1980s. The first was Latinos, many of whom were foreign-born. The second was gay White men: newcomers to the city as well as longer-term New Yorkers moving north from Manhattan's historical gay enclave, the West Village, in search of cheaper housing.[13]

There was another piece to this in-migration to Chelsea: the movement of businesses from the West Village, along with art galleries from SoHo farther to the south. Overall, as these shifts helped displace many of the remaining manufacturers and meat-packers from the area, the changes happening in the High Line's shadow in the 1980s should be understood as a process of commercial gentrification as much as one of residential gentrification.[14]

Given these demographic and cultural changes to the areas around the High Line, the picture for both proponents of reuse and proponents of removal was further complicated in the late 1980s by a series of municipal scandals that resulted in the defeat of three-term mayor Ed Koch by Manhattan borough president David Dinkins, who became the city's first Black mayor in 1989.[15] Koch rose to prominence as a liberal reformer, but as his political career went along, he rebranded himself as a conservative Democrat, deliberately appealing to the city's White working class in the "defended" neighborhoods of Queens, Brooklyn, and Staten Island.[16] Dinkins, as a liberal with a Manhattan base that included left-leaning wealthy Whites, was well positioned to challenge a scandal-plagued incumbent; he won the Democratic primary by nine points before closely defeating Republican Rudolph Giuliani in a general election marked by sharp racial divisions.[17]

Dinkins would remain in office only four years before outerborough White resentment propelled Giuliani to victory in their 1993 rematch. While in office, Dinkins's primary contribution concerning the High Line came in January 1991, when the city issued a permit allowing the demolition of five blocks of the High Line at its southern terminus.[18] This action was pursued by the Rockrose Development Corporation, which had purchased that section of the structure from Conrail for an undisclosed price in November 1990 in order to develop luxury apartments at 99 and 100 Jane Street, in an area that had been rezoned from M1-5 (manufacturing) to C6-2A (commercial, with high-rise mixed-use permitted) in 1984.[19] Following this demolition, Dinkins, who had previously stated his support for reuse while serving as Manhattan's borough president, stated that the remaining portion's continued existence "would significantly limit the city's ability to consider other development strategies for the area."[20] Further, the Dinkins administration lent support to a business lobby, Chelsea Property Owners, that was pursuing legal action to force Conrail to abandon the High Line, after which it would presumably be turned over to the city government for demolition.[21]

Giuliani took office on January 1, 1994, and continued on the path toward demolition. Giuliani represented a return to the reactionary politics that had generally characterized the Koch administration.[22] Like Koch, Giuliani enjoyed a base of support among the city's disaffected White communities, where his tenure as U.S. attorney for New York's Southern District in the 1980s—during which he famously served as lead prosecutor in the Mafia Commission trial—provided his law-and-order bona fides, which were germane, given that the city was emerging from two decades of wreckage following the 1975 fiscal crisis and was still experiencing high rates of violent crime. Race was a major factor, of course; after four years of a Black mayor, it was no coincidence that Giuliani was elected the same year that 65 percent of Staten Island's voters approved a nonbinding referendum to secede from New York City.[23] In his rise to the mayoralty, Giuliani also courted the ascendant sectors of the city's economy—finance and real estate. Linking pro-market economic policies with revanchist social policies, Giuliani was a textbook neoconservative.[24]

Like Dinkins, Giuliani was an ardent supporter of demolition. In 1999, nineteen years into the High Line's contentious holding pattern, his administration accelerated efforts to have the structure torn down. Two events portended opposing futures for the space. One was a report from the Regional Plan Association, a prominent advocacy group in the New York area that had been commissioned by CSX—the company that now owned the High Line as a result of acquiring Conrail—to study uses for the structure. The second was a new $150 million lawsuit, filed in federal court by the city government and local real estate developers, that, like the 1991 suit, attempted to force the company to demolish the rail line.[25]

In its report, the Regional Plan Association outlined eight possible uses for the High Line, including making it part of the city's subway system (as an extension of either the 7 train or the L train), a light-rail, or a way of bringing waste to the waste-transfer station at West Fifty-Ninth Street.[26] One of the options considered was to transform the High Line into "a greenway, which would also include a bikeway, walkway, and either a rubber-tire vehicle or a light trolley line."[27]

With gentrification accelerating in the areas around the High Line in the 1990s, the revival of the reuse option was simply not acceptable to the Giuliani administration and his allied coalition of real estate developers. Indeed, the Regional Plan Association's ultimate recommendation was that the structure become "a high amenity transportation corridor," which might resemble a "street in the air" with "retail establishments . . . on the High Line's surface."[28] This was the first serious reuse proposal that did not involve reinvigorating rail traffic, and it intrigued the city's urban-planning groups and local community boards. But Giuliani, who was at the time agitating for a new professional football stadium near the High Line's northern terminus, would not have it. Said Giuliani's city planning commissioner Joseph Rose, "That platform has no right to be there except for transportation, and that use is long gone," and that, given the two-decades-long impasse, the High Line "has become the Vietnam of old railroad trestles."[29] Rose added, "It would be one thing if CSX was saying they would provide the investment necessary to fix this old thing up as a public park. That we would consider, but that is not what they are saying. . . . The bottom line is that the High Line will have to come down."[30]

Renewed calls for demolition encountered a different social geography than that of the early 1980s, when the High Line's closure had prompted pleas for removal so that new development could proceed apace. (The High Line itself had changed, too: the defunct railway was now a blossoming bed of wild grasses and flowers, an unusual green shock in the gray landscape of western Chelsea.) By the late 1990s, Chelsea's identity had become fully steeped in both high art and gay culture. Indeed, while the racial composition of the neighborhood had not changed much since 1980 (with Whites, Blacks, and Latinos representing, respectively, 59 percent, 9 percent, and 23 percent of the population east of Tenth Avenue), intensifying gentrification pressures in the West Village led to the continued northward movement of gay White men.[31] By 2004 the *Times* could remark that Chelsea had become the "epicenter of gay male life in New York."[32] There was significant overlap between this community and the neighborhood's insurgent art world, which by 1999 housed more art galleries than any other neighborhood in New York City.[33]

These identities, while not encompassing the totality of Chelsea's residents or its institutions, had nevertheless become strongly associated with the neighborhood (and indeed formed a powerful "brand" that local boosters sought to commodify).[34] In such a context, particularly given the rising aesthetic fascination with postindustrial buildings and infrastructures since the late 1970s, a disused railway could take on a new and different significance.[35] Though the High Line had long been a real barrier and a frequent dispenser of "pigeon shit," residents new to the area could consider that the artful reuse of this industrial object could further develop Chelsea's reputation as an arts district and add a public amenity to the former industrial center.[36]

Following the publication of the Regional Plan Association's report in June 1999, the High Line's future became a matter of wider public interest and input. Community Board meetings were held in Chelsea and the West Village, where the Regional Plan Association presented their study and the various options for the High Line. At one of these meetings in Chelsea, the beginnings of the High Line's eventual future were born, when two local residents—Josh David and Robert Hammond—met. Several months later, the two founded the Friends of the High Line with the goal of preserving the space and transforming it into a park. The group was so named because of its "friendly," "neutral" tone, an important consideration given the power of the opposition.[37] In the early months of planning, Hammond enlisted the help of developer Phil Aarons, who had previously worked for the city government under Ed Koch.[38] Aarons quickly established himself as an integral member of the Friends of the High Line team, arranging for meetings with attorneys from CSX and helping to file a lawsuit against the city to prevent the High Line's demolition.[39] With this initial period of organizing, the Friends of the High Line established for the public that if the High Line was to be saved, its future would not be as a part of the city's subway system or a new light-rail—it would be as a public park.

As the pro-reuse movement was gaining momentum, the pro-demolition effort suffered a major blow: the federal Surface Transportation Board again ruled against the city and the Chelsea Property Owners group in July 1999.[40] With the Giuliani administration still firmly opposed to the park proposal, the impasse continued.

At least it did until September 11, 2001, when the city's World Trade Center towers were attacked. In the previous two years, the nascent Friends of the High Line had generated all manner of support for their vision; they had raised funds, built alliances with other nonprofits and community groups, and acquired pledges to back the project from the mayoral candidates who were aiming to replace Giuliani after he finished his eight years in office. But in the immediate aftermath of September 11, it was unclear what New York's future would look like, let alone a fledgling park project.[41] As Friends of the High Line cofounder Robert Hammond would later recall, "selfishly, my first thought when I realized the towers had fallen was, Well, there goes the High Line. Who's going to ever care about the High Line when we have a disaster on this scale?"[42]

Soon after September 11, the Friends of the High Line were faced with a bleaker fate than merely being forgotten: Giuliani was attempting the unprecedented move of extending his mayoral term by three months, given the city's crisis.[43] He went so far as to secure support for his plan from the two major-party candidates, Republican Michael Bloomberg and Democrat Mark Green, threatening, just weeks before the election, that if he did not obtain their blessing he would consider running for a third term on the Conservative Party ticket, a clear violation of local term-limit laws.[44]

Giuliani ultimately abandoned this hope, as it hinged on the approval of the Democrat-controlled state assembly. Facing his final months in City Hall, and despite the real political challenges encountered after September 11, Giuliani found no score too small to settle. In December 2001, with just two weeks left in Giuliani's term, the state Supreme Court overturned the Friends of the High Line's restraining order that was preventing the city government from moving forward with demolition.[45] When Giuliani signed the eleventh-hour demolition papers, it appeared that two years of organizing had been for naught; despite incoming mayor Michael Bloomberg's previously stated support for the park project, it was unclear if the decision could or would be reversed.

• • •

Billionaire business mogul Michael Bloomberg was sworn in as mayor of New York on January 1, 2002. A Republican like Giuliani, Bloomberg had campaigned on his business acumen— as someone with the experience and the technocratic skill set needed to engage the private sector and get the center of global capitalism running more efficiently. Though seemingly more receptive to the High Line's transformative possibilities—and, most important, its potential to stimulate economic growth—one month into his term a spokesperson nevertheless indicated that the new mayor was "still familiarizing himself with the issues" surrounding the potential park.[46] In the Friends of the High Line's quest to secure the new mayor's firm support, it helped that two of their earliest supporters had recently assumed positions of power in city government. Amanda Burden, a wealthy and well-connected member of the City Planning Commission, was named chair of Bloomberg's City Planning Department, and Gifford Miller, a close friend of Hammond's, was elected speaker of the New York City Council.[47]

These connections enabled the Friends of the High Line to obtain an audience with Dan Doctoroff, Bloomberg's deputy mayor for economic development. In their initial meetings, the Friends of the High Line emphasized to the administration that redeveloping the High Line as a park would be an economic boon to the neighborhood. Enlisting the help of real estate developer John Altschuler, David and Hammond presented the city with a rosy financial picture. Hammond recalled that Altschuler "figured out how to frame the argument . . .: parks increase the value of nearby real estate, and thus the addition of a new park on the High Line could create an economic benefit for New York City."[48] They projected that the properties adjacent to the High Line would receive an increase in value between 6 and 13 percent. For an estimated cost of around $100 million, the city would see $262 million in new revenues over the park's first twenty years.[49]

Bloomberg was sold. The administration believed that the redevelopment of the High Line would help the city's bid for the 2012 Summer Olympics, which was a project of great interest to

Doctoroff.[50] Bloomberg revived Giuliani's plans for a new sports stadium atop the West Side Railyards, which was to be the centerpiece of the bid. While any new tourist attraction would likely be of service to winning the Olympics, the High Line's location, which ran north to the site of the prospective stadium, made it especially appealing. The Bloomberg administration had additional plans to encourage development in the neighborhood, including deregulating zoning codes in the former industrial district. The mayor hoped that the three plans—stadium, High Line, and zoning deregulation—would coalesce as a single push for economic growth on the Far West Side.[51]

Bloomberg also saw a revitalized High Line as part of his broader agenda for parks and public spaces in New York. Bloomberg believed that civic amenities were an important piece of attracting the "creative class" to cities, and he therefore sought to enhance all kinds of public spaces, including parks, bike lanes, promenades, and other recreational features. He included a parks plan in his 2001 campaign materials, and his much-touted 2007 master plan advertised "a greener, greater New York" on its cover and boasted of plans for "the largest expansion of our [parks] system since the New Deal."[52] This park creation was to rely on the conversion of former industrial sites, brownfields, and underdeveloped public lands, particularly along the city's expansive waterfronts. While termed a "five-borough development strategy," much of the real planning resources went to Manhattan and gentrified areas of Brooklyn, with the tourist-friendly High Line, Brooklyn Bridge Park, and Hudson River Park standing as the administration's top priorities.[53] The Bronx, Queens, Staten Island, and outer Brooklyn were worth Bloomberg's attention to the extent that they could facilitate corporate expansion. As argued by Doctoroff, the administration needed "to develop areas outside the traditional central business districts of Midtown and

Lower Manhattan so that companies that need to diversify or need lower cost alternatives can be accommodated within the five boroughs."[54] By building what Bloomberg's master plan termed "destination parks," new residents, businesses, and visitors could be drawn to these newly lucrative sections of the city.[55]

This parks program was also an extension of the privatizing trends that had been present in the city's parks since the early 1980s. As New York was bottoming out in the throes of the urban crisis, developers used that crisis as an opportunity to remake the city's public spaces. While "Fear City" grappled with the realities of increased violent crime, rising poverty, and depopulation—and the insecurities that resulted—developers set to shoring up the privately owned public plazas that lined upper Park Avenue, the financial district, and other areas where skyscrapers were built using a 1961 zoning revision: developers could be awarded more height for their buildings if they created public spaces at street level.[56] Such so-called "bonus plazas," which were built to be more hospitable over time as middle-class Whites repopulated the city, ushered in a model for privatized public space—one that was consumerist and securitized.[57] On a more institutional level, this trend was intensified by the creation of private park corporations, most notably the Central Park Conservancy, in the 1980s. With public-sector retrenchment leading to disinvestment in the city's Department of Parks and Recreation, private groups stepped into that financial and organizational void to shore up parks located in or adjacent to wealthy neighborhoods. As this arrangement become more popular in the 1990s and 2000s—and indeed celebrated by neoliberal political leaders, who could outsource parks funding and management to donors and volunteers—alliances between the city government and conservancies (and even business-improvement districts) became commonplace.[58]

Given that political-economic context, and with Bloomberg's support secured, the Friends of the High Line ramped up their efforts to accumulate private philanthropic dollars for the park. David and Hammond, the two cofounders, were new to the nonprofit world when they started their enterprise, but they were far from ignorant about how to generate buzz and financing for their proposal. They tapped into their personal networks, which were extensive and well resourced: both were Ivy League–educated, longtime Chelsea residents; as creatively inclined gay White men, they were well positioned to represent the "new" Chelsea—and many of their early supporters shared these demographic traits. As Josh David would note, "Gayness ultimately became an identifying characteristic of the organization and, to some degree, of the park itself."[59]

Delving into these networks along with Aarons's business contacts, David and Hammond sought the support of elites from Chelsea's art world and New York's traditional philanthropic networks. "I thought nonprofits were run and funded by Upper East Side women," remarked Hammond, "but they weren't interested."[60] Instead, their fledgling group found willing deep pockets among the old-money philanthropists' well-heeled children. Joining forces with their group of young professionals and longtime Chelsea residents were wealthy blue bloods with surnames like Rockefeller, Van Wyck, and von Furstenberg.[61] Adding a further dash of glamour to their support base, David's partner was a Hollywood talent agent and partner at the prominent Gersh Agency.[62] In short order, celebrities such as Edward Norton, Martha Stewart, and Kevin Bacon (whose father Ed was an esteemed urban planner in Philadelphia) threw their financial and promotional support behind the Friends of the High Line.[63] What emerged from these early years of organizing was a rather formidable advocacy group—one with the economic resources and cultural capital to be a forceful part of the redevelopment project, ensure Bloomberg's continued support, and have a say in what architectural form the park would ultimately take.

Part of that partnership with the city government meant reckoning with the interests of the Bloomberg administration and the motives of the financiers and real estate developers that the Friends of the High Line had courted in its early days. Indeed, while community members saw a redeveloped High Line as a sort of dreamscape, whose final form was open to the interpretation of the beholder—a vision that the group carefully cultivated, by allowing picturesque photos of the High Line in its blooming state of disrepair, rather than architectural renderings, to speak for the park's future—there were other motives that, if not necessarily in conflict with the Friends of the High Line's open-ended efforts to preserve the unique mix of green plants and gray infrastructure, certainly diverged.[64]

For key members of city government, especially Burden and parks commissioner Adrian Benepe, the High Line was a signature park, one that Benepe described as "not just a park. It is a work of art."[65] For Mayor Bloomberg, the High Line was the linchpin of developing other sites on the Far West Side; after the stadium proposal died its last death in 2005, his focus moved to a new use for the West Side Railyards: "12.4 million square feet of commercial, residential, recreational, and cultural space," all propped up by $1 billion worth of columns that would allow this development to sit atop the active railyards.[66] And for the developers enthralled with the project from its inception, the High Line was a rare real estate opportunity. Once the zoning codes were lifted in the part of Chelsea west of the High Line, the lightly populated former manufacturing district would become a virtual free-for-all: with none of the usual suspects in the area to cry "not in my backyard," developers would be able to take their pick of the old, low-rise industrial buildings to be demolished and redeveloped as luxury housing. Arguably, it was precisely this evolving mix of motives that enabled the park project to keep rolling through the aftermath of 9/11 and the economic recession of 2007–2008.

In the final years of the redevelopment process, these differing visions for the High Line were each reflected, to varying extents, as the park progressed and the surrounding cityscape took on new forms. In 2004, architects were hired—a team led by James Corner, Liz Diller, Ric Scofidio, Charles Renfro, and Piet Oudolf, whose vision of a minimalist, wild garden won over both the city government and the Friends of the High Line.[67] In 2005, the Surface Transportation Board ruled in favor of the redevelopment proposal, and most of the manufacturing area to the west of the High Line was rezoned for commercial and residential use.[68] In 2006, construction on the park began (the first act: deracinating the wild plants that had made the railway an intriguing site for a park). As progress on the park continued, speculative new development started popping up around the High Line, including luxury apartment buildings and offices designed by famous architects like Frank Gehry.[69] And further bolstering Chelsea's claim to art-world centricity—and the High Line's new place in it—in 2009 the Upper East Side's Whitney Museum of American Art purchased land from the city government (at a reduced price of $18 million) at the park's southern terminus with the intention of building a new home for its collection.[70]

In June 2009, ten years after the Regional Plan Association formally proposed building a greenway on the High Line, the park opened. At a cost of $152 million, including $108 million in public funds, the stretch of the park from the southern terminus at Gansevoort Street to West Twentieth Street was complete.[71] While the plan was eventually to adapt the entire 1.45-mile railway, opening part of the park before the rest could be built (indeed, in 2009 there was still some question as to whether the northernmost half-mile would be preserved, as it formed half the circumference of the Hudson Yards project) offered a strong argument: public excitement grew, and rave architectural reviews poured in—as did more philanthropic money for the Friends of the High Line. The new park merged together a distinct mix of green landscapes, industrial aesthetics, and towering views of Chelsea, Midtown, and the Hudson River. Its tight corridor also provided opportunities for commerce: artists, artisanal food vendors, and a restaurant lined wider sections of the park, along with a space for visitors to purchase park memberships from the Friends of the High Line and to buy High Line–branded memorabilia.[72]

Although public funds had largely financed the park effort, and the city's Department of Parks and Recreation was part of the broader redevelopment team, moving forward the park was to be under the institutional supervision of the Friends of the High Line. As the organization pivoted from park advocates to park managers, Josh David and Robert Hammond remained in leadership roles. The growing organization would be responsible for the majority of the park's operating expenses; it also had the freedom to craft event schedules for the park (including renting out sections to private groups), regulate the businesses that operated in the park, and set rules and restrictions for the space.

It's difficult to overstate the admiration that the new park received in the initial months after its opening. Cynical architectural and cultural critics rolled out their highest praise, with the High Line drawing frequent comparisons to Central Park, the city's grandest park and a foundational achievement in landscape architectural history. Nicolai Ouroussoff of the *Times*, while admitting his fear that he might see Carrie Bradshaw (fictional protagonist of television's *Sex and the City*) out for a stroll, nevertheless called the High Line "one of the most thoughtful, sensitively designed public spaces built in New York in years."[73] Longtime *New Yorker* architecture critic Paul Goldberger termed it "a miracle above Manhattan," "one of the most innovative and inviting public spaces in New York City and perhaps the entire country."[74] Beyond critical success, the High Line was a popular triumph as well. As a signifier of the distinctly New York nexus of all things gritty, nostalgic, and sophisticated (as admittedly in-conflict as such concepts seem), it was an immediate phenomenon, an instant draw to residents of Lower Manhattan and beyond. Three hundred thousand people visited the park in its first month of existence; more than two million visited in its first year. That number that would reach five million by 2014, solidifying the park as one of the city's top tourist attractions.[75]

On one level, the successful re-creation of the High Line was the logical conclusion of the privatization of park development in New York City. Like other new or redeveloped spaces, such as Bryant Park, Union Square, and Brooklyn Bridge Park, the High Line was a triumph of capital: built with substantial private funds, managed by a private group, and catering to the recreational, aesthetic, and consumption preferences of the creative class and wealthy tourists. But the High Line's distinct geography—sandwiched between a cultural epicenter and a postindustrial district that was ripe for development—coupled with the park's glamorous benefactors and ties to the art world more generally, brought a heady mix of cultural and economic capital that would be hard for any other American city to replicate (indeed, it would be hard for even Manhattan to replicate the conditions that made the High Line such a dynamo). In these respects, the High Line was an archetype—of both a public space and an engine of capital.

But in 2009, plenty of American cities had disused railways and other underdeveloped spaces that could theoretically become homes to High Line–esque greenways. Certainly, the cultural prestige the High Line embodied could be enough to inspire city leaders elsewhere to build their own replicas; a good deal of urban parks history in the United States is exactly that—mayors and other city boosters seeking their own version of Central Park.[76]

More lucrative still than cultural prestige was cold, hard cash. Even the High Line's greatest detractors couldn't deny that— least of all Edison Properties, the parking-lot company behind the Chelsea Property Owners and two decades of efforts to demolish the High Line. In 2014, the company sold its primary West Chelsea lot—an entire block bordering the High Line between West Seventeenth and Eighteenth streets—for $800 million.[77]

4

"NO MORE BAKE SALES, MAN"

WHILE the Bloomingdale Line had no mythic early patron like Peter Obletz, it nevertheless entered a similar state of decay and unplanned plant growth after its closure to rail traffic in the 1990s. For Chicago's planners, the Bloomingdale Line offered a clear opportunity to improve transportation infrastructure and public space in a section of the city underserved in both respects.[1] While the park project that eventually took hold atop the railway would take significantly longer to realize than the High Line, redevelopment ideas were nevertheless percolating around the Bloomingdale Line within a few years of its closure. While early supporters of reusing the High Line imagined a range of possible futures for the space, backers of the Bloomingdale project coalesced around the idea of turning the former rail line into a linear park.

If any city was positioned to become home to an innovative public park in the twenty-first century, it was Chicago. The city's Latin motto was "*Urbs in Horto*"—"the city in a garden." Chicago had a long history of distinguished public parks, designed by venerable landscape architects like Frederick Law Olmsted, Calvert Vaux, and Jens Jensen. It also had the nation's oldest and largest city park organization, the Chicago Park District.[2]

The Chicago Park District—created and funded by the State of Illinois and nominally independent of the city government— had once been a towering public institution. Founded in 1934 as a consolidation of twenty-two independent park districts across Chicago, it benefited greatly from an influx of New Deal and urban-renewal funds over its first three decades. During the height of the Democratic machine's hegemony at mid-century, it was one of the great sources of patronage jobs.[3]

This state of affairs changed significantly by 1990. Beyond Chicago's economic decline, a series of corruption scandals and renewed attention to the organization's racist park policies reduced the Park District's patronage power.[4] The latter point gained attention during the 1983 mayoral election, won by Harold Washington, who became the city's first Black mayor. Washington ran as a reformer and specifically targeted the Park District and its longtime Superintendent, Edmund Kelly.[5] In the preceding decades, not only had years of activism and advocacy by Black Chicagoans been required for the Park District to build even the most modest green additions to Black communities, but once parks were built in Black neighborhoods—or once Black people started using "White" parks as they moved into neighborhoods that Whites were vacating— public investment slowed to a trickle.[6] In the 1940s and '50s, when the Park District unveiled its richly funded and much touted "Ten Year Plan" to build new parks throughout the city, only two of the thirty-one parks created under the plan were built in areas that had more than a handful of Black residents at the time of construction.[7] By mid-century, as Black Chicagoans became the primary users of the South Side's Olmsted-designed Washington Park, the Park District defunded this onetime "crown jewel" of the park system. Per-acre expenditures in the White North Side's Lincoln Park were *seventeen times* the comparable investments in Washington Park in the 1940s and '50s.[8]

However, the organizational independence of the Park District, coupled with massive resistance to Washington's administration in the city council (and Washington's unexpected death in 1987), limited reform efforts.[9] Slightly more effective was a May 1983 federal consent decree obtained by the U.S. Department of Justice, which charged the Park District with failing to provide equal resources for parks in communities of color under the terms of the Housing and Community Development Act of 1974, resulting in increased (but still limited) capital investment to such areas.[10]

The net result of Harold Washington's actions and the federal consent decree was not a wave of park reparations but rather a power vacuum in Chicago's parks sphere—to be filled in 1989 by Richard J. Daley's son, Richard M. Daley, who ascended to the mayor's office. Daley II's penchant for implementing neoliberal reforms translated in important ways to Chicago's parks.[11] While Daley's lineage suggested a return to old-school machine politics, the decade of scandals had altered certain levers of influence in the city, specifically through the creation of "legal restrictions on lower end patronage jobs," which enabled Daley to broker deals independently of the Democratic machine.[12]

From the early days of his administration, Daley was committed, as his father had been in the 1950s and '60s, to shoring up Chicago's economic fortunes by once again redeveloping the Loop—this time to put Chicago on the map as a "global city."[13] Such plans took the form of the broader post-1990 tilt toward urban entertainment districts, a planning strategy that in large measure included parks and public spaces.[14] The Loop, which housed most of the city's major cultural institutions and one of its "crown jewel" public parks, Grant Park, was missing the key element of "spectacle" that elites saw as important for establishing a global urban brand.[15] And the Loop had a perfect site for such a project: the underdeveloped space above the Illinois Central railyards. This open-air space was functional, but an eyesore for tourism-minded downtown interests. If it could be capped, it would suddenly provide the city with twenty-five acres of open public space just north of Grant Park.

Indeed, Daley envisioned Millennium Park—as the $484 million space ($310.5 million in public money and $173.5 million in private donations) would be called—as the cultural *pièce de résistance* of his mayoralty.[16] Built between 1998 and 2004, Millennium Park was conceived as a space for the arts, culture, and commerce: its design and uses revolved around spectacle (including numerous public art installations, most notably Anish Kapoor's $11.5 million Cloud Gate sculpture, aka "the Bean") and event spaces, including a music and dance theater and several event pavilions, all built for tens of millions and named for private benefactors.[17]

Orienting park development around profit, branding, and cultural spectacle, Daley's policies carved out a new purpose for Chicago's parks in the twenty-first century. Further, by partly circumventing the Park District and using private funding for park development, Daley also helped usher in a new, neoliberal organizational model for park financing and management.[18]

Millennium Park thus laid the public/private, tourist-friendly groundwork for the development of the Bloomingdale Trail/606 in the subsequent decade. Under Daley's administration, which lasted until 2011, preliminary plans for the green conversion of the Bloomingdale Line were drawn up in 1998 and then elaborated upon in 2004 with the support of the city's Department of Planning and Development and Department of Transportation, as well as the Chicago Park District.[19] This early plan discussed the merits of a park (under the working title "Bloomingdale Linear Park"), stating:

> The raised Bloomingdale rail corridor . . . presents an opportunity for the creation of an elevated linear park that includes a trail and passive areas. In addition to providing a new transportation route that could connect to existing bike lanes . . ., the greenway would afford recreational opportunities and improved aesthetics for area residents.[20]

In a city known for making "no small plans," and for a mayor who had just propelled his half-billion-dollar vision of Millennium Park to completion, this initial proposal offered a rather modest and practical assessment: a connection to bike lanes and neighborhood beautification. On the heels of raising $173.5 million in private money for Millennium Park—which included donations from fifteen of the twenty-one wealthiest Illinois residents—modesty and practicality compelled no coffers, public or private, to be opened for the "Bloomingdale Linear Park."[21]

Without funds on the table, it was left to community members—several of whom founded the Friends of the Bloomingdale Trail in 2003—to mobilize local support for the park project.

That, and wait for a new mayor, one who needed his own signature park space to throw his political capital behind.

• • •

What exactly is the 606? And why would a park be called by a number?

The name is half the story. What's uncontroversial is that the railway, which runs along Bloomingdale Avenue on the Near Northwest Side of Chicago, was known as the Bloomingdale

Line from its opening in 1872, through its elevation in 1914, up until 1998, when it was dubbed the prospective Bloomingdale Linear Park by the city government. Highlighting the salience of rails for shaping community boundaries in Chicago, the railway's east-west path was understood to demarcate the border between West Town and Logan Square when, in the 1920s, sociologists at the University of Chicago codified seventy-five "community areas" for the city (instituted as the official definition for Chicago's neighborhoods).[22]

The space was named the Bloomingdale Trail by the non-profit group that initiated the reuse project in 2003 (a nod to its assumed future as a "rails-to-trails" space—a form of conversion that had become popular in suburban woodlands in the 1980s and '90s), and some people, especially the park's early supporters, prefer to call it by that name. "The 606" was unveiled as the redevelopment process was well under way, in 2013.[23] The name referenced the first three digits of all Chicago zip codes. To some of the park's influential boosters in city government, the name represented the idea that the new elevated park space was for all Chicagoans.[24] To many community members, it was a sign of tasteless branding and tantamount to a betrayal of the original vision for the park.

The 606, as much as its name recalls the common practice of using numeric placeholders for yet unnamed public parks, was not a generic "Park No. 606." For the park's downtown backers, the creation of an elevated park for Chicago was an opportunity to announce, especially in the years after the High Line opened in 2009, that as leaders of a true "global city," they too could build a cutting-edge elevated park for the twenty-first century. Whether the 606 name evokes such high-minded aspirations is a matter of opinion; either way, it was a rhetorical departure from the grandiosity of Daley II's favorite park project.

The fact that a park's nomenclature could become something of a lightning rod is partly a product of the park's geographic location on the Near Northwest Side. It was no Millennium Park; it was not in the backyard of the city's downtown elite. Indeed, the Bloomingdale Line was several miles from the Loop, in a section of the city that, like most of Chicago, is primarily low-rise and visually nondescript. Although the railway passed near the heart of Chicago's "neo-bohemia," Wicker Park, it wasn't necessarily a prime location for a tourist attraction.[25] Whereas the High Line, theoretically, offered passage from the Meatpacking District, the West Village, and Chelsea—elite cultural hubs of early-twenty-first-century New York—to Midtown Manhattan—the city's longtime economic center—a repurposed Bloomingdale Line couldn't even take visitors downtown. It was cut off by Ashland Avenue and the elevated Kennedy Expressway (Interstate 90/94) well before it could reach the Loop, or even Old Town or Lincoln Park, the neighborhoods to the east.

Beyond the success of the High Line, what put the idea of an elevated park on the map for Chicago's boosters was the gentrification that occurred in Wicker Park, one of the neighborhoods located in the West Town community area, in the 1980s and '90s. This gentrification, which came in the aftermath of controversial urban-renewal efforts at the neighborhood's eastern end, was incentivized by policy maneuvers that raised property values, including the construction of a shopping mall at Ashland and Milwaukee in the 1980s, the creation of a Wicker Park historic district in 1991, and various infrastructural improvements.[26] These developments helped facilitate the movement of White bohemians—artists, service-industry workers, and other cultural producers—and their commercial accoutrements into what had been, for several decades, a predominantly Puerto Rican area.[27] In 1980, the core of Wicker Park (the triangle formed by Damen

Avenue, Milwaukee Avenue, and Division Street) was 24 percent White; by 2000, it was 59 percent White; by 2016, it was 75 percent White and just 8 percent Hispanic, down from 55 percent in 1980.[28] More than just a "Whitening" of the area, gentrifiers in Wicker Park embraced a particular aesthetic for the neighborhood: a gritty new epicenter for Chicago's creative class, one that would go on to win dubious accolades like being named the "fourth best hipster neighborhood" in America by *Forbes*.[29]

But the Bloomingdale Line extended well beyond Wicker Park, with the 2.7 miles of railway touching a total of four seemingly distinct neighborhoods: Bucktown and Logan Square, which were on the north side of the tracks, with Wicker Park and Humboldt Park to the south. This divide, while materialized by the railway, was culturally constructed—and porous. As several of these neighborhoods have seen their fortunes rise in recent decades, their cultural boundaries have shifted and more territory has been symbolically annexed by Wicker Park, Bucktown, and Logan Square.

The Bloomingdale Line's role in upholding these spurious neighborhood divisions is therefore open to interpretation and subject to change. But another boundary, this one a more clearly racial one, ran north-south on Western Avenue, dividing Wicker Park and Bucktown, which had become firmly White by 2000, from Humboldt Park and Logan Square, which had been showing signs of gentrification (especially in Logan Square) but were still predominantly Latino in 2004 when the city government announced its intention to create an adaptive reuse trail.[30]

Humboldt Park figures importantly in the Near Northwest Side's story of racial tension and turnover in the twenty-first century. From the late 1940s and 1950s, the neighborhood (which, like several others in Chicago, shares its name with the large, eponymous park at its geographic center) had been the major entry point into Chicago for Puerto Rican migrants who arrived by the tens of thousands.[31] Before racialized neighborhood boundaries were invented between Humboldt Park and Wicker Park, the heart of the Puerto Rican community stretched 1.5 miles along Division Street from Ashland Avenue to California Avenue.[32] Known colloquially as *La Division*, the area that would eventually be home to neo-bohemian bars like Phyllis' Musical Inn and the Rainbo Club was, for several decades, a Puerto Rican commercial and cultural center.

As the first wave of gentrification took hold, turning the section of Division between Damen and Ashland Avenues into a bohemian destination by the early 1990s, community organizers in Humboldt Park took action to firm up what remained of *La Division*. Between Damen and Western Avenues were Saint Elizabeth Hospital and Roberto Clemente High School—institutional spaces that served as a helpful buffer. But whether gentrification would soon leap those spaces and move farther west was an open question, as "speculators, developers, and artists [had] purchased and rehabilitated nearly 50 . . . buildings" west of Western Avenue by the mid-1990s.[33] In 1995, two massive steel cutouts of the Puerto Rican flag were erected across Division Street, one at Western Avenue and the other at Mozart Street, thereby marking the neighborhood as a Puerto Rican space.[34]

The half-mile section of Division between the flags was officially dubbed *Paseo Boriqua* (Puerto Rican Promenade), imparting to the space a sense of community permanence that contrasted with the more informal *La Division*.[35] With local Puerto Rican business owners supporting the maneuver as symbols of the hoped-for development of a commodified "Little Puerto Rico" restaurant district along Division (an aspect that helped secure the city government's support for the project), the flags were at once branding and brandishing Humboldt Park's ethno-racial identity.[36]

The flags represented competing conceptions of Humboldt Park's twenty-first-century future: whether it would become a commodified tourist destination or remain a legitimate home to, not merely a symbol of, the city's Puerto Rican community.[37] Many local leaders and longtime residents sought to defend what remained of the Chicago barrio and were therefore on alert to signs that downtown's growth machine had its sights set on the community. Most relevant here were the improvements made by the Chicago Park District to Humboldt Park in the 1990s, which included the long-requested restoration of the park's lagoon, beach, boathouse, and fieldhouse.[38] That such changes coincided with initial signs of gentrification raised suspicions that the city government was hoping to aid in the movement of Whites across Western Avenue.

The redevelopment of the Bloomingdale Line, particularly as the park-building process unfolded, was interpreted by some Puerto Rican residents as evidence of planned displacement: another green improvement intended not for them, but for incoming Whites.[39] If that's what the Bloomingdale Trail/606 came to represent for many locals, it belies the fact that initial supporters of the park project included some of the Latino community's strongest and most populist institutions: the Puerto Rican Cultural Center and the Logan Square Neighborhood Association. Indeed, two of the seven cofounders of the Friends of the Bloomingdale Trail were in leadership positions at those organizations, suggesting that the Friends of the Bloomingdale Trail resembled something close to an inter-neighborhood and interracial partnership at its founding in 2003.

But eighteen years later, the Bloomingdale Trail/606 is arguably the biggest harbinger of the displacement of Latinos from Humboldt Park and Logan Square. While those pressures were in place for reasons well beyond the creation of the park, just as

New York's High Line turned an upper-middle-class neighborhood into a runway for the 1 percent, the Bloomingdale Trail/606 has hastened the upscaling of longtime working-class communities. How did this happen?

. . .

The Friends of the Bloomingdale Trail were undoubtedly central to the construction of the park. Unlike the Friends of the High Line, which spent just two years in the wilderness of an unfriendly mayoral administration before Bloomberg saw the light, the Friends of the Bloomingdale Trail needed to wait four times as long before a sympathetic figure took the keys to City Hall. In that eight-year interim, the Friends of the Bloomingdale Trail raised funds and established a broad base of community support in the neighborhoods surrounding the railway, but most of all, they kept the idea of redevelopment in the public consciousness and in the city's planning conversations.

This was a necessary accomplishment; Mayor Daley had done little more than express milquetoast support for the park project, and if it was to come to fruition, someone else would have to do the work. The Friends of the Bloomingdale Trail was a modestly connected group in comparison to the High Line's early supporters. The seven cofounders—Darren Beck, Josh Deth, Raul Echeverria, Lucy Gomez, Ben Helphand, Tim Lane, and Paul Smith—included a public-space advocate, two craft-beer makers, and two administrators from community organizations, collectively representing both the gentrified areas (Wicker Park and Bucktown) and the still firmly Puerto Rican neighborhoods (Humboldt Park and Logan Square).[40] Tied into more modest circuits of cultural and economic capital than the Friends of the High Line, the group was typical of the community organizations that have formed around the United States in the era of neoliberal park development, which in a time of public-sector retrenchment have relied on volunteers and small-scale philanthropy to beautify parks and conserve local environments.[41]

The Friends of the Bloomingdale Trail's interests were primarily recreational, civic, and cultural—not economic. The group described itself simply as "a grassroots community organization that advocates for the conversion of the Bloomingdale rail embankment into an elevated, multiple use park and trail."[42] Reflexively aware that lack of inclusion vis-à-vis the Latino community could submarine the project, the group's efforts toward interracial and interclass inclusivity presaged the gentrification concerns that would ultimately cause blowback for the Bloomingdale Trail/606 after it opened in 2015. Therefore, the group's organizational structure mandated that its board of directors would "always maintain at least two representatives from each of the four neighborhoods that line the Trail"; further, the group held public meetings and events in Humboldt Park and Logan Square, and many of their community-facing documents were written in both English and Spanish.[43] But inclusive intent may have made little difference, in the end. As the Friends of the Bloomingdale Trail would discover in time, the fate of the park would not rest solely, or even largely, in their hands.

Indeed, to conflate the role of the Friends of the Bloomingdale Trail and the Friends of the High Line would be a mistake. While the groups had similar initial aspirations, the Friends of the High Line was able to access the most important thing— money—while the Friends of the Bloomingdale Trail was unable to seize financial control of the project and ultimately ceded organizational power to the Trust for Public Land, a national conservation group and park builder. The Trust for Public Land, founded in 1972, has become a paragon of neoliberal park development. Though framing its work in classical park terms—around high-minded appeals to the beauty of nature, democratic access, and environmentalist principles—the organization had mastered the art of using financial logics and corporate dollars to put forth businesslike ideas about the form and function of urban parks.[44]

In 2006, with few funds forthcoming from the Daley administration and limited recourse to private fund-raising, the Friends of the Bloomingdale Trail reached out to the Trust for Public Land, which had a national portfolio of park projects in addition to a Chicago field office, where the group had just raised $300,000 to expand Haas Park in Logan Square in 2005.[45] The 2006 partnership with the Trust for Public Land furthered the legitimacy of the Bloomingdale Trail project for Chicago's power brokers. The Trust for Public Land used its networks and experience to institutionalize the project's outreach and fund-raising while permitting the Friends of the Bloomingdale Trail to remain a public face. This partnership more or less morphed the grassroots group into an organizational figurehead: visible but not especially powerful.

Much of the benefit of the partnership came through the critical task of land acquisition. Unlike the High Line, whose access points were created via stairways and elevators to public sidewalks below—and therefore did not require the purchasing of adjacent plots—the architectural plan for the Bloomingdale Trail called for it to be lined by a series of pocket parks. Without them, it was difficult to see the rails-to-trails project as genuinely improving green-space provision in a park-starved section of Chicago. Further, given plans to allow bikes and the reality that the thick, earthen structure required wider access points (something like the High Line's cutout stairways would have been unfeasible from an engineering standpoint), acquiring adjacent land was also central to the trail's intended functionality. The Trust for Public Land's comparatively deeper pockets allowed this process to be realized, albeit in a piecemeal fashion. For example, in 2003, the Friends of the Bloomingdale Trail had targeted vacant lots abutting the railway at 1800–1808 North Whipple and 1805–1807 North Albany as possible access points near the western end of the park and held cleanup efforts to signal the viability of the project and build community support.[46] But these plots remained unacquired by the city government—a problem, given advancing gentrification in the area—until the Trust for Public Land intervened in 2006, purchasing several of the lots for later transfer to the city government. But evidencing the dynamic nature of a sprawling, linear park and the logistical difficulties of purchasing and linking a series of disconnected pieces of land, all while gentrification continued to churn around the railway, one of the lots in question, 1808 North Whipple, was not purchased for inclusion in the project until July 2015, at a price of $260,000.[47]

After the 2006 partnership, governmental actors started to pursue the Bloomingdale Trail project more seriously, with the Chicago Park District committing $2 million in late 2007 as part of the 2008–2012 Capital Improvement Plan.[48] Some local property owners donated vacant parcels adjacent to the railway, and modest private donations also started to accumulate: a March 2007 check from the Rails-to-Trails Conservancy for $20,000 was the fledgling project's largest to that point; community fundraising events targeted donations in the $50–100 range.[49] In 2009, the city's Department of Transportation selected an engineering firm to lead the design process.[50] At the end of Richard M. Daley's administration, the Bloomingdale Trail looked like a real priority; with the Trust for Public Land, there was momentum in terms of a private-sector contribution as well. But with a projected cost of over $75 million, and just a few million raised, park advocates were still very far from making the Bloomingdale Trail a reality.

• • •

"People have been talking about [the Bloomingdale Trail] for years. I told them when I ran for office in 2011, I said I'm going to be for it. No more bake sales, man."

—Rahm Emanuel, July 2015[51]

Richard M. Daley's 2010 decision not to seek reelection after his sixth term opened the door for a new chief power broker—a position that, history suggested, was difficult to turn over. With no obvious successor waiting in the wings, the 2011 election came down to six candidates: several veterans of Chicago politics and one, Rahm Emanuel, whose political experience was primarily at the national level, most recently as chief of staff to another Chicagoan, Barack Obama. With this link to the popular president, Emanuel was well positioned to thread the electoral needle in racially fragmented (but overwhelmingly Democratic) Chicago. Indeed, he carried North Side Whites and downtown elites along with the Black South and West Sides en route to 55 percent of the overall vote.[52]

Campaigning on three primary issues—"safe streets, stable finances and stronger schools"—and backed financially by Chicagoland elites from real estate, banking, and other white-collar industries, once in office Emanuel's priorities turned to enhancing the city's global economic imprint. Taking a similar path to that of his predecessor, Emanuel embarked on an ambitious neoliberal program of attracting outside investment to the Loop, targeting gentrifying areas for redevelopment, and bolstering the city's cultural industries, all while seeking to cut city pensions, close underperforming schools, and implement other austerity reforms.[53]

One of Emanuel's favored buzzwords during his campaign was "world-class": he was deeply invested in getting Chicago the kind of international respect more often afforded to the nation's coastal cities.[54] By the time Emanuel took office in May 2011, not only was the notion of building cities for the "creative class" a truism of twenty-first-century urban governance, but the High Line's opening two years earlier showed that public spaces in general, and elevated linear parks in particular, could be economically generative. Given Emanuel's constituency of "lakefront neoliberals" and his pro-business, pro-branding ideological bent, he quickly targeted the Bloomingdale Trail as a project that could simultaneously achieve cultural, economic, and demographic goals.[55]

Just twenty-three days after Emanuel took office, a press release from the Department of Transportation announced, "Mayor Rahm Emanuel has identified the Bloomingdale Trail as a priority to reach his goals of creating a world-class bike network, improving the pedestrian environment and creating new open space."[56] The vision that Emanuel held for the Bloomingdale Trail more closely resembled the glitz of the High Line and Millennium Park than the Friends of the Bloomingdale Trail's original modest hopes. Indeed, as the project quickly sped up during his first term in office, it was branded as "a backyard-version of Millennium Park."[57] Under Emanuel, the city government assembled key logistical and fund-raising accomplishments for the park between 2011 and 2013. These included purchasing the rail from Canadian Pacific Railway for $1; obtaining $7 million combined from Chicago-based corporations CNA, Boeing, and Exelon; and putting "naming rights" to the viaduct's thirty-six bridges up for sale (prices ranged from $1 million to $5 million).[58]

Emanuel's most important maneuver was acquiring $50 million of the necessary $75 million from the federal Department of Transportation's Congestion Mitigation and Air Quality (CMAQ) Improvement Program.[59] The Bloomingdale Trail had previously appeared on the Chicago Metropolitan Agency for Planning's list of CMAQ projects for 2007 and 2008, but only in the amount of $2.6 million.[60] In an era when public dollars for urban parks were difficult to find, Emanuel defined the same project his administration touted as "the High Line on steroids" as a humble transit project in order to access funds earmarked for bike lanes and the like.[61]

Ultimately, with Emanuel at the helm, the park developers were able to raise the $75 million needed to open the park ($95 million is the eventual expected total for the acquisition of all street-level access parks): $5 million from the local government, $20 million in private funds, and the crucial $50 million from the federal government.[62] For a city government that was becoming cash strapped in the aftermath of the Richard M. Daley administration, this amounted to no small coup—building an iconic rail park, one that might compete with the High Line for acclaim and tourism, with just five million in city dollars.

The arrival of these funds allowed the architectural and engineering workers to ramp up construction early in Emanuel's term. With the mayor's maneuvering came the solidification of his control over the project. Emanuel had a real sense of urgency to see the park opened. Though he swept into office riding a wave of Obama-inflected jubilee, Chicagoans were quickly disabused of the notion that Rahm was a fellow homegrown savant. With an increasingly rocky first term, including battles with the city's teachers' union and scandals involving police violence (heightened by the murder of Laquan McDonald by city police in October 2014 and the subsequent cover-up by Emanuel and city officials), Emanuel came to see a shining new linear park—a fully completed one—as important for his reelection hopes in 2015.

In June 2013, the park development process was fully merged with Emanuel's branding vision and political desire for expediency. Together with the Trust for Public Land, Emanuel unveiled the park's new name. Beth White, Chicago director of the Trust for Public Land, suggested, "As the plans for this project took shape, we realized we were building something much bigger than the Bloomingdale Trail, something that needed a bigger name to reflect the full scope of the project."[63] That name, "the 606," with its reference to all Chicago postal codes, would "draw an immediate connection between the system and the neighborhoods it serves," argued Emanuel.[64] Concocted in consultation with an advertising agency and a design firm, the name change was a clear indicator of the growth machine's vision for the space: not merely the "neighborhood connector" listed in the 1998 Logan Square Open Space plan or the "rail trail" dreamt up by the Friends of the Bloomingdale Trail, Emanuel and his private-sector allies saw the 606 as an iconic space for tourism and economic growth—a new spectacle that would once again announce Chicago's place on the global stage.

This renaming was not met with kindness by the Friends of the Bloomingdale Trail's grassroots supporters. At the public meeting where the city government and the Trust for Public Land unveiled "the 606," which had not been previously shared with the park's design team or neighborhood stakeholders, the name was lustily booed.[65] Echoing the feelings of many of the park's supporters, who saw the Bloomingdale Trail as a local community space rather than a "backyard Millennium Park," Frances Whitehead, one of the park's designers, described the new name as "this abstraction, this cipher, named after what, the Post Office, a dying institution? You're going to name this new $100 million amenity after a dying institution?"[66]

Emanuel's central and growing role in shaping both the space and the identity of the Bloomingdale Trail/606 was also felt, again negatively, by community members who believed that compromises were made in order to finish the park in time for the mayor's reelection campaign. The Bloomingdale Trail, unlike the High Line, was first and foremost an engineering project—and a massive one at that. Speeding up the construction of the park was no mere question of planting a few trees: it involved cutting through the structure's thick concrete basin, building seventeen entry ramps, and shoring up the integrity of the railway's thirty-six bridges and three miles of retaining walls. With Emanuel's political fortunes riding in part on the unveiling of the new park, aspects were compromised: the city government scrapped some of the planned architectural flourishes, along with a sustainability study and pursuit of LEED (Leadership in Energy and Environmental Design) certification. The result, as Whitehead recalled, was that "a five-year project happened in three years."[67]

Whether the impending opening of the Bloomingdale Trail/606 won Emanuel votes or not, in April 2015 he edged out progressive Democrat Jesus "Chuy" Garcia, 55–45, in a runoff election. Two months later, on June 6 (or 6/06), the Bloomingdale Trail/606 was opened to the public. Flanked by reporters, a triumphant Emanuel led a bike parade down the trail and greeted fellow parkgoers.[68] Gesturing toward the park's civic benefits, the mayor noted, "It is essential that all Chicagoans have access to world-class parks and open spaces—including playgrounds for children, gathering places for families, and alternative transportation routes for bicyclists and pedestrians. . . . The Bloomingdale Trail is a major, exciting project that will improve quality of life for many of our residents."[69] Now, whether a three-mile linear park would deliver such widely distributed benefits was doubtful; much in the way that the 606 brand, to critics, falsely suggested a citywide benefit, Emanuel's inclusive rhetoric was misleading. More than likely, the Bloomingdale Trail/606 was positioned to offer neither the tourist spectacle of the High Line nor the populism of Chicago's Lake Michigan beaches. Its benefits were most assuredly local: it would give property values a boost and offer an elevated bikeway for nearby residents.

Despite Emanuel's "world-class" expectations, initial reviews were mixed. Gentrification concerns, which had been bubbling throughout the redevelopment process, cast a long shadow over the park's opening, with one critic wondering if it was "a path to displacement."[70] On the park's design, architectural critic Edward Keegan asked bluntly, "Is that all there is?"—but conceded that the design's simplicity "should ultimately become one of its great strengths. It doesn't suggest that capital 'D' design will solve all our city's problems."[71] Again noting the new park's modesty, Blair Kamin of the *Tribune* appreciatively painted a pastoral scene: "What isn't on The 606, it turns out, matters as much as what is there. No blaring, piped-in music, as at Navy Pier. No shops. No ads. No revving of truck engines or honking horns. You can hear birds chirping, the wind rustling through the trees and the hum of factories along the trail."[72] Drawing the inevitable comparison to the High Line, Kamin argued, in contrast to New York's park, "The 606 is down-to-earth, not otherworldly; modestly designed, not virtuosic; primarily aimed at locals, not tourists."[73]

Such critiques spoke to the tension at the heart of the Bloomingdale Trail/606: the tourist-friendly, corporate-branded vision of Emanuel and other downtown interests versus the community space imagined by the Friends of the Bloomingdale Trail and their local allies. While both perspectives, in an age of "green gentrification," might have led to a similar outcome—one that privileged particular kinds of park users and park uses—it was Emanuel's involvement that not only allowed the park to be built, but magnified its symbolic value in hopes of generating economic growth. In an area of the city with rising property values, the Bloomingdale Trail/606 presented Chicago's growth machine with an opportunity to further cash in. While the mayor's political support and ability to access federal funds allowed the initial community vision for a rail trail to be realized, in the process the park was branded with sky-high expectations and flooded with outside funds and ulterior interests. As a representative from the Trust for Public Land flatly commented in response to the growing concerns about the displacement of the Latino community from the western portion of the trail, "We are not in the business of housing."[74] Such a sentiment evinces the top-down vision for the park: the goal was to create a space with high symbolic value; it would necessarily be dressed in the guise of aiding the "community," as most all urban parks are, but who that community would be was up to the fluctuating fortunes of the local housing market.

While initial architectural reviews suggested that perhaps Emanuel's hopes for a "backyard Millennium Park" had fallen flat, the Bloomingdale Trail/606 can still be a foundational piece in the Near Northwest Side's new symbolic economy.[75] The Bloomingdale Trail was never going to be the High Line, despite Emanuel's efforts to bend the site to his will. With less than half the budget of the High Line, with the viaduct's narrower passageway limiting the design possibilities, and with the site offering nondescript vistas of a low-rise cityscape rather than monumental views of the Empire State Building and the Hudson River, the same degree of spectacle was simply not possible. Nor was the Art Institute going to relocate to the new park's knee. But in a city whose identity is tied more to grit than to glamour, such modesty might, in the longer run, better serve the purveyors of Chicago's particular urban "brand."

Regardless of one's interpretation of the Bloomingdale Trail/606—as a harbinger of displacement, as an architectural disappointment, as just the right fit for the Near Northwest Side, or perhaps as all three—it was undeniably an achievement of another sort. In the aftermath of the High Line's runaway success in 2009, boosters in many cities were drawing up plans for "their" High Lines. Park advocates in Chicago, by virtue of having the necessary disused railway in a valuable part of the city and having had reuse plans on the table since 1998, were among the first to actualize one. Given persistent intercity competition in the United States, for those keeping score of such things, that counted for something. While it might not have met Rahm Emanuel's grandiose expectations, the park was enough of a success for the project's director on the Trust for Public Land side, Beth White, to move to Houston, where another group of park advocates was moving forward with another linear park project.

5

"A PIECE OF CRUD"

NOT every city has the rail infrastructure of New York or Chicago. In the absence of rails, city boosters seeking their own version of the High Line must get creative in the search for an underutilized public space that can be transformed into a linear park. Indeed, in a Sunbelt city like Houston, where roads have been the dominant mode of transit, elevated rails are rare.

Houston didn't have the same density of rails, but it did have bayous: 2,500 miles of them within city limits. Its challengers for Texan cultural supremacy, Austin and San Antonio, both had waterfront walks—the parks along Lady Bird Lake and the Riverwalk, respectively. While these public spaces had their supporters, and more than a few tourists, they weren't exactly in the High Line's tier: they weren't the sort of spaces that screamed "global city!" In Houston, a city that had risen with minimal outside fanfare to become the nation's fourth largest by 1990, making statements about its economic and cultural power mattered to the local growth machine. Efforts to drive the city's high-culture reputation can be seen in the establishment of downtown theater spaces in the late 1960s, the Rothko Chapel in 1971, the Menil Collection in 1987, and the branding of the "Museum District" in 1989.

Despite such efforts, however, compared to other large American cities, Houston's boosters were well behind in mobilizing cultural resources in the 1980s and '90s.[1] Part of the problem was the city's own history: with oil profits, Jim Crow, and rapacious real estate development standing as the foremost historical priorities, Houston lacked not only the older cultural institutions of New York and Chicago, where major art museums and the like had been founded upwards of a century earlier, but the legacy of large, picturesque public parks that were a hallmark of nineteenth-century urbanism. In Houston, where the dominant green spaces are private lawns, where leisure activities are often air-conditioned, and where pedestrian street life is minimal, parks are less vital to the public culture of the city.

Houston's largest park is Memorial Park, a 1,500-acre public space (nearly double the size of New York's Central Park) on the West Side. The site was originally home to Camp Logan, a venue that also served as the flashpoint of a race riot in 1917.[2] Sold to the city government by the Hogg family in 1924 after the camp closed following the end of World War I, Memorial Park was carved into functional recreational spaces, including a WPA-financed golf course, an exercise trail built in 1978, and the Houston Arboretum.[3] The park was also nearly approved for a drilling operation by Brownco, the oil company headed by George R. Brown, in 1976.[4] The city's other large open space within the "inner loop" (defined by locals as the circumference of Interstate 610) is Hermann Park, a 445-acre site donated to the city in 1914 that has been underdeveloped since its beginnings. It was conceived as a picturesque-style park with water features that would link to nearby Brays Bayou, but the plans were never fully actualized as a result of changing municipal priorities.[5] Rather than a Central Park for Houston, Hermann Park became a container for statues, parking lots, and a golf course. Located adjacent to

Rice University and the Texas Medical Center, more than one hundred acres of the park's onetime footprint had actually been eliminated by new streets, new hospitals, and the Baylor College of Medicine.[6]

Large parks in Houston have never been the pleasure grounds dreamed up by landscape architects like Frederick Law Olmsted. While even Olmsted's prized creations have witnessed the intrusion of buildings, through streets, and other interlopers that ran counter to the original plans, Houston's landscape-architectural achievements were limited, so encroachments on park spaces and modernist revisions to park purposes were not treading upon widely beloved or venerated spaces. Memorial Park and Hermann Park, then, had all of the familiar post–World War II "improvements" found in New York's Central Park or Chicago's Jackson Park, but little of their preserved antecedents—neither the undulating pastoral fields nor the picturesque nooks and crannies.[7]

Houston had smaller parks, too; the city's original parks master plan, devised by Bostonian Arthur Comey in 1913, called for an even distribution of parks across the city's existing and presumed future footprint. For Comey, Houston was already "far behind" in parks planning in 1913 compared to other U.S. cities, but he hoped that because much of Houston's environs had not yet been developed, it was "possible at the start to adopt a plan adequately meeting future requirements."[8] Based on 1910 data, Houston, with just 115 acres of parkland (much of which had only been acquired, not developed) had 685 people per park acre; this compared unfavorably with similarly sized (at the time) cities like Oklahoma City and Hartford, which had populations per park acre of 36 and 73, respectively.[9] The parks that did exist in old Houston included Sam Houston Park, located downtown, and Cleveland Park, located two miles west along Buffalo Bayou (the region's central waterway, which led to the Gulf of Mexico).

Emancipation Park, a four-acre space in the Black Third Ward, was initially the only park accessible to Houston's Black population; ultimately, only three additional "Black" parks would be opened before the end of Jim Crow in the 1950s.[10]

Houston's leaders did not share Comey's foresight that the small but rapidly growing city should plan for park development in anticipation of future expansion. Many of the parks he called for, including a system of "continuous bayou parks," were never built.[11] Nor did the city government engage in serious park building in subsequent decades, when first WPA and then urban-renewal funds enabled the ambitious expansion of parks systems in many cities, notably New York, Chicago, Minneapolis, and Cincinnati.[12] Given that Houston's leaders were focused on building and annexing a suburbanizing metropolis, and particularly since the power elite's anti-federal-government posture led to comparatively little use of such funds for anything besides highways and flood control, adding green spaces to the core of the city was low on the civic agenda. As a consequence, the parks landscape in the core of Houston was largely unchanged between the 1920s and the 1980s.[13]

• • •

While Houston's parks were neglected for much of the twentieth century, a different form of environmental planning was taking place. Flood control became one of the city's primary urban-planning tools, given the city's precarious ecology—a situation that grew more hazardous over time as urbanization created more impervious surfaces.[14] In addition to the creation of the Addicks and Barker reservoirs to prevent downtown flooding, such efforts meant the concretization and channelization (straightening riverbanks to increase draining speed) of many of the city's bayous.

By 1950, the Army Corps of Engineers and the Harris County Flood Control District had already channelized 1,260 miles of local waterways.[15] While this policy's efficacy as flood control was debatable, the aesthetic transformation it made to the city's ecosystem was less so. The green sites Comey had envisioned as recreational amenities were reconceptualized as gray infrastructures. In many cases, not only were bayous concretized, but highways were often built to parallel the waterways, a decision that seemingly foreclosed future recreational transformation. Such highways included Interstate 10 along White Oak Bayou, Interstate 610 along Hunting Bayou, and two parkways, Memorial Drive and Allen Parkway, that boxed in Buffalo Bayou as it ran between downtown and the West Side.[16]

In the late 1960s, local governmental entities (the Harris County Commissioners Court and the Harris County Flood Control District), joined again by the Army Corps of Engineers, were expanding their flood-control plans in response to urban growth. One location targeted by these plans was a stretch of Buffalo Bayou on the West Side, just outside of the 610 beltway, in an area into which middle-class Whites had moved en masse in the 1950s and '60s: the Memorial Villages, a collection of several newly built residential communities that would ultimately avoid being annexed by Houston despite their location, just nine miles from downtown and well inside Houston's eventual western boundary.[17] Local residents learned only after construction was under way that the Flood Control District was concretizing and channelizing the path of Buffalo Bayou.[18] The project was a logical extension of the channelization that had been completed in the 1950s in the stretch of the bayou just to the east, between Shepherd Drive and downtown.[19] Led by Terry Hershey, a nearby resident who would emerge as one of Houston's foremost conservationists, along with other locals including then-Congressman

George H.W. Bush and oilman George Mitchell, the Buffalo Bayou Preservation Association thwarted the plans, leaving a large stretch of the bayou in its natural state.[20]

This successful preservationist movement announced that Buffalo Bayou was no longer simply a body of water to be manipulated for purposes of flood control and commercial shipping, that the bayou might actually be an aesthetic amenity (or this particular stretch of it, at least—east of downtown, it became the heavily industrialized Houston Ship Channel). In the years following the victory of the Buffalo Bayou Preservation Association, the first trails around the bayou were built with funds from 8F member Gus Wortham, and in 1977 architect Charles Tapley created a master plan for a park-centered redevelopment of the Buffalo Bayou area.[21] By 1986, Mayor Kathy Whitmire founded the Buffalo Bayou Partnership. This private nonprofit successor to the original preservation group was granted official oversight of the section of the bayou between Shepherd Drive and the Port of Houston turning basin, nine miles to the east.[22]

With preservation achieved in the late 1960s, and with official plans by the late 1970s to use the downtown section of Buffalo Bayou for recreational purposes, why did Houston require four more decades before opening Buffalo Bayou Park in 2015? In those intervening years, much of the land that would become Buffalo Bayou Park was an underdeveloped green space: a park called Buffalo Bayou Park, but one that was not particularly inviting—so much so that it was home to an annual canoe race called the Reeking Regatta.[23] The 2015 redevelopment reflected the first time that major resources went into the park. Like Chicago's Bloomingdale Trail/606, plans for Buffalo Bayou Park centered on a linear walkway that would connect a series of surface parks and public spaces. When Tapley's master plan was first actualized in the 1980s, initial planning efforts focused not on the trail itself, but on a twenty-three-acre park sited at the downtown terminus of the future trail, Sesquicentennial Park, built between 1987 and 1998.[24]

As the first project to enter the broader framework of the Buffalo Bayou redevelopment, Sesquicentennial Park was intended to complement the older generation of downtown cultural spaces built in the late 1960s. These included the Alley Theater, Jones Hall (home to the city's symphony orchestra), and outdoor amphitheater Jones Plaza (the latter two named for 8F godfather Jesse Jones).[25] Sesquicentennial Park also offered a green centerpiece to a broader swell of downtown redevelopment in the 1980s. Although conceived around the time that Houston was entering a five-year recession caused by falling oil prices in 1982, the cultural turn in urban branding led local leaders to promote the area around Sesquicentennial Park as a theater district, highlighted by the 1987 opening of the Gus S. Wortham Theater Center, adjacent to the park.[26] Other nearby development further asserted this section of downtown as an entertainment hub, particularly the redevelopment of the city's former convention center as a dining and entertainment complex called Bayou Place. The related naming of the Lyric Centre, a new office tower, played off of the area's revitalized brand; developers placed David Adickes's thirty-six-foot-tall sculpture of a cellist at the building's front entrance.[27]

Compared to the more nature-centric plan that would be realized along Buffalo Bayou in the 2010s, Sesquicentennial Park embodied the cautious embrace of public spaces by growth coalitions across the United States. Like many of the 1980s wave of tourist-friendly public spaces, such as San Francisco's redeveloped Embarcadero and Baltimore's Harborplace, Sesquicentennial Park invited bodily movement and visual spectacle.[28] The park featured a small hill, brick and stone promenades, and neoclassical architectural flourishes. Built as a public-private partnership, boosters touted the park at its 1987 groundbreaking as a "major waterfront attraction that will bring people to downtown and commemorate Houston's heritage."[29] Such statements belied the fact that the park essentially provided a side yard and aesthetic garnish for the postmodern monumentality of the Wortham Center. With downtown's White population plummeting (the once nearly all-White area was just 29 percent White in 1990), neither the park nor the broader "cultural fix" could remedy the increasing desolation and racial anxieties of downtown Houston; boosters were forced to work diligently to attract the desired clientele by hosting an after-hours concert series and other events throughout the late 1980s and 1990s.[30]

This strategy of bulwarking downtown represented elites' counterreaction to Houston's decentralization (which had been celebrated by city boosters for decades, until the balance of economic power started to tilt away from downtown).[31] By 1990, two other economic centers had been developed within the city, suggesting a more diversified economy (or at least a more geographically fragmented one) as the city awakened from the 1980s oil recession. The first was the Texas Medical Center, a post–World War II creation, which underwent a $1.3 billion expansion led by the $95 million St. Luke's Medical Tower and the $21.5 million Texas A&M University Institute of Biosciences and Technology. In 1990, with downtown vacancy rates at an all-time high, these were the only high-rise buildings under construction anywhere in Houston.[32] In 1999, Skidmore, Owings, and Merrill created a new fifty-year master plan for the medical center, ushering in another building boom—again totaling over $1 billion—with projects including new buildings for MD Anderson, Memorial Hermann, Houston Methodist, and Texas Children's Hospital.[33] By the mid-2000s, fanciful new towers lined Main Street, creating a medical approximation of the Las Vegas strip.[34]

The other economic hub to rise within Houston's city limits was the Uptown business district, located eight miles west of the central city. Like other "edge cities" that grew as White flight accelerated—such as Stamford, Connecticut or Rosemont, Illinois—Uptown prospered as downtown Houston's fortunes were fading; but, unlike other edge cities, this new center was still within city limits.[35] Located near the über-rich enclave of River Oaks along with the wealthy White communities that had avoided annexation—West University Place, Southside Place, Bellaire, and the six Memorial Villages—Uptown was geographically primed to usurp downtown. Spurred by the construction of Interstate 610 along Post Oak Road in 1964, which led to a real estate boom, developer Gerald Hines sought to secure the area's fortunes.[36] In addition to a number of smaller properties, Hines's strikes against downtown came with the 1970 opening of the Galleria shopping mall (expanded in 1976, 1979, 1986, and 2003); the 1982 opening of Post Oak Central, an office complex consisting of three high-rises; and the 1983 opening of the sixty-four-story Transco (now Williams) Tower, a neo–Art Deco monolith.[37] Views from the fifty-first floor's observation deck pointed not east, toward downtown, but west, over the vast expanse of prairie. Other private investment followed, and by 2015 Uptown would grow to become the seventeenth-largest office district in the United States.[38]

This decentralization, coming at the expense of entrenched downtown interests, could not be wholly combated in a city with little in the way of centralized planning. Equally as damaging as the flight of corporate offices to Houston's edge cities was the fact that some of the post-oil-recession recovery proved to be a smoke-and-mirrors economy. The economic elites guiding downtown around the turn of the twenty-first century were led by Ken Lay, founder and chair of Enron, who had become known as "Mr.

Houston" for his business and philanthropic endeavors, including leading the construction of a new downtown baseball stadium, Enron Field.[39] The infamous 2001 collapse of Enron, whose efforts to financialize the oil and gas industry turned out to be a sham, ended with Lay and CEO Jeff Skilling convicted of fraud, conspiracy, and insider trading; but other leaders of downtown's resurrection, including real estate moguls Joe Russo (builder of the Lyric Centre), John Ballis, and Harvin C. Moore, along with banker O. Dean Couch, also saw their runs of power end in prison time.[40] Effectively replacing these once and former power brokers was a group with deep philanthropic pockets and political influence, especially ex-Enron billionaires Rich and Nancy Kinder and John and Laura Arnold, and George Mitchell, the "father of fracking," all with interests in building Houston's global reach.[41]

For this generation of downtown leaders, combating decentralization increasingly took on a cultural complexion, with the revitalization of Buffalo Bayou to be one of several downtown anchors. Another was the creation of Discovery Green, a Millennium Park–style festival space atop longtime parking lots at the eastern end of downtown. Built between 2005 and 2008 at a cost of $125 million, the twelve-acre Discovery Green featured artworks, a restaurant, performance spaces, and other familiar touches of privatized public spaces. Driving Discovery Green was Democratic Mayor Bill White, who spent his tenure working diligently to make downtown Houston an entertainment destination, along with private groups, including the Kinder Foundation and the Brown Foundation. Built with a plan for private management from the very beginning, as the park was to be operated by the Discovery Green Conservancy rather than the local government, the park effectively offered a town square for the George R. Brown Convention Center and the high-end hotels and luxury apartments that quickly lined the perimeter.

• • •

In that context, plans for Buffalo Bayou Park accelerated around 2011, three years after the completion of Discovery Green and two years after the High Line's opening.[42] As a linear park, Buffalo Bayou Park would be a connector; but what was it going to connect to? Extending a public space outward into neighborhoods of uncertain economic stability and cultural desirability required a leap of faith for Houston's boosters. This was particularly true because of past infrastructural investments around Buffalo Bayou. Not only was the bayou cut off from easy pedestrian crossings by Memorial Drive and Allen Parkway—both six-lane parkways that clogged its northern and southern edges (and Memorial Drive offered no crosswalks at grade)—but a massive concrete interchange of Interstate 45 at the would-be park's eastern edge, along with the Historic Oaks of Allen Parkway Village, one of the city's privately managed public-housing complexes, stood as a significant racial-spatial barrier.[43] Further, once in the park, park users would be walking below three six-lane overpasses that crossed the bayou at Shepherd Drive, Waugh Drive, and Montrose Boulevard. By conventional planning wisdom, the site of Buffalo Bayou Park was about as unlikely as any to draw significant pedestrian traffic.[44]

Because the development of Buffalo Bayou Park was clearly tied to elites' desire to "Whiten" downtown and the surrounding neighborhoods, the renewed vision for Buffalo Bayou Park was complicated by the fact that the eastern half of the park would traverse areas that had been solidly non-White for decades. On the southern bank, the old Fourth Ward, historically home to Freedmen's Town after the abolition of slavery, was 63 percent Black and 98 percent non-White in 1990.[45] On the bayou's north side, the eastern edge of the planned park again encountered a neighborhood that was 88 percent residents of color in 1990.[46] By 2010, with gentrification from predominantly White Montrose spilling over and leading to the rebranding of some of the old Fourth Ward as "Midtown," the area on the southeastern side of the planned park had grown from 2 percent White to 28 percent White in the previous twenty years. North of the bayou, it was a similar story as gentrification emerged in the Sixth Ward's Washington Avenue corridor and the White population jumped from 12 percent to 64 percent.[47] Since the neighborhoods near the western end of the planned park—Rice Military, River Oaks, and Montrose—were solidly White and middle to upper class, the racial transformation of the zone between wealthy residential areas and downtown's entertainment district was critical to the acceleration of plans for Buffalo Bayou Park.

In this question of how the park would fit into existing social geographies, Buffalo Bayou Park encountered a similar set of issues as the High Line and the Bloomingdale Trail/606, but in a different political context. This was not a bottom-up process driven by an energized local group; it was a top-down project mobilized by elites committed to building the downtown area, who had already seen, with the High Line's opening in 2009, what a highly touted linear park could accomplish. On a local level, the elite-led creation of Discovery Green, which had spurred more than $1 billion in new development, offered further evidence of urban parks' economic power. Unlike the High Line's redevelopment, there was no contentious divide between competing groups, as there had been during the days of Giuliani and the Chelsea Property Owners. Unlike the Bloomingdale Trail/606, the Buffalo Bayou development did not involve the co-optation of a grassroots movement by political elites. Rather, as with most civic projects in Houston's history, the story involves the mobilization of resources by private elites with the money and influence to dictate the terms of the project, with little in the way of public involvement or sustained opposition.

The official financial tally was that Buffalo Bayou Park, redeveloped primarily between 2011 and 2015, cost $58 million: $30 million from the Kinder Foundation, $23 million more in private donations raised by the Buffalo Bayou Partnership, and $5 million of engineering work completed by the Harris County Flood Control District. (This figure does not include the $81 million over thirty years for ongoing park maintenance to be paid from the city's Tax Increment Reinvestment Zone #3.[48] Other contributions, often obscured in official calculations, include that of the Houston Parks and Recreation Department, which contributed to a pedestrian bridge near Montrose Boulevard, with assistance from Tax Increment Reinvestment Zone #5.[49])

What emerges is a highly privatized public space: a park that received 91 percent of its initial funding from private groups. Few urban parks in the United States have been built with such a dramatic proportion of private investment. While the space is technically owned by the city, the park's construction was guided by the Buffalo Bayou Partnership, a private group, and the Tax Increment Reinvestment Zone funds help offset the costs of a private maintenance and security staff.[50] Although public-private partnerships have been used routinely for financing neoliberal civic projects, this degree of private influence would likely raise more than a few eyebrows in cities where parks and public spaces have figured more centrally in local culture, and where the burden of financing public-private partnerships tends to fall much more heavily on the "public" side of the equation. In Houston, a city that is promoted as an entrepreneurial, free-market metropolis, private funding and control of public spaces is celebrated as a natural continuation of the city's philanthropic history.[51]

Chief among Buffalo Bayou Park's private interests was the Kinder Foundation and its $30 million contribution. Its chairman, Rich Kinder, became Houston's wealthiest person in the early 2000s as cofounder of energy giant Kinder Morgan. Kinder, like earlier generations of boosters before him, was a firm believer in Houston's founding myth as a city that was, in his words, "built on the back of free enterprise."[52] The former Enron president, along with his wife, Nancy, became increasingly involved in philanthropy in the 2000s, guiding the private-sector contribution of Discovery Green (with Nancy acting as chair of the Houston Downtown Park Corporation), contributing $75 million for the Nancy and Rich Kinder Building at the Museum of Fine Arts, Houston (opened 2020), as well as rebranding Rice University's Institute for Urban Research as the Kinder Institute for Urban Research for $15 million in 2010, and, controversially, the city's High School for the Performing and Visual Arts as the Kinder High School for the Performing and Visual Arts in exchange for a $7.5 million donation.[53]

Following the development of Discovery Green, the Kinders set their sights on the Buffalo Bayou project.[54] The project had been unfolding outward from downtown after the creation of Sesquicentennial Park; the next stage was the creation of the Buffalo Bayou Promenade (since renamed the Sabine Promenade) in 2006, which forged a path from Sesquicentennial Park to Sabine Street. A 2002 master plan, developed in concert by the city government, the Harris County government, the Harris County Flood Control District, and the Buffalo Bayou Partnership, set the scope conditions for the eventual 2015 redevelopment. This plan introduced a rebuilt Buffalo Bayou Park—a two-mile stretch between Sabine Street and Shepherd Drive—as the eventual centerpiece of a broader bayou parks plan. As the document described, in 2002 the site of Buffalo Bayou Park was "an underutilized—even undiscovered—recreational resource," whose "waterfront areas lack basic pedestrian amenities—benches, lights, and signs" and with an overall "poor public image."[55]

This new master plan called not only for the full development of recreational green space along the stretch of Buffalo Bayou between downtown and Shepherd Drive, but for an eastward extension through downtown and all the way to the Houston Ship Channel's turning basin. This redevelopment was to be the heart of an even broader project, one that would seemingly realize Arthur Comey's vision: 150 uninterrupted miles of waterfront parks along the city's bayou system. The banner for this ambitious citywide project, eventually termed Bayou Greenways 2020, was to be carried by the Houston Parks Board: though the name suggests a governmental entity, it is, in fact, a private group (one that hired Chicago's Beth White as president and CEO, and reported $68 million in assets to the IRS in 2016).[56] This arrangement was made in 2013, when the Kinders committed a $50 million donation to the Bayou Greenways project with the stipulation that the city council turn over future maintenance and management to the private group.[57]

Realizing this citywide project required momentum. The key to building it would be the successful completion of Buffalo Bayou Park, which would model—at the high end—a revitalized urban waterfront for the rest of Houston. The Buffalo Bayou Partnership was already accustomed to the financial and architectural challenges of the site; led by Anne Olson since 1995—the year it switched from a volunteer group to a professional organization—the group had raised more than $100 million toward bayou-related projects, most notably the Buffalo Bayou Promenade and updates related to Allen's Landing and Sesquicentennial Park.[58] Private funding for and control of Buffalo Bayou Park were also facilitated by an ineffectual Houston Parks and Recreation Department, a city government entity that faced significant budget cuts after 2000. The department's lack of serious inclusion in prominent new projects like Discovery Green and Buffalo Bayou Park was not exactly contested by the parks department. Joe Turner, the department's director from 2004 to 2017, in fact celebrated the privatization of the city's parks: "The combination of public and private dollars has always been a part of our department's philosophy. . . . Partnerships create an 'ownership' feeling that involves individuals in the stewardship and preservation of parkland."[59]

Rich and Nancy Kinder's $30 million contribution to Buffalo Bayou Park, announced in 2011, marked the largest contribution to date to a Houston park project and encouraged other private investment—noteworthy since the Buffalo Bayou Partnership was only a few years removed from raising $15 million for the Sabine Promenade.[60] Per Anne Olson, Buffalo Bayou Park "was so visible that everyone wanted to be part of it. There was a sense in Houston that green space mattered."[61]

The Kinders' investment, as with their $50 million commitment to the Bayou Greenways project, came with important strings attached. Here the demand was not private management— a fact long secured by the Buffalo Bayou Partnership—but a financing agreement that would keep the public sector responsible for funds through 2043 via a tax increment imposed upon the northwestern half of downtown and any revenues stemming from park spaces themselves.[62] Rich Kinder, not wanting to open up the possibility that a city government of the future might opt for different spending priorities, noted at the park's opening in 2015: "The last thing we wanted is for this to turn out the way it is right now and then three or five years from now it turns into a piece of crud because some future administration says, 'We've got other things to do with our money.'"[63] Tax increment financing, a growing strategy of neoliberal municipal governance, allows city governments to "securitize projected increases in property tax receipts and create bonds similar to structured asset-backed securities (e.g. mortgage-backed securities)" and places budgetary discretion in the hands of unelected economic development officials.[64] In this instance, it was two billionaires' necessary condition for beginning the massive redevelopment of the two-mile stretch of Buffalo Bayou.

Indeed, the project required not only the architectural talents of SWA and Page, the firms hired to design the park, but the Harris County Flood Control District's engineering work. Plans for the grand opening were pushed back several months as a result of major flooding around Memorial Day 2015—evincing rather quickly that the new park had a function, as flood control, that was not shared by the High Line or the Bloomingdale Trail/606.[65] While park backers held that the design withstood the initial test, the flood event pointed toward the difficulty of maintaining a lushly landscaped, tourist-friendly green space in the core of a floodplain—a fact that would be more grimly realized in August 2017, when Hurricane Harvey's one trillion gallons of water devastated the park, causing several million dollars' worth of damage.

Despite questions of the park's financial and physical sustainability, Buffalo Bayou Park has been received as a resounding success since its official reopening in 2015. With the Buffalo Bayou Partnership projecting about one million visitors per year, the park has drawn tourists and locals seeking various forms of active and passive recreation across its 160 acres.[66] Appreciative critics lauded the park not only as an indicator of Houston's newfound embrace of being "fanatically green," but as a worthy culmination of Arthur Comey's original vision.[67] The *Chronicle* declared the site transformed "from weedy to wonderful"; *Houstonia* went so far as to dub it "Houston's Central Park."[68] Rich and Nancy Kinder were named "Houstonians of the Year."[69] In 2017, the Urban Land Institute selected it for one of thirteen Global Awards for Excellence.[70] Meeting boosters' hopes of spiking new development in the vicinity of Buffalo Bayou, the park's warm reception has incentivized the construction of a long-delayed, privately built megaproject, Regent Square, as well as catalyzing newly announced plans by Houston developers DC Partners for a $500 million mixed-use site adjacent to the south side of the park.[71]

The park's primary spaces, an interweaving series of trails at different elevations, provide opportunities for the same kinds of activities that take place at the High Line and the Bloomingdale Trail/606: walking, running, and biking, with the added opportunity for canoeing and other uses of the slow-moving waterway. Accessing these forms of recreation, which are thought to appeal especially to the White "creative class" that Houston's elites hope to lure downtown, is difficult for those not living within walking distance of the park. There is limited street parking near Buffalo Bayou Park, and in car-centric Houston, this restricts access to what has been heralded as a "destination" park for the entire city. Further, lack of pedestrian entryways has proved to be an issue, with limited grade-level access on the north side of the park and, on the south side, a one-mile gap between a pedestrian crosswalk at Montrose Boulevard and an elevated pedestrian bridge—a problem highlighted when three pedestrians were hit by cars on Allen Parkway in a two-day span around the time of the park's opening.[72]

Beyond accessibility issues, it is an open question as to how "public" the public space actually is. Fostering wealthy patrons' "ownership" of public spaces—an act celebrated above by longtime parks chief Joe Turner—is furthered by the use of a private security force, considerable reliance on volunteer labor for park maintenance, and commerce at several park sites, including the Cisterns—an underground former reservoir that is host to art exhibitions ($10 entry), tours ($5), and meditation classes ($7)—as well as the Dunlavy, a trendy restaurant with a high-end event space for weddings and other private rentals, which serves as a regular meeting place for the park's private donors.[73] Many places within the park have been branded, from the Kinder Footpath and the Wortham Foundation Grove to the Scurlock Foundation Overlook and the Kathrine and John P. McGovern Cascade.

While such privatization is a growing phenomenon in cities across the United States—both the High Line and the Bloomingdale Trail/606 involved significant private funds and private control—in Houston, where parks have not historically been a valued civic resource, privatization has unfolded more rapidly. There are several reasons for this. First, there is scant legacy of highly esteemed parks; while contemporary boosters might dispute this, and might proclaim the beauty and prominence of Memorial and Hermann Parks, there is no question that over the years, city leaders have gladly siphoned off park spaces for more economically generative purposes—whether adding acreage to the Texas Medical Center or prospecting for oil. The fact that an older parks master plan dates to 1913—and that it called for a system of bayou parks—allows contemporary boosters to conveniently reclaim this mantle of ecological foresight. But these waterways over the years have served as infrastructural, not recreational, spaces: home to publicly funded engineering projects that enabled Houston's sprawling urban form to take shape across environmentally precarious floodplains. The renewal of these infrastructural spaces, a process that accelerated only after the High Line demonstrated the newfound economic value of linear parks, speaks to the motives that underlie Houston's green reinvention.

Parks privatization in Houston has been facilitated by a comparatively weak public realm. Whereas the Chicago Park District and the New York City Department of Parks and Recreation remain powerful institutions despite recent privatization in their respective cities, the Houston Parks and Recreation Department has been defunded in recent years at the same time that boosters have sought to portray a new green image for Houston. Public oversight of public spaces is therefore easily obviated.

The irony of boosters' celebration of the private sector's benevolence—in the words of Rich Kinder, its willingness and ability to do what "the public will not or cannot put the money up for"—is that the city government could have easily paid for Buffalo Bayou Park without any of these philanthropists.[74] Between 2005 and 2017, public funds for parks were consistently reduced in real dollars. If the Houston Parks and Recreation Department's funding had been maintained at 2005 levels (when the budget was $98.6 million in 2017 dollars) through 2017 (when the budget was $85.3 million), the city would have spent an additional $174 million on parks over that twelve-year period—an amount that would have paid for Buffalo Bayou Park three times over, with $20 million to spare.[75] This retrenchment thus creates the political space where private elites' rescue of park projects presents to the public as the only viable option.

6

PARKS FOR PROFIT
OR FOR PEOPLE?

COLLECTIVELY, the High Line, the Bloomingdale Trail/606, and Buffalo Bayou Park represent a transformation in park form, financing, and purpose. These multimillion-dollar linear parks, built with varying levels of public and private funds, have created a compelling model for urban boosters elsewhere who are hoping to join the current parks renaissance. Indeed, while the High Line's initial economic impact seemed singular a decade ago, the Bloomingdale Trail/606 and Buffalo Bayou Park have demonstrated that architecturally interesting linear parks do not need to be located in the epicenter of global capitalism to raise property values and attract visitors. To hear boosters and visitors tell it, these parks are brilliant contributions to the social conditions of contemporary cities. On the surface, that seems hard to dispute: even critics must admit that the parks have an undeniable appeal, offering needed public spaces and unique vantage points on urban landscapes.

In one sense, there is nothing new about the elite-led production of urban public space: the grand picturesque parks of the nineteenth century were also built with wealthy White visitors in mind, and corresponding hopes for real estate gains and cultural prestige.[1] While park reforms associated with the Progressive movement and the New Deal offered a more populist vision, the decades leading up to the creation of the High Line, the Bloomingdale Trail/606, and Buffalo Bayou Park witnessed the creeping privatization of urban parks: first, with groups like the Central Park Conservancy assuming stewardship of prestigious parks in response to public-sector retrenchment, and later, with business improvement districts using parks as profit centers.[2]

The High Line, the Bloomingdale Trail/606, and Buffalo Bayou Park remain embedded in an unequal parks landscape in the twenty-first century. The ongoing retrenchment of public parks funding actively harms poorer communities, where local private resources cannot offset such defunding. The other side of retrenchment, privatization, thus directs resources to parks in wealthy neighborhoods and parks with tourist appeal. These inequalities are further clarified when we consider that at the same time that many public park districts fade into the background, public funds still underwrite these elite linear parks. The High Line received $144 million in public money for construction; the Bloomingdale Trail/606, $55 million; and Buffalo Bayou Park, $5 million—not including that some version of "the public," via tax increment financing, will be responsible for approximately $81 million over the next thirty years.

Private management rules the day at both the High Line and Buffalo Bayou Park (the Bloomingdale Trail/606 is under the purview of the Chicago Park District). Given the tourist orientation of these parks, it is probable that few visitors care or even know about the private control. Visitors who are able-bodied, middle class, and White are not likely to find their spatial practices impeded by private security or surveillance. But what about those who don't fit these privileged categories? While the very location of these three parks within gentrifying social geographies raises questions about how broadly accessible they are, more concretely the discretionary powers granted to private management allow the Friends of the High Line and the Buffalo Bayou Partnership to decide on park rules—rules that can and do differ from those of city-run parks.[3] With scrutiny toward the kind of "quality of life" violations that infamously cleansed urban public spaces of homeless people in earlier decades, the gaze of private security falls more heavily and more frequently on people of color and poor people who visit these spaces.[4] (Evincing the revanchist turnaround of these three spaces, those are indeed the kind of folks who used to inhabit the disused railways and under-developed bayou banks).[5] Again, while the racialized policing of public spaces is nothing new, consider that at the height of Jim Crow in Chicago, when Black parkgoers were routinely harassed and attacked for using "White" parks, there were political mechanisms of redress: groups like the Urban League and the Chicago Commission on Human Relations could take abuses to the Park District and other governmental authorities, and sometimes did find justice.[6] Do such channels exist in the twenty-first century? Can outsourced private security firms, like Citadel Security (the High Line) and U.S. Security Associates (Buffalo Bayou Park), be scrutinized or challenged in the same way?

While criticism of the unequal impacts of these parks has emerged, the elites who build them are unperturbed. On one front, city boosters have moved forward with proposed improvements to parks in communities of color. In Chicago, this has taken the form of developing similar parks in Pilsen (El Paseo) and the Far South Side (Big Marsh) in an effort to make park building appear equitable. In New York, organizers have initiated plans for Queens's answer to the High Line, QueensWay, a project billed as "a gateway and introduction to New York City's most diverse communities."[7] In Houston, the Kinder Foundation gave $3 million to the Emancipation Park Conservancy, private keepers of a local symbol of Black freedom.[8]

On the other front, political leaders and private elites plow forward with plans for new or revamped high-end parks. In Houston, where private influence seems to hold the most sway, philanthropists like the Kinders have only been emboldened by the apparent success of their creations: since the opening of Buffalo Bayou Park, Rich and Nancy Kinder have granted $70 million to the Memorial Park Conservancy.[9] Plans for another linear park, this one atop a soon-to-be disused elevated freeway, may be the lubricant for a World Cup hosting bid.[10] In New York, billionaire High Line donor Barry Diller has taken a similar tack, battling various opponents to develop a $250 million privately managed park, Little Island—aka Diller Island—in the Hudson River.[11] All of this suggests that, in the neoliberal park era, there is no shortage of eager elites wishing to shape public spaces in their own image. It also suggests that there are few modes to contest rampant privatization.

Or, it suggests that people feel no reason to oppose these parks. And therein lies the genius of the contemporary power elite's newfound love affair with parks: spending millions on green spaces offers many benefits to the billionaire ego—flattering media coverage, naming rights to a favorite park bench or meadow, and a public perception of benevolence—while offering an opportunity to forcefully reshape contemporary cities. It recalls the political strategies honed by twentieth-century master planner Robert Moses, who knew that rallying the public to support his park projects was easy, given all of the social goods that they represented (never mind that his were usually connected to highways and other disruptive infrastructural projects). For Moses, "parks symbolized something good, and therefore anyone who fought for parks fought under the shield of the presumption that he was fighting for the right—and anyone who opposed him, for the wrong."[12] Park symbols remain a powerful means of suppressing dissent.

III

GARDENS IN THE MACHINE

7

DEFECTIVE LANDSCAPES

A T the same time that Rich Kinder was pouring $150 million into Houston's parks, his company, Kinder Morgan, was on the cusp of drilling a $7.4 billion pipeline through Alberta and British Columbia.[1] The pipeline, scheduled to open in 2020, would pump 890,000 barrels of crude oil per day from the Tar Sands oil fields, through Native lands, and out to the Vancouver metro area for global export. That the same person could be backing the revival of nature in one context, while profiting from its destruction in another, speaks to the dissonance at the heart of social constructions of nature. What makes one site—the banks of Buffalo Bayou—worthy of beautification, and another site—the plains and mountains of western Canada—worthy of extraction?

"Nature" and its referents are new buzzwords for Kinder and urban boosters across the world.[2] For one, the present and future realities of climate change mean that urban engagements with nature have become existential: to survive sea level rise and other effects of global warming, people must learn to live with nature, not triumph over it as in the past. Part of living with nature in contemporary cities means to bring nature *back into* cities. This is widely seen as a good thing: the revival of green spaces as important parts of urban life.

What's new about the High Line, the Bloomingdale Trail/606, and Buffalo Bayou Park is not only their private influence and economic power. What makes these parks different from the parks that came before them, and also different from other newly built, heavily commercialized public spaces, is their strange aesthetic mix: an imbrication of built and natural environments, combining industrial spaces—railways, highways, and outmoded buildings—with apparently wild nature.

Postindustrial parks break the historical rules of landscape architecture and diverge from traditional park forms, thereby calling into question older ontologies of cities and nature. Historically, planners sought to separate spaces considered "urban" from spaces considered "nature." The visual unity of green and gray forms in these new parks suggests a changed relationship: one of hybridity. And despite their aesthetic novelty, the High Line, the Bloomingdale Trail/606, and Buffalo Bayou Park remain a continuation of parks' long-standing ideological purposes—specifically, the use of nature as a benign guise to soften master plans and control social space.

Revisiting the New York, Chicago, and Houston cases, this section examines the forms of nature, conceptions of urban space, and cultural power embodied in these three parks. Imbricated spaces, while initially products of disinvestment and depopulation, have become culturally valuable as urban boosters envision them as important aesthetic components of postindustrial cities and have made them accessible and appealing to wide audiences through parks like the High Line, the Bloomingdale Trail/606, and Buffalo Bayou Park. While at the same time, postindustrial parks are connected to what parks have always been about: cultural power and social control.[3]

• • •

When Frederick Law Olmsted, the preeminent American land-scape architect, visited the Chicago site that he would transform into South Park in the late nineteenth century, he condescended that "The first obvious defect of the site is that of its flatness."[4] As a fellow Yankee, I had to agree with Olmsted's lament when I arrived in the city for the first time in 2012. My biases about nature were well honed by the time I reached the Midwestern prairie. As a fledgling urban sociologist, I moved to Chicago with a picture of the city in my head, as it had been the site of many influential studies. But I did not anticipate the flatness.

Olmsted, though, had an altogether different task; no mere flaneur, he was hired by the South Park Commission to reshape one thousand acres of marshy prairie according to the dominant style of the time: "the picturesque." The picturesque, which linked painting, philosophy, literature, and landscape architecture, had been developed in England beginning in the late 1700s.[5] Popu-larized in the United States in the 1840s and institutionalized by early urban parks like Olmsted and Vaux's Central Park in the 1850s, the picturesque was a very particular, idealized vision of nature and of natural landscapes. It emphasized rough edges: uneven, rocky terrain, meandering rivers and waterfalls, elevation changes, and other broken, weathered representations of nature's forces. The picturesque had other implications, too: in the context of urban growth, it constructed the countryside as under threat. More than a catchall for rural plant life, nature in its picturesque form became representative of a romanticized premodern social life—of tight community bonds rooted in the rhythms of the natural world.

As a product of the politically and economically dominant British Empire, the picturesque transformed the landscapes of rural England into a cultural cudgel. While less violent than military power, the cultural power that came to be associated with the picturesque nevertheless colonized and domesticated frontier landscapes.[6] As the picturesque entered new geographic contexts, it meant that nature, if it was to be culturally valuable, would have to be transformed—flatness most definitely included.[7]

Olmsted's plan for South Park therefore called for a major transformation of the Chicago landscape. Believing that the adjacent Lake Michigan was the site's only "object of scenery . . . of special grandeur or sublimity," and that "artificial means" could make it "no more grand or sublime," Olmsted called for water to enter the park through a series of lagoons, thereby producing visual coherence between the park and the lake.[8] And although the plan was never actualized to Olmsted's liking—remaining only partially developed through the end of Chicago's 1893 Columbian Exposition, which was held on the park's grounds—South Park, subsequently renamed Washington and Jackson Parks, embodied core urban park concerns of the nineteenth century. Like other grand picturesque parks, South Park created a representation of nature as pure, sacred, and vast, thereby demarcating it from the broader "city" beyond park walls—an urban context that was generally seen, in an era of rapid industrialization and urban migration, as dirty, dangerous, and diseased.[9]

As Chicago grew in the second half of the nineteenth century, local elites believed that cultural prestige could validate the city's impressive wealth—and parks, like art museums and symphony halls, became vehicles for such cultural accumulation. That the South Park site was not endowed with the rocky topography of rural England was irrelevant: Chicago needed a park, and it needed to be prestigious, and therefore, it needed to be picturesque.

• • •

Much in the same way, the cultural prestige bestowed upon New York's High Line has accelerated the transmission of its form to new contexts, such as Chicago and Houston. While the landscapes of these and other cities may not be "defective" in the way that Olmsted considered Chicago poorly suited to picturesque transformation, different places have different ecologies, different histories of constructing nature, and different meanings around urban parks in general. The picturesque's totalizing vision of nature does not hold in the present, as ideas about cities and nature have changed over the past 170 years.[10] Seemingly in the picturesque's place is this new and ascendant "imbricated" vision, where the decay of industrial environments has created a "second nature" of sorts, where cities' legacy buildings and infrastructures create the topography upon which postindustrial parks are built. Contemporary landscape transformations are not concerned with converting Midwestern prairies to stony English fields (and these days Chicagoans are busy restoring the prairies that were destroyed to make way for the picturesque), but a similar impulse to create universal visions of a new urban nature nevertheless persists.[11]

8

IMBRICATED SPACES

PARKS take the shape demanded by the cultural concerns of their time. Once parks are in place, they are no inert stage—their purposes and meanings are made and remade by planners and by park users. Moments of park creation are particularly telling, however, for they reveal and actualize ideas about nature and its relationship to urban society. Indeed, what distinguishes a park from the broader category of public space is the representation of nature that parks are meant to embody. Public spaces include parks, concrete plazas, sidewalks, even indoor atriums. Parks typically have trees, grass, and other plants as their central features. When entering a city park, people often imagine a sharp separation from streets, cars, and buildings. There's a reason for that: traditionally, park designers attempted to create such a feeling by planting tall trees at park boundaries, building stone walls, and constructing other means of partition. What's behind this idea is not only landscape architects' desire to design aesthetically suggestive park spaces, but a much longer history of Western thought that envisions cities and nature as antithetical spaces and oppositional forces.[1]

Parks, more than any other social space, materialize social constructions of nature. Through human interactions with parks, "natural objects are transformed from things into symbols."[2] This social construction of nature allows trees planted at a park's perimeter to become much more than trees: they become symbols of nature's majesty—and of the need to protect it, to partition it from urban intrusion. Our aesthetic preferences around nature— which landscapes we admire and which ones we detest—are socially constructed by our past experiences with landscapes, social influences, and cultural products like art and literature that shape our tastes for certain forms of "nature."[3]

But parks have a tendency to conceal the social relations of their production: trees, grass, and other plant materials have a way of making the most engineered landscapes appear "natural." Despite the obvious cultivation at work in cutting lawns, clearing trails, and grooming flowers, the powerful symbolisms of nature have a way of obscuring the human hands active in parks, not only in the course of ongoing maintenance, but in site histories. When visitors enter a grand urban park like New York's Central Park, they cannot easily conceive of its pre-park past, when it was a mix of undeveloped woods and a settlement known as Seneca Village.[4] Thus, the first fiction of traditional, picturesque park landscapes is that they appear in large part as a product of nature's forces.[5] Which is why postindustrial parks—where the human-made landscapes of railroads and buildings are celebrated and central to park aesthetics—are so curious. Where did these new landscapes come from?

• • •

Urban parks as we know them today date to the nineteenth century, when urban growth in Europe and North America prompted efforts to channel that growth in socially and economically productive ways. Plans for street grids, public works, and urban parks were created in rising numbers after 1800. Early urban plans, such as New York's 1811 Commissioners' Plan, sought to force new development along geometric lines.[6] As urban growth became realized in later decades, however, the limits of such plans became apparent. Grids did not account for topographical variation and treated nature as a blank slate to be worked according to the needs of capital.[7] This approach faced problems when new development encountered waterways and elevation changes. Furthermore, as grids encouraged very dense development, it was evident by the middle of the nineteenth century that cities needed to be ventilated by public spaces.[8]

Parks became an opportunity for city leaders to achieve this ventilation, while at the same time developing terrain that was not palatable to residential or commercial settlement—such as marshes and rock formations—by creating simulacra of "the wilderness" within city limits. But early urban parks were more than just representations of nature. In the way they related to their surrounding cityscapes, parks also materialized ideas about the urban. In the nineteenth century, factories, slaughterhouses, and railroads shaped an arresting urban landscape.[9] Nineteenth-century park designers like Frederick Olmsted saw urban space as something to be kept at bay, often complaining about the banal and negative aspects of cities: their crowded spatial conditions, which were thought to harbor disease and represent a threat to public health, and their crowded social conditions, whose stimuli taxed urbanites' collective psychology.[10]

Parks were thought to remedy each of these: through regular contact with nature, city dwellers could mentally and physically recharge. Often termed "the lungs of the city," parks were cast as having a biotic in addition to a social importance.[11] These ideas became emplaced within parks: landscape architects built circuitous walking paths (a rebuke to the angularity of city streets), expansive sight lines, and elevation changes, all meant to offer respite for park visitors and create a vision of nature in line with picturesque rural landscapes. Despite being fully a part of cities, early urban parks were the most anti-urban of urban spaces.

Ultimately, in the 170 years following the initial creation of picturesque parks, urban parks' cultural power and their symbolism as nature slowly deteriorated as parks became less crucial to urban fortunes. Over time and in many contexts, park symbolisms proved tenuous as elites divested from parks, as marginalized groups contested elite park purposes, and as planners envisioned a wider range of uses for parks. This long decline in parks-as-nature is evident in the aesthetics and planning of urban parks in the twentieth century:

Parks built in the early twentieth century tended to depart from grand, picturesque visions.[12] Unlike earlier motivating concerns about overdevelopment and the loss of countryside, the creation of early-twentieth-century parks addressed the working and housing conditions of tenement districts in cities like New York and Chicago.[13] A growing belief among reformers that public spaces could solve issues of overcrowding prompted what was known as the "small parks" movement. In contrast to pleasure grounds like Central Park and South Park, small parks were targeted interventions rather than large-scale development projects. Their purpose had less to do with nature and beauty and more to do with improving the lives of industrial workers.[14] Their smaller size prevented designers from incorporating typical picturesque landscapes: rolling vistas and water features were traded for playgrounds and fieldhouses.[15] Apart from size and aesthetic differences, small parks differed in that they were more functionalist spaces: areas for sports like baseball or swimming became permanent features.[16]

Related to these changes in park form and function were changes in the demographics of park users. A considerable, if often hidden, aspect of the creation of picturesque parks was the fortification of intersecting raced, classed, and gendered privileges. As nineteenth-century cities colonized new territory and became more ethno-racially diverse, picturesque parks' representations of nature were explicitly connected to creating safe spaces for White elites, particularly White women and children.[17] Early parks' social privileges extended as well to economic ones—i.e., property values—as parks served as anchors of broader upscale development projects: once picturesque parks were built, middle- and upper-class housing was often built next door, as in the case of New York's Central Park and Chicago's South Park. In the case of the latter, Olmsted explicitly envisioned that "a really populous and wealthy district" would grow around the park.[18] Parks may have been originally envisioned as sites of nature within cities, but they were also created as sites of Whiteness within a "racially othered" urban fabric.[19]

Small parks did not undo these associations between picturesque parks and White power structures. Instead, they were part of the simultaneous spatial and demographic expansion of Whiteness: they were most often built in the neighborhoods of White ethnic groups like the Irish and Italians during the time that these groups were becoming fully a part of the White racial category.[20] While earlier landscape architects sometimes made gestures toward the idea of democratic access to nature, small parks seemed to make good on this promise, providing White workers with immediate park access rather than a suburban retreat (large picturesque parks tended to be built very far from poor and immigrant neighborhoods). Thus, small parks were more egalitarian, but far from utopias: they weren't built in Black neighborhoods, and Jim Crow laws and racist violence kept Black people out of nearly every park in nearly every city.[21]

• • •

Subsequent park development in the United States intensified these "denaturing" trends, which continued until postindustrial parks brought a sharp reversal.[22] Beginning with New Deal construction programs in the 1930s and continuing through post–World War II urban renewal, mid-century parks, under the rubric of architectural modernism, became more streamlined, more geometrical, and more functionalist. That is to say, they lost many of the trappings of "nature" that had been essential to the historical definition of urban parks.

Urban parks were moving in two directions at mid-century: first, city park districts—which were becoming important social service organs in many cities—built new parks, often with federal funds, to serve the nation's "baby boomers"; second, with suburbanization taking hold, many older, symbolically valuable parks went into a period of decline as political and cultural power moved from central cities to suburbs.

City park districts everywhere from Minneapolis to Dallas were engaging in the most ambitious park building in their histories, thanks to the influx of WPA funds in the 1930s and urban renewal funds in the 1940s, '50s, and '60s.[23] Particularly in cities with strong ties to the federal government, public dollars for park building worked alongside monies for public housing, highways, and flood control to reshape urban landscapes.[24] This period of park building was not focused on creating new "crown jewels" with high cultural value, but rather on mass recreation: new neighborhood parks in outlying communities, new playgrounds

near schools, and new lawns to accompany public housing complexes. These changes also impacted older picturesque spaces
as park districts nationwide imported the small-park model of
permanent recreational facilities, turning nineteenth-century
meadows into tennis courts, golf courses, baseball fields, zoos, and
fieldhouses.[25]

The diminishment of urban park symbolisms was tied closely
to White exodus. Between 1940 and 1970, White populations in
older cities disproportionately moved to the suburbs or otherwise moved farther away from historical urban cores. At the same
time, Black communities finally and firmly broke the boundaries
of longtime "Black belts," moving in large numbers into neighborhoods—and into parks—that had been exclusively White for
decades. This was not a passive act: significant civil rights organizing went into racially integrating urban parks during this
time.[26] This racial double movement meant that the crown jewels of urban park systems—whether Brooklyn's Prospect Park,
Detroit's Belle Isle Park, Atlanta's Piedmont Park, or Chicago's
South Park—were being used increasingly, and in some cases,
predominantly, by people of color by 1970.[27]

But because parks' cultural power was tied to their symbolism as nature, and because maintaining the powerful symbols of
nature required money and political clout, and because White
people continued to control both of these forms of capital, White
communities were able to create new symbols of nature and establish new, culturally powerful spaces in the suburbs. As sprawling
residential developments and private lawns obviated the desire
for grand public spaces, in their place were country clubs, shopping malls, and nature-oriented cultural institutions. In Chicago,
for example, 1972 witnessed, after three decades of White flight,
the opening of the four-hundred-acre Chicago Botanic Garden,
named for the central city but located in the wealthy suburb of

Glencoe, twenty-five miles north of downtown and thirteen miles from city limits.[28]

Urban parks in mid-century America therefore became new kinds of public spaces, with more diverse uses and users than the parks that came before. Racialized transformations in urban and suburban spaces depreciated the same parks once valorized as nature; these parks were now more embedded in their urban contexts and, in many cases, were re-racialized as their visitors shifted from White to non-White.

• • •

By 1970, park symbolisms had sharply eroded in many cities by the time the consequences of urban disinvestment and suburban growth were fully realized. In cities in crisis, parks were incorporated into an imaginary of "the urban," particularly as such ideas extended to racialized tropes of crime and disorder. Nationally, nothing punctuated this shift better than the sensationalist coverage of the 1989 Central Park jogger case: five Black and Latino teenagers were accused and convicted (in 2002, their convictions were vacated) of beating and raping a White woman who was on an evening run in Central Park; a media firestorm erupted, enflamed by future president Donald Trump, who took out a full-page ad in the *Daily News* that called for their execution.[29] While not every city had such a high-profile crime, many urban parks had become sites of real and imagined danger. In Chicago, for example, the 1968 riots in Grant Park at the Democratic National Convention, coupled with uprisings throughout Black neighborhoods after the killing of Martin Luther King, did much to suggest chaos in Chicago's parks and public spaces. Two years later, Olmsted's onetime South Park became home to a scene out of *The Warriors* when a powerful local gang, the Black

Stone Rangers, held an outdoor tribunal in the park—without police interference—for a Woodlawn man accused of rape and murder.[30] More generally, with depopulation and disinvestment ravaging parks of all shapes and sizes, parks emerged as relatively unwatched spaces, free from the "eyes on the street," where crime could take place.[31] Particularly from the "standpoint of the out-of-towner" and White tourists, parks represented one of the most "out of control" types of urban spaces.[32]

The net result of parks retrenchment in cities across the United States was that parks, particularly those in Black and Latino areas, appeared weedy and overgrown—hardly the symbols of pristine, sacred nature that parks had once embodied.[33] The second path in this early neoliberal period was driven by private park corporations, which filled the void in public funding with private monies for the beautification and securitization of valuable parks. For prestigious but neglected spaces like New York's Central Park, groups like the Central Park Conservancy led a cultural and economic bifurcation of park landscapes, allowing park patrons in wealthy, White, and tourist areas to begin rebuilding the aesthetic prestige and cultural power that had been dormant for over half a century.

While White elites were initiating this rebuilding of symbolic sites of nature, another process of "greening" was taking place. In the cracks of disinvested communities, the same weedy disorder that had catalyzed park conservancies was taking a different hue. In poor neighborhoods, vegetal overgrowth in newly vacant lots and between sidewalk cracks was becoming a marker of poverty and retrenchment. Community block groups and other social organizations fought this decay, as many had for decades, since many residents associated visual disorder with social disorder, such as crime and other undesirable activities.[34]

But in communities undergoing the early stages of postin-dustrial gentrification, such unplanned plant growth was not criticized—at least, not by everyone. Vacant lots and other over-grown green spaces became part of the broader postindustrial fabric, "serv[ing] to heighten the drama" for gentrifiers entering the new urban "wilds."[35] This form of "nature" didn't resemble urban parks at all; it didn't resemble suburban lawns. It was the nature of poverty and disinvestment. Unplanned plant growth in former industrial spaces suggested the passage of time, as it takes time for plants to grow and to take hold of a space. Much like the antique charm of lofts, the patina of age suggested by untamed plants lent an air of ruin, romanticism, and authenticity to the surroundings—particularly because in manufacturing-cum-arts districts, greenery was alien. Most industrial areas were segregated from residential communities; city governments had little to no impetus to build parks in these areas, as very few people lived in them prior to their residential conversion.[36] Manufacturing activities had minimal use for lawns of any size; thus, buildings were typically built out to the lot limits. So, whether in New York's Meatpacking District, Chicago's West Loop, or Downtown LA, these sections of cities had very little green space to begin with. So, the plants that grew during periods of postindustrial decline were not only unusual, but indicators of something fertile, feral, and illicit.

When left uncultivated, plants can do more than sprout between sidewalk cracks; as happened with the High Line, the Bloomingdale Line, and the banks of Buffalo Bayou, plants can fully take over a neglected social space, creating an entirely new aesthetic form.[37] Beyond the spaces that have been redeveloped and reproduced as parks, the visual marriage of industrial decay and growth of the natural environment offers a new powerful image of nature—one that now rivals the classical picturesque during its nineteenth-century heyday. As a new symbol of nature, it too has an ideological basis. The picturesque romanticized rural landscapes, mourned the loss of nature, and rebuked urbanization. Imbricated spaces instead romanticize industrial landscapes, and, rather than rebuking urbanization, celebrate (a particular perspective on) the city's visual qualities. Now, as postindustrial park developers have reproduced this new vision of urban nature through projects like the High Line, the Bloomingdale Trail/606, and Buffalo Bayou Park, it has moved from the avant-garde to the mainstream and has reestablished the cultural power of urban parks.[38]

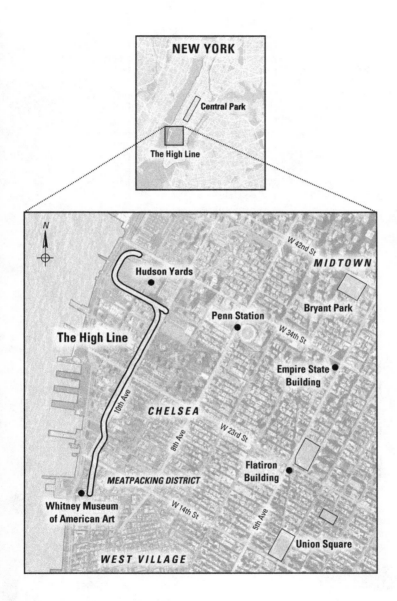

MAP 1 New York and the High Line

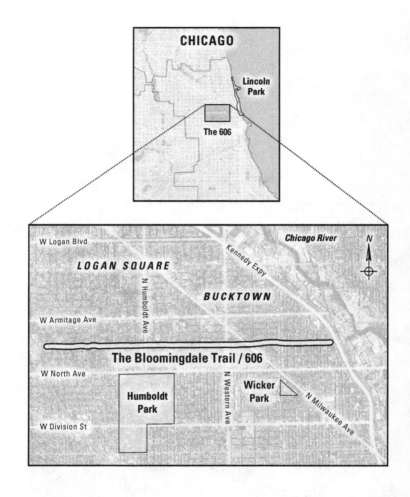

MAP 2 Chicago and the Bloomingdale Trail/606

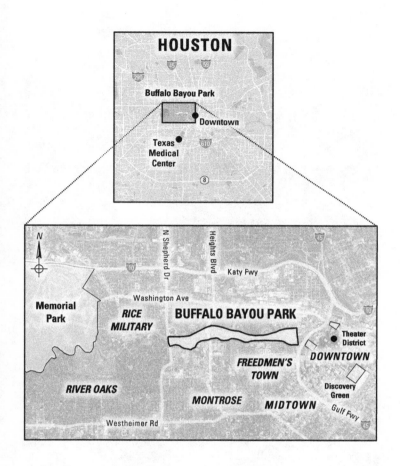

MAP 3 Houston and Buffalo Bayou Park

FIGURE 1 The High Line after redevelopment (photo by author, 2011)

FIGURE 2 The High Line's Tenth Avenue Square as seen from the street (photo by author, 2011)

FIGURE 3 Shopping for art on the High Line (photo by author, 2011)

FIGURE 4 Taking photos on the High Line (photo by author, 2011)

FIGURE 5 Entering the High Line from the street (photo by author, 2011)

FIGURE 6 One of the seventeen ramps designed to make the Bloomingdale Trail/606 more accessible than the High Line, looking "slippery" after a light snowfall (photo by author, 2017)

FIGURE 7 A bicyclist on the Bloomingdale Trail/606 (photo by author, 2016)

FIGURE 8 A billboard advertises luxury apartments—"Life on the 606"—next to the Bloomingdale Trail/606.

FIGURE 9 Down the street, one of the steel Puerto Rican flags on El Paseo Boriqua/Division Street (designed by architects DeStefano & Partners in 1995) announces the area's historical identity. (photos by author, 2017)

FIGURE 10 "Wild" landscape on the Bloomingdale Trail/606 (photo by author, 2016)

FIGURE 11 View of Humboldt Boulevard from the park (photo by author, 2016)

FIGURE 12A & 12B Buffalo Bayou Park, dry and wet: (a) the same space photographed from trail level (2016) and (b) from above, days after Hurricane Harvey. Note the water level on the streetlights (2017). (photos by author)

FIGURE 13 One of Buffalo Bayou Park's "word sculptures" (photo by author, 2020)

FIGURE 14 Walking through Buffalo Bayou Park (photo by author, 2016)

FIGURE 15A & 15B Buffalo Bayou Park's (a) picturesque and (b) sublime qualities (photos by author, 2016)

9

CONSTRUCTING
ENVIRONMENTAL AUTHENTICITY

WHAT kind of nature is this? Postindustrial parks are a kind of death show, with their zombie plants and railroad corpses. This urban-environmental necrophilia, where the past is not mourned as it was but rather eroticized for its rich visual palate, is strange enough; but the parks fit so seamlessly into contemporary urban plans that it's easy to miss just how strange these parks are.

Social constructions of nature, once transformed by the decline and renewal of industrial neighborhoods, have provided postindustrial parks with an aesthetic and ideological basis much in the same way that paintings and philosophical reflections on the English countryside supplied a generative image for the first generation of urban parks in the nineteenth century. Despite the long decline of the picturesque, it was never really supplanted as the dominant cultural image of nature in the West, even as many picturesque parks (spatial representations of this image) were disinvested. The "small parks," playgrounds, and other twentieth-century park forms, while they were built in great numbers and had an ideological basis, were not attempting to tie down an ideal form of nature—or any kind of "sacred" cultural image, for that matter.[1] Their instrumental purposes did not reject the cultural power of the picturesque; rather, they interjected a new kind of recreational space into the urban landscape.

Postindustrial parks are not only the first parks since the nineteenth century to have a strong symbolic basis as "nature," but, just as crucially, postindustrial parks in many ways subvert traditional park themes and traditional ideas about nature, especially nature's relationship to "the urban." But at the same time, traditional ideas about landscape remain central to postindustrial parks, despite their architectural novelty. Taken as a whole, the architecture of the High Line, the Bloomingdale Trail/606, and Buffalo Bayou Park reveals a new understanding of city and nature: as imbricated and sustainable, but also romantic and pastoral; at once a rejection and a reification of old ideals of nature, combined with an historically new, direct embrace of the urban.

· · ·

A central theme in the architecture of postindustrial parks is the re-creation or restoration of a particular essence of the sites. At Buffalo Bayou Park, the goal was to restore the natural beauty of the bayou and its banks and harmonize them with the broader urban context; at the High Line and the Bloomingdale Trail/606, the goal was to cultivate a version of the uncultivated plant life that had bloomed as the structures decayed. Because of this nostalgia, it's helpful to have a more explicit sense of the aesthetics of these three spaces prior to their redevelopment.

The High Line, in large part by virtue of its location in Chelsea, where the railway's 1980 closure coincided with the ascendance of intersecting gay and arts scenes, has the most florid past—or at least, its decades of abandonment have the most admirers. At the High Line, the post-closure combination of uncultivated plant life and furtive industrial space, largely invisible to those below, created a sense of visual ruin and social mystique. Rumors of illicit activities that took place on the structure in the 1980s and '90s have become essential to the narratives of the park's creators. As Friends of the High Line cofounder Josh David wrote of his early memories of the High Line:

> It was about thirty feet tall, and you couldn't see what was on top of it, but the rusting Art Deco railings gave it a sense of lost beauty, and the spaces underneath were very dramatic; they had a dark, gritty, industrial quality, and a lofty, church-like quality as well. . . . I didn't know what the thing was called. . . . My friend John told me it was a sex spot—coming out of the Spike or the Eagle, he'd ducked underneath it with a trick more than once. There was sex to be had up top, too, and there were parties up there, raves, along with some homeless encampments.[2]

David recalled that the High Line's salacious past similarly captivated the park's architects, who "described the High Line as a ruin, a found object. Liz Diller used the word illicit: you had to crawl under a fence, and you entered a forbidden, secret area that had an aura of past sex and drugs. [They] loved the High Line's dark and mysterious quality, which I was also drawn to."[3]

The Bloomingdale Trail/606's years of disuse are similarly memorialized with tropes of sex and drugs. One Logan Square resident remembered her teenaged visits to the closed railway, where she and her friends would "go drink a few beers, smoke some weed and do your paint, do your graffiti on some of the old rail cars that were on the tracks."[4] Josh Deth, a cofounder of the Friends of the Bloomingdale Trail, recalled:

> There were lots of hypodermic needles up there and beer cans and broken bottles. There was a homeless encampment at Kimball.

> One homeless guy at Leavitt hooked up electrical wires to the
> local power grid and had a TV in there. . . . Part of it is that you're
> in this space where there's no rules, because the cops didn't really
> go up there. . . . There was an old piano up there at one point. I
> don't know how the hell someone got a piano up there, but they
> sure did.[5]

This romanticization extended less so to Buffalo Bayou Park,
where the space's decay did not produce the same sort of fascination for those who frequented the bayou prior to redevelopment.
In part, this could be because Buffalo Bayou Park was already a
(disinvested) park; plants were an expected presence, not curious
visitors. But it's also because the overgrown, unkempt plant life,
when mixed with the built specter of highway overpasses and
skyscrapers, more closely resembled the landscapes of urban mar-
ginality than those of postindustrial cultural production. And, it's
because the romantic collective memories being shaped around
the High Line and the Bloomingdale Trail/606 have been nar-
rated by individuals who were either involved with, or benefited
from, the redevelopment process.[6]

Because there's little question that the same kinds of activities romanticized at the High Line and the Bloomingdale
Trail/606—sex, drug use, parties, etc.—were happening on the
banks of Buffalo Bayou prior to redevelopment. Indeed, on the
northeast corner of Houston's future "crown jewel," an encampment of more than two hundred homeless people endured from
1982 through its removal by city police in 1996—a community
described in patronizing tones by the *Chronicle* as containing
"a superb view of downtown's skyline, half a dozen well-built
shacks and his and hers outdoor toilets."[7] Accounts described
the space generally as "wilderness: degraded, maybe, and trashy,
but unmanaged and untamed," where washed-ashore debris and

other "flotsam could linger as long as it pleased, keeping company with snakes and raccoons."[8] Rich Kinder, the principal private donor behind Buffalo Bayou Park's transformation, claimed that the space "was tremendously, really a disaster. I used to run there, and you never knew what was around the next turn, whether it was a syringe or a beer bottle or whatever."[9] So rather than nostalgia for the site's more recent history, as was the case with the High Line and the Bloomingdale Trail/606, in the redevelopment of Buffalo Bayou Park, the nostalgia called all the way back to 1913, to Arthur Comey's citywide, bayou-centric parks plan.

Postindustrial parks thus bring together nostalgias for danger, sex, and drugs that align with narrative tropes around postindustrial environments more broadly, which have a tendency to fetishize and sexualize the excitement and/or fear that gentrifiers find in "discovering" furtive places.[10] Different narrators have different takes on whether these historical aspects are good (as they are for Josh David) or bad (as they are for Rich Kinder), or morally ambiguous.[11] What these narratives reveal across the board, however, is that these imbricated spaces were, in their decades of institutional abandonment, as intriguing *socially* as they were *spatially*. That is, for many of the people who came from the outside to "discover" these spaces, their appeal was rooted not only in the strange mix of overgrown nature and decaying built environment, but in the equally outcast kinds of people and activities that existed in the spaces.[12]

• • •

Romanticism for sex and drug use can only go so far to mobilize park development. History suggests that city governments are far more likely to clear such spaces than celebrate them.[13] The broader appeal for redeveloping these spaces as public parks, while connected to this nostalgia for the illicit, was ultimately driven by the shock of nature and its newfound relationship to the built environment—an appeal that, given the historical novelty and heretofore obscurity of this aesthetic, needed to be cultivated. Especially at the High Line, the first of the parks to be developed, artful photographs of the site's uncultivated plant life were central to soliciting public support. Taken by Joel Sternfeld between 2000 and 2001, a series drawn across New York's four seasons was used frequently in the Friends of the High Line's promotional materials and allowed the wider public, prospective philanthropists, and the city government to see what was on top of the old railway.[14]

What was up there, in the words of Friends of the High Line cofounder Robert Hammond, was "another world," an unused railway teeming with grasses and flowers.[15] He wrote of his first visit to the High Line during its time of decline:

> You walked out and you were on train tracks that were covered in wildflowers. I don't know what I had expected. Maybe just gravel, stone ballast, and tracks—more of a ruin. . . . I just didn't expect wildflowers. This was not a few blades of grass growing up through gravel. *The wildflowers and plants had taken over.* We had to wade through waist-high Queen Anne's lace. It was another world, right in the middle of Manhattan.[16]

For the Friends of the High Line and their partners in the Bloomberg administration, recapturing the magic of the site guided their search for an architectural team. The winners of the park's design competition, a collaboration among James Corner, Liz Diller, Ric Scofidio, Charles Renfro, and Piet Oudolf, won over established firms like Skidmore, Owings, and Merrill and designers like Michael Van Valkenburgh, who had been commissioned for several other parks in New York City at the time (and whose firm would go on to codesign the Bloomingdale Trail/606). At the time of selection, James Corner was an architectural professor known for his efforts to bridge traditional landscape architecture and postindustrial Urbanism. His partners in the High Line design, Liz Diller, Ric Scofidio, and Charles Renfro, had been producing high-concept abstract architecture—in the form of installations and pop-up buildings—since the 1970s, but had relatively few building credits to their name (though the firm had just won the commission to redesign New York's Lincoln Center prior to winning the High Line competition). The team's landscape designer, Piet Oudolf, was a horticulturalist considered one of the foremost experts on cultivating wild-looking grasses.

From a design perspective, the High Line was one of the first parks to present intentionally as an imbricated space. The Coulée Verte in Paris—the first park built on an elevated railway, opened in 1993—despite its postindustrial location, offered a traditional botanic garden as its form of nature. The High Line, in contrast, offered a simulacrum of the plants that had existed in the space in the 1980s and '90s. Whereas previous brownfield interventions, like those at the Coulée Verte, had tended to demolish existing sites and plop a traditional park (whether a playground or a garden) in their place, the design of the High Line, in contrast, elected to celebrate and reproduce the space's origins.[17]

For the city government, transforming the "old" High Line into a safe, usable public space required removing the site's original railbeds and plants. In their place, the park designers sought to reconstruct as many of the old elements as possible: reusing pieces of the original rails for aesthetic effect, developing a rail-inspired planked walkway, and cultivating wild-looking plants. These design elements would communicate to park visitors a sense of environmental authenticity: for locals, it would communicate nostalgia for the High Line in its disinvested state; for tourists, it would communicate nativity—that this was a less cultivated site than a typical park, and that the nature on display was indeed "natural."

Key to the commingling of plant life and built environment was the concrete planking system that defined the park's walkable area. This recalled the wooden planks of a railroad and enabled the park's plants to mix with built material, as the architects devised a series of openings between planks, presenting the illusion that the plants were breaking through the surface. Architect Ric Scofidio remarked:

> Rather than pouring a hardscape or a macadam path, [we designed] a planking system that could feather into the landscape. Actually we looked at concrete sidewalks, where the concrete had been broken and the grass was forcing its way through, and there was incredible tension between the green and the concrete.[18]

Landscape designer Piet Oudolf rejected the tightly mowed grasses of typical urban parks and the ornateness of botanical gardens. His planting philosophy illustrated the same sort of nostalgia and melancholy that the High Line itself had come to represent, arguing that "the skeletons of the plants are . . . as important as the flowers."[19] In designing the High Line, Oudolf considered how visitors' experiences of nature would flow from one end of the linear park to the other, and how the park's landscape would change with the seasons, describing his work "as a process, . . . a performance in place."[20]

What was new about the High Line's design was not only this illusion of wild nature; it was also the way the park seemed to embrace its urban context—both the rail structure itself and the broader cityscape. The visual union of the park and its surroundings was done explicitly, as the park's designers drew out elements of the High Line's industrial qualities in artful ways. At the "Tenth Avenue Square," for example, part of the structure was removed to provide parkgoers with a glass-enclosed view to street traffic below. Such spaces created visual exchanges between park users and people on the outside; they also made mundane aspects of urban existence visible to people on the High Line—domestic aspects, too, as the High Line's elevation offered views into many of the apartments that lined the park. Bringing the High Line's aura of sex and voyeurism full circle, when the park opened in 2009, visitors were memorably greeted with live sex scenes courtesy of guests of the Standard Hotel.[21]

Whereas bringing city views into a park would have been anathema to Frederick Olmsted and other nineteenth-century park designers, the High Line's architects instead celebrated the city and its convergence with the natural environment. At the "viewing spur" at Twenty-Sixth Street, the park's architects designed a metal frame to mimic a billboard that had previously occupied the same space. This offered a focal point for park users to look out into the city and vice versa. Architect Ric Scofidio explained:

> There's this wonderful moment . . . where there's always been a billboard. In the restoration process, everything was ripped down, and that history would be gone. But we thought it would be nice to keep the memory of it, so at 26th Street we have that frame, but it also becomes a frame back to the city.[22]

Beyond incorporating new urban views and nostalgia for the High Line's past, the designers held a vision of the park's broader social and political significance: cities like New York were seen as communities with interesting histories and contemporary environmental and recreational needs, which encouraged the reuse of former industrial spaces in the name of sustainability. Architect James Corner commented on how the High Line fit within his ideological approach toward cities and nature:

> The whole environmental agenda is something that landscape architects have been trained in and have worked on for years. . . . Cities are beginning to invest in new parks, new public spaces, new waterfronts, and the transformation of many of these postindustrial inheritances from the 20th century. . . . With the shift . . . to a service economy, a lot of land is abandoned and derelict. No one knows what to do with it. The High Line is a great example of making something new.[23]

The High Line was something new, indeed. The architects' intentions for aesthetic novelty were validated upon the park's opening in 2009. Much as the park's immediate economic impact was toasted by the media and the High Line's supporters, its cultural impact—as a new type of urban park—was likewise celebrated. The High Line's unusual form of nature, and the new relationship to the urban that it symbolized, were one of the central themes raised by architectural critics. Nicolai Ouroussoff wrote that the High Line represented "a subtle play between contemporary and historical design, industrial decay and natural beauty. . . . Those gardens have a wild, ragged look that echoes the character of the old abandoned track bed when it was covered with weeds, just a few years ago."[24] Paul Goldberger further situated the High Line's historical newness in relation to traditional parks:

> Parks in large cities are usually thought of as refuges, as islands of green amid seas of concrete and steel. When you approach the High Line . . ., what you see first is the kind of thing urban parks

were created to get away from—a harsh, heavy, black steel structure supporting an elevated rail line that once brought freight cars
right into factories and warehouses and that looks, at least from a
distance, more like an abandoned relic than an urban oasis.[25]

In contrast to the parks of generations past, the High Line
embraced "the urban" rather than rejecting it, while still—and
simultaneously and paradoxically (at least to the old way of
thinking)—asserting the space as a site of "nature." Nineteenth-
century parks that presented nature in its picturesque form were
designed to oppose cities and their symbolisms. Twentieth-
century planning placed parks deeper into the urban fabric and
brought more aspects of modern urban life into parks (to the
effect of diminishing parks' symbolism as nature). In embracing nature and the urban all at once, the High Line flipped these
historical trends on their head. While there was nothing radical about the park's political-economic basis—a product of the
urban growth machine par excellence—its cultural aspects indeed
marked a turning point: embracing the avant-garde form of
nature favored by postindustrial gentrifiers and taking it mainstream through a park that initially cost $152 million to build.

Aesthetically, the park's designers recaptured the "old" High
Line by maintaining the appearance of urban decay and insurgent nature even as the "new" High Line's spaces were carefully
constructed by architects.[26] The designers sought to reorient people's visual relationship to the city and intended the High Line
to serve as a model for green-urbanist interventions—one that
would live with and embrace nature's forces, rather than dominate them.[27] The High Line indicates that part of postindustrial
parks' appeal is the suggestion that nature had a hand in creating
the space. In contradistinction to the manicured plants of traditional public parks, it seems from both the architects' intentions

and the critical reception that plants in imbricated spaces must appear "authentic"—that they are part of the native fabric of the parks, even when the original plants have been removed and the new ones cultivated.

A certain authenticity is demanded of the built environment as well. The patina of age suggested by the deterioration of buildings and infrastructure contributes to the aesthetic appeal, as decay conveys the passage of time and produces the desired sense of nostalgia. As with other spaces where industrial decline has been fetishized, the High Line's relic industrial materials present not as transportation infrastructure but as art objects.[28] These art objects, hollowed out of whatever original purposes and meanings they had, are more-than-suitable vessels for consuming the landscape.

• • •

The prospect and pressure of creating something new loomed over the production of Chicago's Bloomingdale Trail/606. The High Line had been declared an architectural triumph by critics and visitors. Chicago's version needed to do the same thing— build a critically acclaimed linear park on top of a defunct railroad viaduct—while being sufficiently different from the New York version. Inevitably, the Bloomingdale Trail/606, opened in 2015, would be received in direct comparison to the High Line.

Some of the Bloomingdale Trail/606's backers embraced this inevitability and chose to raise the stakes. Rahm Emanuel's deputy mayor, Steve Koch, declared in 2013 to an assemblage of the city's elites that Chicago's answer to the High Line would "transform the city . . . [and] make it a fundamentally different place. A lot of people are familiar with the High Line—[the Bloomingdale Trail/606] is a concept far beyond that truly transformative project."[29] Others sought to mark a distinction in the

Bloomingdale Trail/606's purpose. Beth White, Chicago director of the Trust for Public Land, contended that " 'The Secret Garden' was the theme of the High Line[.] Our theme is connection. It's connecting four neighborhoods. It's connecting this part of the city with bike routes and transportation routes."[30] As Mayor Emanuel attempted to clarify at the opening of the park in 2015, "I don't have anything against the High Line, obviously, but [the Bloomingdale Trail/606] brings neighborhoods together and neighbors together who didn't know they were neighbors."[31]

That these power brokers would make such claims and clarifications speaks to the importance of postindustrial parks' "branding" in a post–High Line world, where, for park boosters, a park's brand—its official motto, its press coverage, its marketing—is as important as its design (though obviously a well-received design can enhance all of those things). Clearly, it is not enough to build a linear park tailored to the local needs of Chicago. Urban boosters' quest for economic growth and cultural prestige demands trumpeting parks like the Bloomingdale Trail/606 in grandiose terms—or, if acting with more modesty, splicing the right mix of buzzwords together to suggest a fundamentally unique park project.

The tension between the local growth coalition's desire to brand the Bloomingdale Trail as the 606 and the designers' desire to implement their own vision influenced the park's reception, as critics' and visitors' and boosters' expectations had been ratcheted up by Emanuel et al.'s promises. The tension affected the production of the park—with Emanuel accelerating its opening to aid his reelection hopes—and informed the designers' intentions for the space. All this unfolded in the shadow of the High Line's cultural and economic impact.

• • •

It has been tedious to have to talk always about the 606 through
the lens of the High Line.

—Frances Whitehead, lead artist, Bloomingdale Trail/606.[32]

Much of what makes the High Line *the High Line* has nothing to do with design at all. Rather, it's the park's location in a
dense, urbane part of New York City. Being "first" in the global
race for an iconic postindustrial park helped, of course: the first
High Line is likely assured a better reception than the twentieth
High Line. But swap designs with the Bloomingdale, and probably it's still "an economic dynamo"; probably it's still a "miracle
above Manhattan."[33] The High Line didn't need brash boosters
to make it iconic (though it needed them to survive demolition
threats); once its fate was settled by the Bloomberg administration, its fortunes were linked to the already ascendant Chelsea
and Meatpacking District.

The park designs still matter because they articulate new
understandings of nature in the postindustrial period—and
because architectural accolades establish distinction, which
helps the parks, the neighborhoods, and the cities accumulate
cultural and economic capital.[34] And while counterfactuals can
hypothesize the interchangeability of linear park designs, there
are important differences between the High Line and the parks
that have been built in its image. Booster branding is one thing,
but the site of the Bloomingdale Trail/606 ensured that Chicago's park would be different from the New York version. It was a
concrete basin filled with old earth, not a viaduct on stilts. Some
of what made the High Line so visually enmeshed in the city—
like the Tenth Avenue Square, which disassembled part of the
viaduct to create a new perspective—was less possible. Further,
the Bloomingdale Trail/606's built surroundings simply lacked
the verticality that provided High Line visitors with picturesque

vantage points.[35] (In these respects, Chicago once again was a victim of its "defective landscape," as Olmsted had complained of South Park in the 1800s.)

Charged with the tall order of overcoming such "defects" and creating aesthetic novelty at the Bloomingdale Trail/606 was the design team of Collins Engineers, artist Frances Whitehead, and landscape architects Michael Van Valkenburgh Associates. Collins Engineers, an international, Chicago-based firm with experience in civil and transportation engineering, had become a major private partner of the Chicago Department of Transportation in 2012 and served as the primary contractor for the Bloomingdale Trail/606 project.[36] Frances Whitehead, a professor at the School of the Art Institute of Chicago, had previously been artist-in-residence with the City of Chicago. Michael Van Valkenburgh had been one of four finalists in the High Line's design competition, and the Bloomingdale Trail/606 presented an opportunity to display what had been denied in New York. Van Valkenburgh's vision was a rawer form of nature than that displayed by Corner, Diller, Scofidio, Renfro, and Oudolf. The Van Valkenburgh proposal for the High Line, which was publicly displayed in 2004, was described by the *New York Times* as:

Willowy aspens, swaths of mustard flowers and sunflowers and an alternating rhythm of miniature forests and meadows. . . . Over time, the [Van Valkenburgh-led TerraGRAM] team maintains, sunflowers and mustard seed can restore the High Line's impoverished soil to full life-bearing capability. Entering the park, visitors would climb a stair from the gritty streets, pass through a trap door and pop up into a "forest of trembling Aspens—like Alice in reverse," Mr. Van Valkenburgh explained. "I fell in love with the contradictory power of this enduring industrial structure living in combination with the in-vitro natural landscape," he said. . . . This design is romance for the postirony crowd: a thousand flowers bloom, but they're shooting up out of 20 inches of gravel and debris.[37]

This approach to postindustrial park design—one that might rehabilitate the fertile ground of an old railbed, rather than simply reanimate the ghosts of plants past—was led at the Bloomingdale Trail/606 by MVVA architect Matthew Urbanski, and was a viewpoint shared by lead artist Frances Whitehead. Whitehead too argued that postindustrial park aesthetics should work in the service of an ecological mission—a mission that she held in contrast to her opinion of the High Line's design:

> I think it's overwrought. It's over-designed. . . . If you go back to the original . . . Friends of the High Line motto, . . . their motto was "keep it wild." That was the ambition: "Keep it wild." Well I would say they failed. There's nothing wild about it. . . . And I'm a fan of the landscape concept of the urban wild. I'm very interested in wildness inside the city.[38]

The design team's interest in "wildness," or taking an approach that emphasized ecological impact and locality, took several forms. For one, the designers sought to highlight the geospatial location of the Bloomingdale Trail/606 in terms of its relationship to Lake Michigan, by placing "three enigmatic compass rose-like 'medallions' that indicate the [park's] East/West axis" at each mile marker.[39] This was done to enable an authentically Chicago-style way of seeing the land, where Lake Michigan often serves as a point of orientation from anywhere in the city:

> The unusual East-West arrows turn convention on its head, reorienting the viewer towards the Lake. These transgressive mapping elements eschew the convention and abstraction of the north

arrow, and send the viewers' attention along the axis of the biore-
gion reconnecting to the reality of place."[40]

The presence of the lake had another effect on the design, captured in the park's "Environmental Sentinel." For the designers,
this element allowed the park to serve as a hybrid cultural/eco-
logical model akin to Japan's cherry blossoms, following from the
idea that "sustainability and climate change are cultural problems[,] not technical or biologic problems[,] and that cultural
strategies can be used to make these issues and phenomena tangi-
ble and legible to the public."[41] Of the design, Whitehead wrote:

> Running the full length of the 606, [the] Environmental Sentinel
> is a climate-monitoring artwork and landscape intervention. The
> planting will consist of a line of 453 native, flowering trees *Amel-
> anchier grandiflora* (Apple Serviceberry), whose five-day bloom
> spread will visualize Chicago's famous Lake Effect. These temper-
> ature-sensitive plants will serve as environmental "sentinels" for
> Chicago, bio-indicators of microclimate change.[42]

Beyond gestures to the local environmental ecology, the design
of the Bloomingdale Trail/606 provided two architectural
aspects that literally staked out new ground: elevation changes
and "access parks," both of which attempted to maximize the
Bloomingdale site. Prior to the elevation changes, Urbanski
found the Bloomingdale inexorably flat and thus "relentlessly the
same."[43] The solution was to create undulations by removing the
structure's earthen materials in one place, and often reusing them
elsewhere for access ramps and the park's "Observatory" at its
western terminus.[44] Urbanski recalled:

> What that did was give us ups and downs, revealing the walls,
> and that worked nicely with the found-object quality in revealing

the structure. It also started to vary the environment, literally, of the trail. You had different kinds of conditions, sloped conditions, high conditions, low conditions. One way of looking at the top from an ecological perspective is that it was very consistent to begin with, and by varying the grades, we started to vary the ecology of the top. That led to the idea that for a whole three-mile walk or bike ride, it would be nice to have some variety of planting along the length of it. And it could start to respond to these different conditions that are created.[45]

Access parks, another architectural piece that differentiated the Bloomingdale Trail/606 from the High Line, represented an effort to, in the words of the park's official plan, "balance trail and park aspirations."[46] The four access parks—Julia de Burgos Park, Park No. 567, Churchill Field Park, and Walsh Park—provided ramped entry points onto the trail and offered the kinds of permanent recreational facilities found in urban parks built in the twentieth century: playgrounds, a baseball field, and basketball courts. These four parks, ranging in size from 0.33 acres to 2.2 acres, effectively grounded the lofty ambitions coming from the mayor's office: they were modest, useful, and local—not global tourist spaces. (Attesting to the messiness of the renaming of the Bloomingdale Trail, the official designation is that these separately named parks are nevertheless part of the 606.) If nothing else, the access parks seemed to ensure—given the planning maxim that "people don't climb stairs to get to open space"—that the 606, as a whole, would continue to draw local users even if the luster of elevated parks were to wear off in the future.[47]

So, while the designs and the geographic contexts of the High Line and the Bloomingdale Trail/606 are indeed different, ultimately the parks have more in common as they materialize the same urban-environmental aesthetics and ideology. Much like the High Line and other newly glamorized postindustrial sites, the Bloomingdale Trail/606 displays apparently wild, untamed plant life. Though the Bloomingdale Trail/606's comparatively deeper soil allowed for more and larger trees than the High Line, the same tall grasses and understated flowers predominate. Like the High Line's Tenth Avenue Square and Viewing Spur, the design of the Bloomingdale Trail/606 positions certain vantage points as contemplative sites. By virtue of their elevation, these parks have views from everywhere; at the Bloomingdale Trail/606, the "prospect" at Humboldt Boulevard likewise attempted to deepen the visual exchange between park visitors and the city beyond:

> The design concept for the prospect at Humboldt Boulevard is to create an architectural communal seating area and sense of place, focused on the views of the historic boulevard below, which marks the south end of the Logan Square Boulevards District. A symmetrical bank of stepped wooden stadium bleacher-style seating is . . . picking up the formal geometry of the historic site and these important, dramatic views. These clean stepped forms without architectural reveal or bull nosing lend a modern feel to the historic context. Four rows of petite purple smoke trees extend the median strips below, as if the greenspace is flowing up and over the trail from the street.[48]

These concepts of environmental authenticity and of a visual union between city and nature extended beyond the park's immediate setting to the urban scale. Like the designers of the High Line, the Bloomingdale Trail/606's architects upheld a similar ideal of adaptive reuse, one that reimagined outmoded industrial objects and transformed them into useful civic spaces. In words that echoed James Corner, Bloomingdale Trail/606 architect Matthew Urbanski framed the questions as:

> How do you take this piece of industrial infrastructure and turn it into a public amenity? . . . With these infrastructural elements in cities, and converting them into public space, my fundamental question is, what do you keep and what do you change? Because you can't change everything, and you can't keep everything, because it's made for trains. . . . What we realized was that there was this volume of soil here—unlike the High Line in New York, which is a bridge—there was this volume of soil. . . . What we'd like to do is re-grade that between the bridges, which would give us ecological gradients and then also facilitate access, and then start to reveal the structure as a giant "found object."[49]

Chicago's park is therefore an extension not only of the High Line's architectural styles, but of a new urban-environmental ideology that offers green spaces as fixes for the intertwined problems of climate change, brownfields, and urban growth. Yet as spaces for the urban future, they are curiously backward looking. Extending Frederic Jameson's observation that postmodern architecture is the built equivalent of "late-night reefer munchies," in postmodern, postindustrial parks the brownies are served with a comforting glass of warm milk: nature, despite its funky new facade, continues to appear as pastoral and salubrious as it ever did.[50] At the High Line and the Bloomingdale Trail/606, the radical architecture is cut with plaintive plant life: re-creations of long-dead grasses and flowers, whose melancholia is further boosted by the parks' consecration of industrial heritage and, to a lesser extent, the spaces' more recent histories of sex and drugs.

But there's amnesia at work in building these collective memories. They say these spaces are "found objects"—found by whom?

Did the Bloomingdale Line disappear from the mental maps of the Latino communities who lived alongside it for decades? Did the meatpackers forget the sights, sounds, and smells of the High Line? These industrial objects were in place long before intrepid gentrifiers and architects and park developers found them. Yet these sites draw out the persistent narrative of "discovery" that erases both the past and local subaltern perspectives.[51]

Most of all, postindustrial parks are presenting a useful illusion. In claiming that the parks have environmental benefits, the parks are positioned as having a broader purpose than mere recreation. Reflected in the brand identity of "the 606" that alleges a citywide benefit, the architectural and booster narratives stake out a scale of impact that far exceeds the small footprint of these linear spaces. Postindustrial parks are striking symbols of a new and powerful urban ideology, which proposes that cities—as dense, communal, carbon-friendly spaces—are humanity's best hope of surviving climate change, and that green space development is a key part of making cities more sustainable.[52] For consumers, the beauty of this approach is that is soothes the already substantial cognitive dissonance between consumption practices and environmental crisis: the heavy symbols of nature are entrusted with doing the hard work of carbon reduction, relieving any ecological guilt arising from air travel habits and new MacBooks. For governments, this sleight of hand is even more effective: postindustrial parks offer nice symbols—but what's their real environmental impact compared to, for example, imposing regulations on polluting industries? Corporations, too, benefit from this ideology: by donating to park-building efforts, corporations "greenwash" their polluting ways—recall that Boeing donated millions to the Bloomingdale Trail/606; Coach and other fashion companies (an industry notorious for its environmental waste) did the same for the

High Line; and Buffalo Bayou Park was built primarily with oil-money largesse.

The result is that the radical potential of socio-spatial transformation is snuffed out by the ruling urban ideologies.[53] When linear parks facilitate the expansion of White middle-class territory and reinforce a very specific kind of recreation (favoring the passive over the active, the intellectual over the bodily) and a very specific representation of nature (favoring the symbolic over the real thing), cultural power expands, further tying nature and environmental sustainability to urban economic growth. That proponents of this ideology have chosen *this* aesthetic—of a romantic, agentic, wild nature—is no accident. Beyond its association with earlier waves of postindustrial gentrification and discovery narratives, the plant life makes it seem that the parks are truly natural sites within unequal urban landscapes.

This new aesthetic is not merely a replica of the plant life that existed in two defunct railbeds; indeed, since the opening of the High Line in 2009 it has become institutionalized as the preferred representation of nature—in other parks, and in any site where developers and architects are advancing postindustrial aesthetics. Architectural styles are always copied, but the Friends of the High Line have attempted to effectively trademark the park's aesthetic through the creation of the High Line Network, a consortium of thirty-seven postindustrial parks (which includes the Bloomingdale Trail/606 and Buffalo Bayou Park) that spreads the gospel of adaptive reuse.

But how far can this new ideology be stretched? So far, I have argued that these parks are not really about nature, but about money and branding and prestige—and that even their "nature" is more often about aesthetics than ecology. In theory, then, this style of park could be built just about anywhere. But if the political-economic impetus is necessary, is it also sufficient?—particularly when taking this new representation of nature into Houston, arguably America's most unnatural metropolis? Given all of the efforts to massage the High Line's and the Bloomingdale Trail/606's authenticity, how did the creators of Buffalo Bayou Park attempt to inscribe nature and postindustrial aesthetics in a site without rails and in a city with few collective concerns about nature, parks, or sustainability? In other words, when it comes to postindustrial parks' authenticity, is it as simple as letting the grass grow?

• • •

On August 30, 2017, Buffalo Bayou Park was under water. The $58 million linear park, opened just two years prior, drowned in the trillion gallons of water that had fallen on Houston during Hurricane Harvey's four-day deluge.

And it was disgusting. The floods stuck around, and they stank, in the searing Houston heat. Draining Buffalo Bayou Park was not like pouring out a bucket. Harvey had not brought a massive storm surge like those that wrecked New Orleans and New York during earlier storms, which made landfall and then receded, laying bare their destruction. Rather, the flood in Buffalo Bayou Park was a clogged toilet, a slow-moving drain full of debris and sewage sitting out for a week in hundred-degree temperatures.

Visiting Buffalo Bayou Park in the immediate aftermath of Harvey, it was hard to picture what was beneath the rotting brown stew. The water had nearly reached the top of the bayou's high banks and had flooded out the two roadways that ran parallel on either side of the park. Below that waterline was millions of dollars' worth of architectural and horticultural work—materials that had been intended to function as aesthetically pleasing flood control, given Houston's long history of flooding. Harvey, a supposed "five-hundred-year storm," put that aesthetic infrastructure to a stiff early test.

Harvey's impact on Buffalo Bayou Park presented an interesting new wrinkle in postindustrial parks' representations of nature. In the aftermath of the storm, it was clear that "nature" in Buffalo Bayou Park was going to be more than a social construction, more than a simulacrum of postindustrial plant life. This was the other side of nature: material environmental forces revealing that, in the age of climate change, "all that is solid" may not "melt into air" but certainly at some point will be under water.[54]

The designers of the new Buffalo Bayou Park understood the site's purpose in this dual way: at once pastoral recreation and flood control. Balancing those two objectives was—as had been the case with the High Line and the Bloomingdale Trail/606—a collaboration between firms: architects from Page and landscape architects from SWA Group, two companies with long-standing footprints in Houston and other Texas cities. SWA had previously designed the Sabine Promenade, opened in 2006 at the eastern end of the new Buffalo Bayou Park, and therefore had key experience with the site conditions. Larry Speck, principal at Page and lead architect on the Buffalo Bayou Park design, explained the challenges:

> This is a place that is absolutely constrained. Buffalo Bayou is the floodway for . . . the central part of Houston, and for many, many decades it just has been the way that water evacuates when there's a hurricane or a big rain or a flood. But . . . the 99 percent of the time when it's not being used as a floodway, could it be . . . inhabited as a park space? . . . Everything was constrained. Everything was limited by thinking of that moment when there would be a flood.[55]

That moment came, and Harvey, devastating though it was both for the park and the city, was therefore the expectation, not the exception. With landscape architect Scott McCready anticipating that the entire park that rested "below the very tops of the slopes will go under water relatively frequently— at least a couple times a year," Buffalo Bayou Park's designers approached the tension between beautification and utility in several ways.[56] First, they constructed a hardier landscape than the one that preceded it: the previous lawn area was reduced by 50 percent, and more than thirteen thousand water-absorbing trees were planted within the park's 160-acre footprint.[57] For the new buildings established within the park's boundaries, the architects understood not only that water would inevitably rise, breaching the foundations, but that the flood events would have a directional flow. As Larry Speck explained, regarding the building that housed the park's restaurant and other amenities:

> We had to make the building so stout that even when the rushing waters come and maybe there's a log coming down the water, it can ram into that concrete pier of the building and do no damage whatsoever. We even made the finish of the concrete a kind of textured, board-form concrete, so if gets a little nick or scratch in it, it's just patina and it looks just fine. But everything in the building is understanding that there's going to be a flood, and it has to be able to withstand that.[58]

Such concerns went well beyond the park's handful of buildings: every path, every stair, and every flower was going to be under water at some point. Just as the builders of the High Line and the Bloomingdale Trail/606 favored a rugged aesthetic, in Buffalo Bayou Park similar kinds of durable plant life and sturdy built materials had aesthetic benefits but were also ecologically necessary. Scott McCready explained:

> Early on, our first efforts . . . addressed some of the most challenging portions of the project by building trails and adjusting grades and vegetation and dealing with the hydraulic issues to reconnect . . . west of downtown to downtown itself, we wanted to get people connected back up to the more bucolic landscapes. . . . [We] developed a vocabulary that is very specific to this environment, with these heavy guardrails and light fixtures that can withstand going under water and systems of planting that are robust enough to withstand the frequent inundation.[59]

In this way, the aesthetics of flood protection and of postindustrial landscapes conveniently coalesced in Buffalo Bayou Park. As with the Chicago and New York models, in Houston the landscape architects turned toward local ecologies and the idea of "native" plants. Removing lawns and replacing them with regionally appropriate ground cover and trees habituated to wet conditions reflected the designers' efforts to restore the site to something approaching its original state (or at least an approximation of what it might have been, had the Flood Control District and Army Corps not straightened the bayou's banks and had highways not been built over top and along both sides). So if not getting back to the site's long-gone "first nature," at least something more "natural" in the eyes of architects than manicured lawns—something that could be better harmonized, visually and ecologically, with the contemporary urban environment.

Indeed, while the park's visual transformation—and the official rhetoric coming from the park's boosters at the Buffalo Bayou Partnership—may have suggested to the public that the bayou's nature had been restored, the architects themselves were well aware that this was fiction. Landscape architect Scott McCready noted that the site had long lost its original ecological conditions and that what his team was building could not and would not bring it back. He acknowledged that Buffalo Bayou's channelization in the 1950s had "straightened out a lot of the sinuousity of the channel and resulted in a landscape now that is very far from its original, natural state. Even though Houstonians as they view it, see it as natural."[60] Nevertheless, the landscape architects made efforts to bring the park's ecology within a regional, if not exactly site-specific, environmental authenticity:

> We . . . structured the planting in ways to really bring forth the unique character and ecology: using cypress and cottonwoods and sycamore trees that are more associated with the riparian corridor of the bayou and bring them to the forefront. . . . The species diversity and the plantings that replaced a lot of the areas that were maintained by mowed turf in an effort to restore the ecology and really restore the character.[61]

For the architects, restoring the bayou's character went along with reeducating Houstonians on how to "use" nature. In a city without a rich tradition of urban parks, McCready argued that the technocratic changes to Houston's bayous had "really denuded people's relationship with the land and the most significant natural feature of the Houston landscape."[62] In a touch that would have been out of place in park-rich cities like Chicago or New York, the Buffalo Bayou Partnership emplaced six "word sculptures"—large, all-caps commands—at various points in the park, compelling visitors to "EXPLORE," "PAUSE," "REFLECT," "LISTEN," "EMERGE," and "OBSERVE."[63] McCready termed these additions "art that instructs—in case you've forgotten how to enjoy nature," but more broadly held that Buffalo Bayou Park provided "the cultural education and the ecological education of Houstonians so that they understand not only the beauty of this park but also the impacts of all the development decisions in the surrounding region as well."[64]

Like the High Line and the Bloomingdale Trail/606, Buffalo Bayou Park was visually enmeshed in the city in a way that was historically new. Though Houston's park was always a green space—albeit more of a wasteland than an amenity—the redevelopment process, in transforming the site into a more prestigious form of nature, nevertheless performed the same sort of 180-degree turn from past perceptions of the space. Derelict railways share much with overgrown waterways: both types of spaces were nuisances to many locals. Although the banks of a bayou are more symbolically a part of nature than a railway could ever seem to be, the fact that Buffalo Bayou Park—two green banks along an urban waterway—had to be remade to become "nature" illustrates how nature is socially constructed: there is nothing inherent about the perception of a site as nature; rather, it is produced by the creation and maintenance of a certain aesthetic. In twenty-first-century cities, that aesthetic is one that can be transposed from railway to bayou, so long as a park project's boosters have the funds to take what is in that moment "natural" and make it "nature."

So there are variations on this emerging universal theme: environmental authenticity demands that the architecture in postindustrial parks be attuned to the social and ecological needs of a site and its city. The preciousness of the High Line would be ill suited to a floodplain; Buffalo Bayou Park's rugged texture would have been out of place on a high-fashion catwalk (and its "word sculptures" would likely have been ridiculed in New York). But culturally, they share many things as linear postindustrial parks: a social and visual connection between park spaces and cityscapes;

themes of aesthetic if not ecological restoration; romantic views of the sites' pasts and a longing for the sites to develop the patina of age; a portrayal of nature as insurgent, agentic, wild, native; and a celebration of a particular prospect on cities and urban life, to view shimmering downtown skylines and postindustrial infrastructural grit from the refuge of the hip edges of Chelsea, Wicker Park, or Montrose—to see American cities' post-urban-crisis rebirth like perennials rising from the dirt.

Buffalo Bayou Park was geographically well situated to achieve this. It's notable that this section was the first and most glamourous piece of bayou to be developed out of the prospective 150 miles of planned park transformations promised by the privately funded $220 million Bayou Greenways 2020 project. Not only building a physical connection from the gentrified west side to downtown's tourist spaces, visually the park offers a level of technological sublimity (in the Burkean sense, of moments that evoke terror, but safely, "at certain distances") matched only by the High Line.[65] Close to downtown, the height and density of the built environment inspire awe, while creating lush vegetation and a moody, brooding landscape below. From other perspectives, the crisscrossing overpasses of streets and highways horizontally delimit the park's landscapes, making things, in places, as picturesque as an Olmstedian ramble.[66] So there is a real alchemy of gray and green in Buffalo Bayou Park that precedes the site's recent architectural interventions.

Buffalo Bayou Park, like the High Line and the Bloomingdale Trail/606, is a prominent example of how ideas about nature have been adapted to the urban conditions of the twenty-first century. These parks reject the ecological traditions of urban parks, eschewing universalizing types of lawns and trees that have made past generations of parks everywhere look very much the same. In their place are plants deemed better suited to local ecologies:

plants that can thrive in a shallow railbed, a deep concrete basin, or a floodway; plants that have long histories in these regions, long enough to be considered native.

The architects and planners ultimately build a vision of what kind of nature might have existed, had an old bayou not been channelized and planted with the "wrong" grasses and trees, or if elevated railroads had been left well enough alone. But their interventions raise the question, Was what existed at these sites, and still might exist had the sites been left to rot in peace, nature? Though humans have convinced themselves that nature is some external thing, external from society and the objects of human engineering, human creations become part of the ecological fabric all the same, built with materials that were once earth. Technological interventions—railroads, factories, highways, channelized bayous—cocreated the real and present ecological conditions of these three sites. In time, if the new plantings take hold and the waters don't rise, these new interventions will too create the sites' real and present ecological conditions.

So if the "old" versions of the High Line, the Bloomingdale Trail/606, and Buffalo Bayou Park were the products of nature, why have so much ink and concrete and dirt been spilled to create new and different versions within these same sites? Why, for all the emphasis on ecological locality, do the three parks' representations of nature look curiously the same?

What the parks are doing, despite their radical visual break from parks of generations past, is repurposing and reasserting the values of the picturesque. Contemporary architects' preferred aesthetics—for wild-looking plant life—assert an authenticity to postindustrial displays of nature that very much recalls picturesque architects' efforts to tie down a slice of "wilderness" within urban space. So while postindustrial parks resist the picturesque's ecological traditions—of sprawling green lawns and visions of the English countryside and the deployment of this landscape into any and all local contexts—they do not reject its point of view.[67] The reincorporation of nature and beauty and most of all, of perspective, into urban parks retrofits the picturesque for contemporary use. Though in the twenty-first century the objects of admiration are different—the same buildings, streets, and elevated train tracks that would have been out of place in pastoral landscapes—they remain framed in a romantic lens, projecting cultural authority and sublimity onto the urban built environment.[68]

In reframing how parks intersect with urban space, another universal impulse emerges in postindustrial parks: to visually center high-rise cityscapes and offer close connections to low-rise, gentrified enclaves. The old picturesque was keeping out a particular idea of the urban—loud, dirty, smelly—and the racialized people who inhabited these working landscapes. The postindustrial picturesque, in bringing in "the city," doesn't necessarily invite those kinds of outcast urban places or people. It is difficult to imagine Buffalo Bayou Park being built at the foot of East Houston's oil refineries, or to imagine the park becoming reinhabited by a homeless encampment, as it was during the 1980s and '90s. Postindustrial parks visually consume those old industrial spaces, and even quaff the nostalgia of more dangerous times, but only with the sanitizing view of the present upon the past. Postindustrial parks do not gaze upon the actual working landscapes of contemporary cities—which still exist, but are pushed to the urban periphery, far from downtown views; recall that the High Line served as the final eviction notice for the Meatpacking District's meatpackers. Park visitors are instead treated to industry's corpses, juxtaposed with the towering breath of global cities.

What does all this accomplish? It makes these landscapes powerful for reasons that go far beyond the political and economic forces that spurred their redevelopment. This cultural power is primed to persist even after the initial wave of investment and tourist excitement dissipates, because postindustrial parks have been built as bridges between the historical authority of the picturesque—which, in the hands of urban elites, planners, and architects, determined which landscapes were valuable and which landscapes were not—and the present and future of cities. The picturesque is persistent; it has been institutionalized for centuries. It fundamentally shapes how people (in the West, if not globally) interpret and value landscapes. Every great park, every landscape painting, every picturesque cultural object that has ever been consumed has been culturally hardwiring people to see picturesque landscapes not only as beautiful, but as natural, and as best. Postindustrial parks take on these qualities, and architects' appeals to local, native forms of nature, and assertions of fidelity with local history and collective memory, only further naturalize these spaces within contemporary urban landscapes, dictating that these spaces are not *just* the creations of capitalist growth machines, but ecologically appropriate spaces with unimpeachable cultural authority.

10

SPATIAL PRACTICES AND SOCIAL CONTROL

POSTINDUSTRIAL parks invite walking. More than that—in many of them, it's not just an invited activity but the primary activity that can comfortably take place within a ten-foot path. Walking is a central spiritual, cultural, and political activity: Zen masters practice walking meditation, flaneurs wander alleys and sidewalks, and protestors march through city streets. Friends of the High Line cofounder Josh David likewise considers walking an ideal type of urban ambulation:

> In Italy there's a traditional walk called the *passeggiata*. In small towns and big cities, people come out in the early evening to do a leisurely, theatrical promenade through one of the main streets or a central plaza. When we started working on the High Line, I held in the back of my mind an image of the High Line as a place where something like the Italian *passeggiata* could happen—a place where people would come to stroll just for the sake of strolling, to be among their fellow citizens, to smile and flirt, to check out one another's outfits, to walk with parents after an early dinner, or to meet up for a date.[1]

This kind of walk is venerated not only by David; this form of passive recreation has been prescribed as the preeminent park activity going back to the days of the picturesque—a romantic, slow stroll in the peaceful refuge of a park. Frederick Olmsted wrote that "a park as a work of design should . . . be a ground which invites, encourages and facilitates movement, its topographical conditions [should] make movement a pleasure."[2] But in practice, whether in Central Park or on the High Line, this invitation for a walk is accompanied and undercut by an invitation to submit to various kinds of surveillance, as park designers and park authorities share a compulsion to control public space: to make parks easily surveilled and safe.

This tension between freedom and control is not only central to architectural decisions and policing strategies, but it underlies every inherently political question about how parks should be used (e.g., should officials allow the homeless to sleep in parks? Yes—freedom; no—control).[3] How those politics play out is a dialectic of repression and resistance, one observed over space and time: in Chicago, in 1919, in Washington Park; in Houston, in 1978, in Moody Park; in New York, in 1988, in Tompkins Square Park; to name a few.[4] Victories in either direction, freedom or control, are never permanent, as securing either requires ongoing political and cultural work.

On the side of control, police violence is the most powerful way for governments and other institutions of power to control public space. With the police holding, as Max Weber put it, a "monopoly" on the legitimate use of violence, this force is difficult to resist—evidenced, to take one example, by the NYPD's swift midnight clearance of Occupy Wall Street protestors from the privately owned Zuccotti Park in 2011.[5] The mere threat of police intervention can be sufficient to repress popular claims on public space and create the kind of order desired by local governments and private elites. As indicated by the High Line, the Bloomingdale Trail/606, and Buffalo Bayou Park, which are tightly controlled yet generally lack the visible signs of policing, order can be created by design.

Order in urban parks is often created by design by necessity, as representations of nature tend to conflict with visible signs of policing. It's precisely in the social construction of nature as visually open and untouched by human hands that quickly runs into official desires to make parks safe for visitors and legible to the authorities. Getting visitors to buy into the prospect that parks are indeed "nature" relies on imparting a particular phenomenological experience: to enter a park and to viscerally feel that they have entered a new kind of space, one that, in one way or another, invites them to leave urban things behind.

This tension calls back to the central historical fiction of urban parks: that they are spatially and symbolically distinct from cities. In picturesque parks, where landscape architects demarcated parks from urban space more broadly, the fiction depended on the evacuation of the visible built environment, away from overly "architectural" architectural interventions, which were signs of the fiction.[6] Even something as mundane as a restroom could remind visitors that they weren't really in "the wilderness," but in a simulacrum. In postindustrial parks, where urban forms are central to the aesthetics and public appeal, architecture is made to commingle with nature. But park designers still seek that same feeling of entering a new type of space—if not wilderness, then a space that is at least more bucolic than the streets, a space where the *passeggiata* can take place.

The overt presence of police and signs of surveillance—cameras, locks, gates, harsh lighting, barbed wire—act as detriments not only to presentations of nature but to the privileged cultural practices that rely on nature—and on an atmosphere of "ease" to take place.[7] Racially privileged park visitors may understand on an intellectual level that the police and "prickly" signs of surveillance aren't there to target them but to protect them (and implicitly, to target racialized "others" and the homeless and other nonconsumers).[8] But for those same privileged visitors, there's also an emotional element tied to the latent anxiety of being in public—crime, terrorism, harassment—anxieties easily triggered by those cameras, locks, gates, harsh lighting, barbed wire. Too many police, too many cameras allow anxiety to slip into racial paranoia.

And for all of the new, twenty-first-century surveillance technologies, today's landscape designers go about securing parks in rather analog ways, using techniques not so different from those of the past. In the earliest urban parks, landscape architects used the design strategies of the picturesque not only to create beauty but also to create aesthetic order: to engineer a landscape that was recognizable to visitors and observable to authorities.[9]

And for all of the new, twenty-first-century fears, what the creation of aesthetic and social order seeks to achieve in postindustrial parks is in large measure a continuation of the past, a contemporary effort to address the issue of racial order—*the* overarching historical issue of park politics, embedded in all contests between freedom and control. Parks are spaces where people's claims on the state and citizenship can be made visible. Racial hierarchies influence who is able to make claims that are seen as legitimate by institutions of power. And in parks, abstract racial fears of crime become very personal very quickly—much more so than other venues for racial paranoias. White worries about home break-ins are mollified by security systems and locked gates; in parks, the body is the imagined target.[10]

• • •

Generalized and racialized fears of crime have long dictated parks' forms of surveillance. In 1871, six years after the end of slavery,

Olmsted worried that the cloistered, intimate areas he favored in his park designs offered a level of seclusion that would-be criminals might find inviting, particularly during evening hours. Such spaces, if left unsupervised at night, could repel "decent people . . . from them, and they [might] become nurseries of crime and immorality."[11] Olmsted countered this architectural problem with architectural security measures, as seen in Chicago's South Park, for example, where buildings divided the park's open lawn from the rambles and lagoons, enclosing the grounds so that park police could simultaneously block visitors from wooded areas and survey visitors across the lawn, where it was deemed "desirable that they should be under special police observation."[12]

But there were aesthetic limits to this approach. Olmsted understood that security and the park's "nature" were in visual conflict; lighting the parks' rambles, which would have perhaps made them more secure at night, was rejected because:

> The tarry vapor which escapes from gas-pipes is poisonous to trees, and grounds which are closely planted, or which abound in shrubs and underwood, cannot be so lighted artificially that their landscape beauty may be enjoyed, or so that those wishing concealment in them can be clearly recognized, and their movements surely followed.[13]

Lights would have aided in security efforts but would have detracted from the well-being of the plants.

Early park developers believed that design on its own would not solve the problem of crime in park spaces; police were present in picturesque parks, and long lists of rules and regulations were common.[14] Perhaps reflecting an expectation that larger social forces of racial and class domination would keep order in parks (by keeping people in their socially prescribed places), architects held that informal social pressure could be as power-ful as the police when it came to asserting control. As Olmsted wrote of park security: "the great body of decent, orderly, tidy, and respectable people" will use the "silent influence of example . . . [to] strongly persuade others to exercise due control upon per-verse inclinations."[15]

• • •

As park authorities and architects revised urban park form in the twentieth century, the design tension between nature and security was resolved in one direction, as representing nature became a low priority for most park districts.[16] As the prescribed park activities shifted from pastoral wandering to more programmatic forms of recreation, harsher forms of surveillance did not necessarily dis-rupt the new aesthetics or the newly favored activities. Basket-ball, baseball, tennis, swimming, and the like all took place within highly confined, highly visible spaces—sometimes indoors, oth-erwise within fences or other physical boundaries. Such activities, when formally organized, involved umpires, referees, and other officials, thus offering additional "eyes on the street."[17]

The architectural turn toward more aggressive social control reflected a racial logic. Parks were, as put simply by the Chicago Park District in its 1947 tome *The Police and Minority Groups*, geo-graphically ripe for tension:

> Nearly all of the small parks of the city are stationed in the paths of . . . moving populations. . . . It is within these public parks that the different minorities are first contacting one another. . . . It follows that these are the significant places in which the different groups must be successfully mediated to one another. The impor-tance of the . . . park policemen cannot be underestimated. They

are, so to speak, at the crossroads of the community, and they are a major resource in the maintenance of peace and civil order during the periods when strange and contrasting nationalities and races are having their initial contacts with one another.[18]

For park districts around the country, managing the conflicts posed by urban migration and neighborhood change required the "continuous attention of the police authorities" in "public parks . . . frequented by both races."[19] Such a strategy was informed not only by local tensions but by race riots and rebellions that enveloped parks and public spaces in cities across the United States in the 1910s, 1940s, and 1960s.[20]

• • •

From a design standpoint, one of the key trend lines of urban parks history is the increasing visibility of park users over time. Surveillance was part of parks' origin story, physically built into nineteenth-century parks during a time when more violent and unyielding racial hierarchies ruled American cities. In the nearly two centuries of intervening racial and spatial upheaval, again and again park authorities' solution has been to increase the visibility of park users so that the police and park workers and park users can all observe each other and everyone else. When the "urban crisis" was raging and city governments effectively abandoned many parks, park authorities turned parks into panopticons. As Sharon Zukin notes of this process:

Playgrounds [we]re fenced in for children and their guardians, and parks [we]re closed at night. Tompkins Square Park in lower Manhattan, site of violent confrontations in 1988 and 1991[,] . . . was closed for two years for extensive landscaping. When the park was reopened, open sight lines permitted children, ballplayers, and elderly bench sitters to keep an eye on each other while using their own spaces.[21]

The dual use of design to both refurbish and redoubt urban parks was a common strategy for park authorities during the rise of neoliberal, consumerist urban economies in the 1980s and '90s. Park authorities greeted the return of White workers with revived public spaces, reprieves from cold concrete that—if not necessarily emplacing grand symbols of nature back into parks— at least offered some measure of aesthetic upgrading: new flowers, trees, and comfortable seating that provided office workers and tourists with an "illusion of tranquility."[22] But often these were surveillance techniques masquerading as improvements. As cases like New York's Bryant Park indicate, revanchism and refurbishment could be simultaneous. When the neoclassical Bryant Park underwent a privatized process of upscaling in the 1990s, the park was both architecturally and programmatically renovated in order to secure the space: "iron fences and high hedges were removed, the balustrades were cut open, entrances were added, and the old ones were lowered" in an effort to open the park up for surveillance while simultaneously making the park seem more welcoming.[23] Located one block east of Times Square, excluding the poor and allowing middle-class visitors to feel a sense of ease were paramount to the park's private overseers. As David Madden describes, this was achieved by taking the park's unstructured—and therefore risky—spaces and making them permanently programmatic:

A carousel was added to increase the number of families with children. A staffed, outdoor lending library was established. Fashion shows and circuses were held in giant tents on the lawn. The park would become home to a bocce ball court, a chess area, a nonsmoking section, wireless internet service, movie screenings, concerts, chairs and benches with plaques that could be engraved as personal monuments. In winter months, the lawn would be given over to ice skating. A good portion of the park was taken over by the Bryant Park Grill.[24]

This strategy—of making spaces more visible, more exclusionary, more programmatic, and more consumerist—can be seen in parks in every city: a surveillance strategy that hinges on a more pernicious form of Olmsted's "silent influence of example" or Jane Jacobs's "eyes on the street," where park users are expected to consume—to buy cups of coffee from the vendor or tickets to the private event—and to be suspicious of nonconsumers, because why else are they in the park—what are their intentions? Racial fear still radiates beneath the surface of refurbished parks, their disheveled pasts not so distant in anyone's collective memory (least of all the private park corporations that make pleasing their donors and "customers" the top priority).[25] Park authorities therefore aim to pack parks with "desirable" visitors (a term explicitly and frequently deployed by the Bryant Park Restoration Corporation) through commercial and events programming that allows parks to be policed without seeming policed.[26]

· · ·

Does the High Line even need police? The Friends of the High Line seem to think so, judging by the private security forces that guard the entrances to the park's private events and the team of maintenance workers who quietly and frequently empty the park's trash cans—which is not an overt act of policing, but nevertheless polices "quality of life crimes," like sleeping in public or picking through the trash.[27] Sometimes there are actual cops on the High Line and in other postindustrial parks, or park rangers, or other private security guards making the rounds; generally, though, the parks seem unguarded. The absence of such outward signs of security and surveillance—with things like frequent garbage collection obvious only to a careful observer—helps facilitate postindustrial parks' "natural" facades. Visitors can focus on plants and postindustrial views, rather than police officers and cameras.

The apparent lack of policing in postindustrial parks is an extension of the panoptic design changes advanced in the 1990s and 2000s in spaces like Tompkins Square Park and Bryant Park, where parks were to be "watched and policed, but not by [park organizations or the police]. Given the right social environment, the public would police itself."[28] But panopticons require radial spaces, where all park users can be viewed from a single vantage point (as was dreamed up by philosopher Jeremy Bentham, inventor of the panopticon, in his efforts to design the "ideal prison" in the late eighteenth century).[29] The long, linear spaces of the High Line, the Bloomingdale Trail/606, and Buffalo Bayou Park elude a central site of observation. What that means for park authorities' security efforts is that surveillance is decentralized: for postindustrial parks to be observed and secured, people need to be continuously moving through them.[30]

With eight million people now touring the High Line annually, the waves of visitors are highly controlled. There are no stampedes on the High Line. There are few protests.[31] There's a creepy uniformity in the way that eight million people use the space. While the Bloomingdale Trail/606 and Buffalo Bayou Park have fewer visitors and more room—and bikes and dogs (both banned on the High Line)—they too are home to crowds that for the most part do what the linear spaces invite them to do, and what park boosters want them to do: move slowly, smell the flowers, and consume.

Like other strategies, design that invites movement can have a benign guise even while serving the interests of surveillance, social control, and security. Walking, when framed as a pastoral park activity or a *passeggiata*, is seen as an ideal recreational fit for the linear spaces of postindustrial parks. The Friends of the Bloomingdale Trail, for example, envisioned Chicago's park as "a walking/bike trail that would be a magnet for leisurely weekend and evening strolls" as well as "an elevated retreat from the hustle and bustle of the streets. . . . A place to dream and stroll."[32] Lead artist Frances Whitehead affirmed that the Bloomingdale Trail/606 would "incentivize circulation with unique, complementary amenities"; that is, upon entering the space, visitors would take in the aesthetic pleasures of one scene while their curious gaze would lead them to new spaces within the park.[33] This ensures that no park spaces remain unobserved for long, even during quieter moments when comparatively fewer visitors are in the parks.

The High Line's designers explicitly wanted to encourage an atmosphere of mutual observation—to the point that imagined exchanges among visitors were fundamental to the intended uses of the park. The fact that the High Line opened in three distinct sections over the course of several years allowed architects to respond to feedback from park users and observe the activities that the previous sections encouraged. For example, at the opening of the park's second section in 2011, landscape architect James Corner described his intentions for how people should use the space:

> Certain things we learned in Section 1 is just how people like to linger on the High Line. That it's not simply about strolling, but it's about seating and just taking in the scene. And so in Section

2 there was an attempt to allow for more seating, to create more nooks and crannies where people can sit and relax and to try to create some settings where you can actually theatricalize the relationship between the viewer and the viewed. For example, the seating steps and the sun lawn is really a big exhibitionist sort of space. Compared to many other spaces on the High Line, it's relatively open and relatively large. And so we expect to see a lot of people sort of showing off, but also being a great people-watching scene.[34]

This idea of mutual observation, while cast by Corner in playful terms, underscores the hypervisibility that comes with being in a linear park and therefore how mutual observation can function as surveillance. Visitors are on display not only to fellow park goers but to people on the surrounding streets and in the adjacent buildings. On this point, the authors of the official plan for the Bloomingdale Trail/606 explicitly hoped, given the number of residences directly abutting the park, that "the oversight of nearby neighbors can make the Bloomingdale safer" by offering eyes on the street.[35] Similarly extending the sphere of surveillance to those beyond the physical park spaces, High Line architect Charles Renfro described the park's Twenty-Sixth Street "viewing spur" as a space of mutual observation:

It's not a one-way activity. . . . It's a two-way activity. It's always about a reciprocity. And so the frame is focusing the people from inside looking out, but it's also focusing the people outside looking in. So while it might be confused with theater, it's actually an inversion, and it turns the city into an actor and the people into actors at the same time.[36]

Of the three parks under study, the High Line's designers most clearly teased out such visual connections, which were reinforced by the site's conditions (the comparatively narrower passageway of the viaduct and the physical density of the surrounding areas) but made explicit by architectural techniques—such as the park's sunken overlook above Tenth Avenue, where part of the structure was cut out to give park users a view to the pedestrian and automotive traffic below. Architect Liz Diller commented, "The sunken overlook is a very strong . . . gesture. Not only setting up a consensual space of observation and performance, but also it frames something that is normally thought of as extremely banal."[37]

"Consensual" is an interesting word—implying that to be in a public park is to opt into this form of surveillance. While the architects' genial view of things seems to argue that this surveillance is benign and even fun, this seems true only for people who fit the presumed privileged identities; no doubt this fun takes a darker turn when park goers' collective gaze fixes on the bodies of racialized "others." In this way, seemingly playful popular surveillance can serve as a barrier to entry for people who do not wish to be subjected to privileged scrutiny and the threat of real police violence that lurks behind that gaze.

By encouraging park users to move continuously, postindustrial park architects share a design logic with of one of the most reviled types of public spaces of the twentieth century: the barren "bonus plazas" developed in the 1970s and '80s, which deployed uninviting design to deter people from lingering.[38] Former director of urban design for the New York City Planning Department Jonathan Barnett argued that such spaces were "often inhospitable, not because their designers were stupid but because the owners of the buildings . . . deliberately sought an environment that encouraged people to admire the building briefly and then be on their way."[39] Although postindustrial parks are major tourist destinations rather than the barbicans of urban citadels, a similar effect is nevertheless observed. Visitors' views are trained on the landscape; stops for conversations or photographs are common, but often brief. The three parks under study offer limited seating, and what is there tends not to be comfortable for more than a few minutes: thin benches, many without backs—seating that better serves a streamlined aesthetic than long-term use. In short, postindustrial park visitors tend to admire things briefly and then be on their way.

The implications of continuous movement become clearer, too, when contrasted with the potential consequences of being stationary in a public space. Absurd as it might seem, being stationary can be viewed as a safety threat and even criminalized; therefore, it is an activity that the developers and authorities of public spaces have in various ways discouraged. Being stationary can be construed as loitering, an activity historically criminalized in public space. (Despite the 1972 *Papachristou v. Jacksonville* Supreme Court decision, which declared vagrancy statutes unconstitutional, police departments such as the NYPD continued to issue summonses for loitering into the 2000s.) Police officers have had wide latitude in determining who and what constitutes a threat to social order (and where and when to use force).[40] In a very different social and spatial context, the movement encouraged by the design of postindustrial parks mirrors police logic in hypermarginalized spaces like LA's Skid Row. As Forrest Stuart documents, officers "enforc[e] perpetual movement" for the homeless individuals who populate the public spaces east of downtown. Commanding denizens to "move along," officers theorize that this technique deters crime; as one opined to Stuart, "It's pretty hard to spark your crack pipe when you're busy walking."[41] It may be so that the three parks under study have not seen many "crack pipes" since before their collective redevelopment in the 2000s and 2010s. No doubt, the developers and authorities of postindustrial parks have very different ways of engaging with their publics than Skid Row police officers. But the process and the outcome are the same: keeping people moving creates order.

· · ·

Before movement and mutual observation can create order, people need to physically enter the parks. That isn't always easy to do: the elevated rails of the High Line and the Bloomingdale Trail/606 sit several stories above street level; the sunken trails of Buffalo Bayou Park lie several stories below. The three parks all have ambiguous entry points when observed from the street: from the blocks of Chelsea or Humboldt Park or along Allen Parkway, you can see into the parks and the people walking through them. But less visible are routes to enter the parks: the stairs, ramps, and elevators that transport visitors from the streets to the secluded public spaces are unevenly located—a first-time visitor might need to wander several blocks to find access—making them prime examples of what Steven Flusty terms "slippery space": "space that cannot be reached, due to contorted, protracted or missing paths of approach."[42] Lack of clear, even access creates another barrier to entry to the three parks.

The history of elevated rails and infrastructures in general is indeed one of separation. These are spaces that were built or organized to be away from city streets and sidewalks: the High Line and the Bloomingdale Line were built to get trains off of street level; development around Buffalo Bayou never symbolically embraced the waterway, which was turned into the Houston Ship Channel in one location and boxed in with highways in another. Accessibility was not the point. And so much of the three parks' slipperiness comes from the architectural teams' willingness to let the site conditions determine the park spaces. Which follows from the ideology of adaptive re-use and environmental authenticity, as creating visual fidelity with the past—to have the park designs evoke the imbrications of built and natural forms that existed prior to redevelopment—drove much of the design of the High Line, the Bloomingdale Trail/606, and Buffalo Bayou Park.

But efforts to re-create "in-vitro natural landscape[s]," as Michael Van Valkenburgh put it, conceal the idea that the parks could have looked very different.[43] The High Line didn't need to exist as a straight-line path. It didn't need to stay within the footprint of the existing railbed; with $250 million invested, acquiring an adjacent lot or two for inclusion in the park was feasible if the city government desired a perpendicular extension (a strategy executed for the Bloomingdale Trail/606's "access parks"—and something that was particularly feasible at the High Line because the city government owned the adjacent land that became the site of the new Whitney Museum of American Art).[44] Nor did the park need to remain gravity-bound to the railbed; it would not have been inconceivable to build the park out vertically. One design, submitted to the High Line's design competition in 2003, proposed that the new park should be one long swimming pool.[45] Another suggested a roller coaster. "These were not realistic ideas," said Friends of the High Line cofounder Robert Hammond, "but they made people think about the High Line in new ways."[46] Such alternatives were thus understood by park developers as preludes to making the park as a walking path—the only choice, from their perspective, that made sense for the space.[47]

Allowing the infrastructural site conditions to determine park design provided the architects and developers a convenient rationale for why the three parks weren't more accessible.[48] At Buffalo Bayou Park, six-lane parkways on both sides enclose the space—leading landscape architect Scott McCready to shift the locus of blame about inaccessibility from the architects to the urban environment: "given Houston's weak examples of pedestrian infrastructure, [the parkways] really made [it] very difficult to even get to this park."[49] Only one piece of the $58 million redesign addressed this major flaw: a pedestrian bridge at Montrose Boulevard and Memorial Drive—the only new pedestrian route over the five miles of parkway that barricaded the park from the neighborhoods to the north and south. It was a point that Frances Whitehead was sensitive to, particularly as she drew a distinction between the accessibility of the High Line and the Bloomingdale Trail/606:

> Just look at the access. When you go to the High Line, it's always hard to find the stairs; like, "how do you get up there?" We spent a huge amount of time and eventually decided that we would, except for the architectural intervention of the big stair at Milwaukee [Avenue], there are no other stairs. It is all ramps, so it's all wheel-friendly. . . . And this became a statement about a democratic space.[50]

The near-exclusive use of ramps likely makes the Bloomingdale Trail/606 more accessible than other postindustrial parks. The High Line, as Whitehead points out, may be the worst offender from an accessibility standpoint: seven elevators currently serve as the only stairless entrances, representing fewer than half of the total entry points, and the park opened in 2009 with just two. But the Bloomingdale Trail/606, despite these efforts, still does not have entry points at every block, whether for reasons of expense, security, design intentions, or other logistical concerns. Access therefore remains slippery. This raises questions about how democratic these linear, off-grade parks can really be, given that they inevitably slice between city blocks and border private property along the way, limiting potential paths of approach.[51]

• • •

Behind the design of any park are assumptions about normative cultural practices: picturesque parks were for flânerie, small parks were for programmatic recreation. These cultural practices are part of a process of social reproduction: parks, in shaping how people spend leisure time, shape who people are.[52] Postindustrial parks are no different. What's become normative in postindustrial parks is walking (a symbolic return to the picturesque park activities of the nineteenth century) stirred with consumption. Walking has become instrumentalized and commercialized in these spaces. It is not to wander curiously through the arcades of old Paris or the rambles of Central Park, but to stride along a conveyer belt, walking in an instrumentalized space but also instrumentalizing the walk, with digital devices tracking steps and cameras to document selves and landscapes for virtual audiences.[53]

Park authorities like the Friends of the High Line and the Buffalo Bayou Partnership use postindustrial parks to create consumers of a particular kind: consumers who wish to signal high status through their consumption of distinguished products and landscapes. That pursuit of "distinction" creates exclusion—using cultural practices to establish social, symbolic, and spatial differentiation from the streets, reinforcing the exclusion put into place by slippery park designs and segregated park locations.

For the High Line's designers, the exclusion of certain quotidian urban activities was seen as critical to cultivating a leisurely scene. As Friends of the High Line cofounder Robert Hammond stated, recalling community meetings where the park design was presented and debated, "People said they didn't want people on bikes up there, and they didn't want it to have lots of commercial activity. The design team had come up with a slogan to define their approach: keep it simple, keep it wild, keep it slow. Most of what we heard from the community supported that idea."[54] In practice, this meant making the cultural and commercial activities found in the park distinct from those on the street—in effect, making sure that walking on the High Line would feel different than walking on the sidewalk. As Josh David noted,

> The design team was protective of the High Line, and they didn't want mundane aspects of everyday life diluting its special qualities. For example, they argued against people being able to get a cup of coffee on the High Line, because there are a million other places in New York to drink coffee. . . . [City Planning chair] Amanda Burden, too, was concerned about differentiating the experience of the High Line from that of life below.[55]

Coffee was ultimately served on the High Line when it opened in 2009. Commercial activity in general is a feature of the park, as it is at Buffalo Bayou Park and the Bloomingdale Trail/606. Visitors to the High Line can purchase not only coffee but espresso, paninis, baos, and paletas from various artisanal food vendors, allowing visitors to consume more "distinguished" fare than that commonly found at sidewalk food carts around the city.[56] A full-service seasonal restaurant offers "an open-air wine bar and cafe boasting impressive Hudson [River] and skyline views, a stellar wine and beer list, and smaller plates. An ideal location for a relaxing lunch, an after-work unwind, or sunset sipping."[57] (Keep in mind that alcohol is officially prohibited by the New York City Department of Parks and Recreation.)[58]

At Buffalo Bayou Park, food vendors camp at the park's eastern end, closest to downtown. This grand entrance to the park includes the visitor center where bike rentals are available (starting at $12) and tours of the park's Cistern (an underground reservoir) start at $5, suggesting to an uninitiated (or "undesirable") visitor that payment might be due upon entry to the park.[59] Kayaks and canoes can be rented up the bayou for $30, at the Lost Lake building, where a privately operated restaurant serves a "Southern Californian style menu . . . accented by refreshingly light dishes such as avocado toast with ricotta and lemon zest."[60] The park's website announces that several of its privately named spaces are open for business, which can cost more than $10,000 for a weekend rental.[61]

All of this revenue helps pay for the park's maintenance, as insisted by Rich and Nancy Kinder as a condition for their investment. The tax increment reinvestment zone, the boundaries of which include part of downtown and all of the internal spaces of the park, ensures that commercial activity will remain essential to Buffalo Bayou Park in the future. The Bloomingdale Trail/606 is similarly open for food and beverage carts and kiosks, though commerce is less of a presence.[62] But privileged forms of consumption still take place: though the park has fewer devoted open spaces to house private events within its footprint, in 2017 park boosters made room by shuttering the eastern portion of the park for a $200-a-plate candlelit dinner hosted by a celebrity chef.[63]

What all of this commerce creates is exclusion in postindustrial parks. Regardless of a visitor's ability to pay for goods and services—from a modest $12 bike rental to a $200 dinner—the fact that things are for sale in public space can give visitors pause. Tellingly, when I conducted ethnographic research on the High Line in 2011, a tour guide told me that visitors' most frequent question was "whether the park is public or private."[64] For visitors who slide through postindustrial parks' slippery paths of entry, they are greeted with opportunities to consume. Importantly, these opportunities differ from those found in traditional urban parks, where hot dog vendors and the like are fixtures. The provisions in postindustrial parks are carefully vetted by the private park corporations—one High Line vendor described to me that, in addition to requiring a $1,000 nonrefundable application fee, the Friends of the High Line tasted all of his company's food and met all of his employees—to ensure that the products (and the people selling them) match the parks' artful, upscale aesthetics and thereby appeal to wealthy consumers.[65]

When considered in conjunction with postindustrial parks' forms of surveillance and architectural exclusion, these cultural and commercial practices achieve a new mode of being in an urban park. Being in a postindustrial park is not completely about recreation, nor is it completely about playing the role of the flaneur or taking in the *passeggiata*, as wistfully described by a Friends of the High Line cofounder. It is about consuming landscapes and products and food and experiences. Being the kind of person who has not only the leisure time to visit a park but the good taste and right disposition to admire picturesque postindustrial views and consume artisanal food and drink. Others can visit the parks, of course, but the layers of privilege and exclusion make it very clear who these spaces are meant for.

This leads to a central political question as postindustrial parks not only persist in their current locations but are developed in new social contexts. In the shadow of the High Line, the Bloomingdale Trail/606, and Buffalo Bayou Park, public and private park groups in New York, Chicago, and Houston have been at work to extend the linear postindustrial park model into other former infrastructural spaces. QueensWay, El Paseo, and the eastward expansion of Buffalo Bayou Park—all in development at the time of this writing—promise to bring these commercialized, tourist-friendly urban parks to neighborhoods that are decidedly less privileged than the gentrified areas where they were first created. While the privatized High Line, Bloomingdale Trail/606, and Buffalo Bayou Park are successfully disciplining park users to bourgeois, consumerist norms of park use, the "potential spatial politics of resistance that might emerge from within them" have yet to be revealed.[66] Given the putative "success" of not only this model of park architecture but this model of park financing, there has been an unsurprising filtering not only of architectural styles but of private influence into other parks—parks in neighborhoods of color that were passed over by past park development, where the parks that do exist have been the result of sustained political struggle. If there is going to be a spatial politics of resistance, it seems that these will be the spaces where it unfolds.

IV
CONCLUSION

11

AFTER THE HIGH LINE

FOR urban elites, the High Line, the Bloomingdale Trail/606, and Buffalo Bayou Park were proof of concept: in twenty-first-century American cities, postindustrial parks could be economic engines. But why build just one High Line when you could build two? Why build a fancy park on only two miles of bayou when there are 2,500 miles of bayou in the city?

This is the urban process under capitalism.[1] The hunger to produce ever greater land rents puts pressure on the built environment: what's already in place is often not as profitable as what could be there. Building parks, homes, and roads fixes capital in place and produces limitations for urban growth coalitions, which cannot respond in real time to market fluctuations. This lag time, between what is and what might be, creates constraints as well as opportunities: developers just need to find the right undervalued spot, tear down what's there, and start building. "Creative destruction." The empty infrastructural spaces that have been redeveloped as postindustrial parks are winning projects in this capitalist rubric because they don't require much to be torn down; they don't displace people from their homes (not immediately, anyway).

But as urban growth coalitions try to transport the postindustrial park model to new social contexts, they do so in a new era of park politics. The economic impact of postindustrial parks on nearby communities tests the universalizing claims that park developers have historically made about urban parks: that along with providing access to recreation and nature, they offer widely distributed community benefits. As Mayor Michael Bloomberg declared at the High Line's opening, the park was "an extraordinary gift to [the] city's future," echoing his earlier statements that the park would be "a great win for *all New Yorkers*."[2] Mayor Rahm Emanuel similarly professed that in building the Bloomingdale Trail/606, the government was "once again reclaiming the public spaces of the city of Chicago for the citizens of the city of Chicago."[3] But the High Line quite clearly does not benefit "all New Yorkers": only certain New Yorkers benefit from rising property values and luxury park experiences. Whiteness engulfs the park, despite its location in a racially mixed neighborhood; it's clear that not even all New Yorkers in the immediate area see benefits from close proximity to the park.[4]

Park developers have become sensitive to claims about parks' communal benefits as they seek to bring the same park model to new neighborhoods. The kind of unifying, grassroots rhetoric that energized early supporters of the High Line and the Bloomingdale Trail/606 in 2003 would ring hollow in 2023, because such rhetoric has proven easily co-opted or simply misleading. In the face of demolition threats or public apathy, grassroots organizing has been critical to the eventual redevelopment of many postindustrial parks, but some early supporters of the High Line and the Bloomingdale Trail/606 were in the end disillusioned by the way that the parks served the real estate industry. Even Friends of the High Line cofounder Robert Hammond acknowledged some self-criticism by 2017: "We were from the community. We wanted to do it for the neighborhood. Ultimately, we failed."[5] In Chicago, the Logan Square Neighborhood Association, a prominent community organization and an early institutional backer of the Bloomingdale Trail/606, later shifted its park-related efforts to helping low-income residents stay in their homes in the face of rising property taxes—a product of the new park's gentrifying powers. Brian Perea, one of the group's community organizers, told me: "We're not opposed to the trail or opposed to development, but I think [the terms are] more: having responsible development, that's not a new condo coming into the neighborhood that's going to cost $600,000 that no one in the neighborhood could afford."[6]

A decade after the first generation of postindustrial parks, the process of mobilizing support for new parks looks much different. It's not a bottom-up process of organizing, it's top-down. Powerful private groups—such as the Houston Parks Board and the Trust for Public Land—or constellations of well-connected local institutions are now doing the initial mobilizing rather than grassroots groups. Indeed, some grassroots activists are now inclined to organize *against* new postindustrial park development, given that these parks can do more harm than good for the people who live nearby.

Park developers are now toeing a delicate line: in order to gain and maintain legitimacy, they make it clear that they care about "equity" and defer to the local "community" (two strategically ambiguous concepts)—even if, in reality, they hope for revanchist outcomes.[7] Park developers can't explicitly criticize the unequal impacts of past postindustrial parks because new postindustrial parks in New York, Chicago, and Houston are going to rely on similar—if not overlapping—networks of public and private backers who politically and financially supported the High Line, the Bloomingdale Trail/606, and Buffalo Bayou Park. Parks have become no different from any other top-down redevelopment scheme coming from mayoral offices, private developers, or planning commissions: likely to be wrapped in neutral, egalitarian buzzwords, and likely to be met with skepticism in communities accustomed to being overrun by big urban plans. This is a strange state of affairs. Historically, not only have urban parks been widely seen as community resources—that is, as unequivocally good things—but they have also been amenities denied to marginalized communities in general and communities of color in particular (and Black communities most particularly). Parks that exist in such communities have been the product of sustained political struggle.[8]

The fact that new postindustrial park projects—like the QueensWay in New York, El Paseo in Chicago, and the eastward extension of Buffalo Bayou Park—bring economic and cultural resources into marginalized communities *without* the kind of grassroots mobilization that, in the past, resulted in small victories like Chicago's Madden Park raises suspicions about the real motives at work: are these investments for the current communities that surround these potential parks?[9] Or are they prospective investments in Whiteness?[10]

At the same time that people accustomed to losing the urban land game have been realizing that parks are a potential existential threat, people who do hold political, economic, and cultural power are also seeing parks in a new light. After the High Line, parks have become a more glamourous cause—one now tied to traditional circuits of "high culture" rather than "mere recreation," given the trading of older parks' New Deal aesthetic for an imbricated one. The conflicts that are now emerging when park projects collide with neighborhood politics do not deter the donor class, which needed some convincing, initially, to get behind the cause of postindustrial parks. Friends of the High Line cofounder Robert Hammond remarked that when he first began fund-raising, the traditional vectors of wealth were closed to his fledgling group: "I thought non-profits were run and funded by Upper East Side women, but they weren't interested."[11] But two decades later, park donors are easy to find, and they are feted by their admirers. The editorial board of the *Houston Chronicle*, for example, declared that city residents "owe a Texas-sized thank you to Houstonians Rich and Nancy Kinder" for their million-dollar donations to the city's parks: "Long after we're gone, our children and grandchildren will look to the trees and the sky in what will then be the third largest city in the nation, and they'll add their thanks, too."[12] Such celebration of postindustrial parks and their benefactors normalizes private influence and the outsized role of individual donors.

Other big-money urban plans, from new stadiums to new transit systems, bring opponents out of the woodwork and undergo substantial public scrutiny. Parks, for now, continue to trade—largely successfully—on the soft-focus symbolism of nature. But factions are emerging, with developers, philanthropists, city governments, and other boosters lining up to finance, build, and celebrate the next wave of postindustrial parks, while people in park-starved communities are forced into a complicated political position: at once desiring park improvements while resisting their own displacement. This latter position was articulated in 2015 by Delia Ramirez, a Chicago activist who spoke to the displacement foreshadowed by the opening of the Bloomingdale Trail/606: "It's a beautiful space. We just want to make sure we're going to be able to stay here to enjoy it."[13]

To what extent the next generation of postindustrial parks poses similar threats will be revealed by new park projects in New York, Chicago, and Houston. Planned to be built not in gentrified or tourist areas, these projects in Queens, Pilsen, and Houston's East Side are primed to test the cultural and economic propositions of postindustrial parks.

On the one hand, postindustrial parks seem to be a politically viable and particularly effective form of urban renewal. Decades after the fall of federal Title I funding and "slum clearance," city governments cannot easily and swiftly redevelop entire neighborhoods, even if they would like to. Linear postindustrial parks, rather than making large cuts in the urban fabric, thread lines of potential redevelopment into communities.

On the other hand, what if there is only so much public appetite for postindustrial parks? Capitalist logics dictate that city governments and private developers will look for new places to build this model of park and stimulate local economies, but that doesn't mean they will be successful. With postindustrial park projects impending in many cities, the assumption among growth coalitions seems to be that if they build it, (White) people will come—that postindustrial parks are now such a paramount urban amenity that they can activate the renewal of entire neighborhoods.[14] But is this really the case?

Perhaps the "success" of the High Line, the Bloomingdale Trail/606, and Buffalo Bayou Park has much to do with their prime locations and architectural novelty—rather than the generalized public-space model of a linear walking path through an imbricated garden. These are singular spaces in their respective cities. They draw tourists and locals, and the amount of money spent on these three parks seems unlikely to be replicated in the near future: QueensWay won't be built with a $250 million budget. On the low end, if all that public and private coffers can produce is a modest paved path and some grass, is a linear park really catnip for gentrifiers?[15]

Shortly after the High Line opened, public-space scholars Benjamin Shepard and Greg Smithsimon wrote that the park seemed destined to become a "dated, under-used white elephant" like other elevated public passageways before it.[16] Perhaps this was the right prediction, but for the wrong space. The economic and cultural impact of the High Line and its immediate successors has created an impression that postindustrial parks are too big to fail—even though the "success" of these parks was anything but assured. As the history of picturesque parks has shown, maintaining elite spaces over time requires sustained political and financial resources; one economic downturn might be all that separates the first wave of postindustrial parks from decline. While the High Line continues to be seen as a major success more than a decade later, the white elephants might yet come into view: little-used green corridors dotting would-be up-and-coming neighborhoods, spread thinner around cities than economic resources and cultural interest can permit.

12

ABOLISH, DECOLONIZE, ROT

Three Proposals for Parks Equity

"Basically, what we're saying is that filth is good,"
Bourdain concluded.
Deuki Hong reappeared with a plate of marbled rib eye. "Korean
restaurants don't usually dry-age," he said. "But we're trying
dry-aged. This is, like, thirty-eight days."
"You see? The rot!" Werther exclaimed. "What happens after
thirty-eight days?"
"Good things," Bourdain said.[1]

HERE is much at stake in the present and future of postindustrial parks: these small, linear spaces crystallize centuries of urban development and cultural ideas about cities and nature. Postindustrial parks are new, they are exciting: for many people, they symbolize a necessary reinvention of urban space in the Anthropocene. Though visually radical, the historical (and, in capitalist contexts, inevitable) marriage of parks and land values means that anything revolutionary in these spaces is compromised as soon as the ribbons are cut and the shovels hit the ground. Redeveloping outmoded, neglected sites like railways and riverbanks is an act dictated and financed by powerful institutions: city governments and private groups that seek to control urban space and shore up their own political, cultural, and economic interests.

There may yet be transformative potential in postindustrial landscapes. While urban growth coalitions are primed to orient new parks toward profit rather than people, a shift away from picturesque hegemony and manicured spaces and toward wastelands and rot can still hold radical promise. Acknowledging rot is not about romanticizing disinvestment and decline or seeing such sites as deracialized, de-historicized venues for new investment; rather, it's about removing the moral lens through which landscapes are typically viewed and questioning the value of highly capitalized, highly aestheticized postindustrial transformations like those wrought in New York, Chicago, and Houston. Should all public spaces rot? Of course not. But perhaps these should.

With all that in mind, I offer the following three proposals for parks equity. The political-economic forces that have made postindustrial parks engines for capital must be disrupted. Any move toward equity is certain to be a cultural process, too.

1. Abolish private park corporations.

There is no role for these organizations in an equitable urban parks landscape. The channeling of private resources to chosen public spaces creates a two-tiered system in which private endowments (no matter how large or small) stabilize and therefore normalize the retrenchment of public monies for park development and maintenance. Because these groups are the clearest beneficiaries, and in some ways also the arbiters, of urban parks' soft-focus aura of nature, they often escape sustained criticism. With names like the Quaker-tinged "Friends" aiding their presentations of corporate self, private park groups can claim, credibly, that they are here to *conserve* the parks, to do what evidently indifferent local governments won't do. This political branding has made it very difficult for the public to see parks—and park corporations—as anything but good. The people who run these organizations, whether they have read *The Power Broker* or not, intuit the credo of American planning's archvillain, Robert Moses: "As long as you're on the side of parks, you're on the side of the angels. You can't lose."[2]

Not every private park group is as powerful as the Friends of the High Line or the Houston Parks Board; nor are all such groups founded in the nefarious mist that shrouded the Bryant Park Restoration Corporation, for example. Plenty of folks have grown tired of uneven, unequal parks investment and have decided to organize. There's nothing intrinsically malicious about organizing volunteers for a cleanup day (as long as that doesn't extend to "cleansing" parks of "undesirable" park users, as it sometimes has in the past). Wanting to improve local park conditions, or having a creative idea for a new green space—concepts that united the Friends of the Bloomingdale Trail, for example—are social and political goals that do not need to logically conclude with the private management of a public space. The history of urban parks "from below" is a story of community and social-movement groups organizing for change: from Progressive-era reformers advocating for "small parks" in the early 1900s to civil rights groups desegregating urban parks in the 1950s and '60s. A key difference between then and now is that the leaders of Hull House and the Urban League were not trying to become the new authorities of the parks they were advocating for.[3] These groups fought for equitable park access, but they never demanded management power. Despite what billionaire philanthropists may think, public institutions must remain in charge of public spaces. No matter how racist or corrupt their histories may be, organizations like the Chicago Park District and the Houston Parks and Recreation Department ultimately must answer to the publics that they serve. The Kinder Foundation and the Trust for Public Land answer to their own masters.

2. Decolonize the links among race, capital, and the aesthetics of nature.

More ambiguous but no less ambitious is the charge to dismantle the dominance of the picturesque and its social and symbolic associations. From its British colonial origins to the way it has been spatialized through urban parks, the picturesque has placed racial, cultural, and economic power into seemingly "natural" landscapes. Prominent urban parks were, and remain, those linked to Gilpin's and Olmsted's visions, to capital, and to Whiteness. Parks like New York's Central Park set a template for "nature" that was not natural at all, but heavily landscaped and expensively maintained. Grounded in wealth, privilege, and prestige rather than ecology, picturesque parks colonized cultural imaginations as well as places: native landscapes in cities like Chicago, Houston, and Los Angeles were seen as less-than and deracinated.

At first glance, the radical aesthetics of postindustrial parks seem to depart from the picturesque. Park designers profess respect for local plants, cultures, and ecologies. The designs are located within, and symbolically embrace, structures that picturesque parks were built to oppose—railways, buildings, and roads. But the ideas that animated picturesque aesthetic philosophy continue to drive park design, and as much as architects claim to be pivoting toward local sensitivities, a universalizing aesthetic has nevertheless emerged in postindustrial park architecture. Echoing the colonizing power of the picturesque, postindustrial park aesthetics bring a model of urbanism that glorifies capital and privileged cultural practices. Postindustrial parks extend the idea that socially superior forms of nature are the province of White elites and their confederates into a new era and into a new park modality. Actually existing landscapes, including other imbricated, decaying, unkempt urban sites, continue to be devalued and continue to be socially constructed as culturally, if not also morally, bad.

3. Let the rails rot.

If postindustrial parks are about a rediscovery of nature inside the urban, the most powerful way to recognize the power and beauty of nature would be to let the rails rot. Boosters and architects claim that turning imbricated spaces into green Disneylands was necessary to make the spaces usable by the masses—that the dystopian, wasted landscapes were too unsafe and too unwieldy for people to visit them in situ, no matter how beautiful and surreal they might be.[4] But disheveled conditions on the High Line, the Bloomingdale Line, and the banks of Buffalo Bayou had not deterred people from visiting them. Years before these spaces were cleared out and redeveloped, people had been using them. Clearing the spaces was a decision that was less about accessibility and more about removing unwanted people and activities in order to prime the sites for economic gain. If it was just a question of accessibility, the humble addition of new stairways, ramps, and elevators could have addressed that concern and invited the wider public in. The dilapidated spaces, while far from pristine, were no less treacherous to navigate than a standard "wilderness" path found in many urban parks (see the trails through the ravine at the north end of Central Park, for example). "Accessibility," when deployed cynically by park developers, justifies grander, more expensive designs, which in turn justifies privatization and the need for ever larger public and private funds. (Claims about accessibility were particularly empty in the case of the High Line, where two elevators were initially the only means of access for people in wheelchairs.)

"Restoration" is another concept that park designers and boosters frequently use to justify redeveloping postindustrial spaces as parks—that is, to remove the rot and put something new in its place. In Houston, Buffalo Bayou Park was intended to restore the ecology of a long neglected and overengineered bayou landscape. Likewise, the designs of the High Line and the Bloomingdale Trail/606 sought to recapture the wild landscapes that had grown on their respective railways. Restoration can be a compelling argument because it promises to remove the remnants of past engineering mistakes or wipe away years of human neglect.[5] "Restoration" asserts a plant-based positivism: the idea that there is one "true" nature out there in need of remediation or rediscovery. That's the ontological argument. The cultural argument is about environmental authenticity: that park conditions should reflect local ecologies and landscapes. These ideas are also typically rooted in the past: they call back to long-ago park plans or imagine what "native" plant life would look like surrounded by the postindustrial built environment. It's nostalgia for something that never existed.

The other argument that park developers make against rot and in favor of grand postindustrial park plans is that postindustrial parks are environmentally friendly. The Bloomingdale Trail/606 was funded by the federal government as a carbon-reduction project, and more generally it is uncontroversially claimed that postindustrial parks are positive carbon actors: that linear green spaces promote walking and biking over driving, that their plants absorb carbon emissions, and in cases like Buffalo Bayou Park, also form resilient infrastructures that can slow the impacts of climate change. But do postindustrial parks really have that kind of environmental impact? It is unlikely that the paved-over wilderness simulacra that were built in New York, Chicago, and Houston have a positive environmental impact compared to rot. Taking down tree cover and replacing weeds with concrete walkways, even while new plants are sown alongside, seems counter to the permacultural ideas implied by postindustrial park design.[6] Left unconsidered, too, are suggestions (like those offered for the High Line in the 1980s and '90s) to reactivate disused infrastructures for mass transit—a move that might produce the kind of environmental benefits that carefully tended weeds and art installations might not.

And that's before considering the energy needed, and emissions and waste created, in building the parks. And the ongoing maintenance. If things rot, then they rot. They don't need maintenance. But fancy parks do, if they are to remain fancy, and this is especially true on the banks of a floodplain, where millions of dollars and thousands of hours of labor were spent to recondition Buffalo Bayou Park after Harvey wrecked it. To continue to pour money into these spaces in the name of the environment seems downright profligate in the face of more floods to come, and when the broader urban parks landscape is so persistently racist and inequitable. Rip up streets, not plants. Let the rails rot.

NOTES

1. SOMETIME IN 2009

1. See Pierre Bourdieu, *Distinction: A Social Critique of the Judgment of Taste*, trans. Richard Nice (Cambridge, MA: Harvard Univerwsity Press, 1984).

2. Joshua David and Robert Hammond, *High Line: The Inside Story of New York City's Park in the Sky* (New York: Farrar, Straus and Giroux, 2011).

3. Richard Florida, *Cities and the Creative Class* (New York: Routledge, 2004). For a critique, see Jamie Peck, "Struggling with the Creative Class," *International Journal of Urban and Regional Research* 29, no. 4 (2005): 740–70.

4. David J. Madden, "Revisiting the End of Public Space: Assembling the Public in an Urban Park," *City & Community* 9, no. 2 (2010): 187–207; Sharon Zukin, *Naked City: The Death and Life of Authentic Urban Places* (New York: Oxford University Press, 2010).

5. Kevin Ward, "Entrepreneurial Urbanism, State Restructuring and Civilizing 'New' East Manchester," *Area* 35, no. 2 (2003): 116–27.

6. Miriam Greenberg, *Branding New York: How a City in Crisis Was Sold to the World* (New York: Routledge, 2008).

7. Michael Sorkin, ed., *Variations on a Theme Park: The New American City and the End of Public Space* (New York: Hill and Wang, 1992).

8. Samuel R. Delany, *Times Square Red, Times Square Blue* (New York: New York University Press, 1999).

9. Gregory Smithsimon, "Dispersing the Crowd: Bonus Plazas and the Creation of Public Space," *Urban Affairs Review* 43, no. 3 (2008): 325–51.

10. On the ideology of New Urbanism, see Jill Grant, "The Ironies of New Urbanism," *Canadian Journal of Urban Research* 15, no. 2 (2006): 158–74.

11. David Wachsmuth and Hillary Angelo, "Green and Gray: New Ideologies of Nature in Urban Sustainability Policy," *Annals of the American Association of Geographers* 108, no. 4 (2018): 1038–56.

12. David and Hammond, *High Line*.

13. Kenneth A. Gould and Tammy L. Lewis, *Green Gentrification: Urban Sustainability and the Struggle for Environmental Justice* (New York: Routledge, 2017).

2. VARIETIES OF URBAN CRISIS

1. Joshua David and Robert Hammond, *High Line: The Inside Story of New York City's Park in the Sky* (New York: Farrar, Straus and Giroux, 2011), 12. I use the term "imbricated spaces" to connote the spatial and symbolic convergence of objects representing "nature" and objects representing "the city" or "the urban." See Kevin Loughran, "Imbricated Spaces: The High Line, Urban Parks, and the Cultural Meaning of City and Nature," *Sociological Theory* 34, no. 4 (2016): 311–34.

2. Richard Harris, "Industry and Residence: The Decentralization of New York City, 1900–1940," *Journal of Historical Geography* 19, no. 2 (1993): 169–90.

3. Robert A. Beauregard, *When America Became Suburban* (Minneapolis: University of Minnesota Press, 2006).

4. Kenneth T. Jackson, *Crabgrass Frontier: The Suburbanization of the United States* (New York: Oxford University Press, 1985); Kevin M. Kruse, *White Flight: Atlanta and the Making of Modern Conservatism* (Princeton, NJ: Princeton University Press, 2005).

5. Herbert J. Gans, *The Levittowners: Ways of Life and Politics in a New Suburban Community* (New York: Columbia University Press, 1982).

6. U.S. Census of Population, 1940–1980. Unless otherwise noted, all census data was accessed via Social Explorer, http://www.socialexplorer.com.

7. Kim Phillips-Fein, *Fear City: New York's Fiscal Crisis and the Rise of Austerity Politics* (New York: Metropolitan, 2017), 201.

8. Phillips-Fein, *Fear City*.

9. Phillips-Fein, *Fear City*, 201.

10. Chris Mitchell, "The Killing of Murder," *New York Magazine*, January 7, 2008, http://nymag.com/news/features/crime/2008/42603/.

11. Joseph P. Fried, "There Are Many Motives, but Chief Among Them Is Profit," *New York Times*, August 14, 1977; Manuel B. Aalbers, "Do Maps Make Geography? Part 1: Redlining, Planned Shrinkage, and the Places of Decline," *ACME: An International E-Journal for Critical Geographies* 13, no. 4 (2014): 525–56; Miriam Greenberg, *Branding New York: How a City in Crisis Was Sold to the World* (New York: Routledge, 2008).

12. Despite these historical and structural causes for the urban crisis, the outsized events of the 1970s led many contemporary observers to find more proximate or cultural causes—such as the Black uprisings of 1964 in Harlem and nationwide in 1967, the rise of Black and Latino political coalitions, and the purported decline of the Black family (the focus of the 1965 Moynihan Report). See Thomas J. Sugrue, *The Origins of the Urban Crisis: Race and Inequality in Postwar Detroit* (Princeton, NJ: Princeton University Press, 1996); Arnold R. Hirsch, *Making the Second Ghetto: Race and Housing in Chicago, 1940–1960* (Chicago: University of Chicago Press, 1983).

13. Greenberg, *Branding New York*, 9.

14. Elizabeth Tandy Shermer, *Sunbelt Capitalism: Phoenix and the Trans-formation of American Politics* (Philadelphia: University of Pennsylvania Press, 2013); on Keynesian-Fordist urbanism (whose namesakes, for clarity, are economist John Maynard Keynes and capitalist Henry Ford), which describes the political-economic foundations of post–World War II New York and other American cities, see David Harvey, "Flexible Accumulation Through Urbanization: Reflections on 'Post-Modernism' in the American City," *Perspecta* 26 (1990): 251–72; Roger Keil, "The Urban Politics of Roll-with-It Neoliberalization," *City* 13, nos. 2–3 (2009): 231–45.

15. Marion Weiss, "Geographical Iconography and Signification: How Space Creates Meaning in the New York City Film," *Journal of Visual Verbal Languaging* 3, no. 2 (1983): 85–89; James Sanders, *Celluloid Skyline: New York and the Movies* (New York: Knopf, 2001).

16. Sanders, *Celluloid Skyline*, 375; see also Mimi Swartz, "Blood in the Streets," *Texas Monthly*, November 1991, https://www.texasmonthly.com/articles/blood-in-the-streets/.

17. Vincent Canby, "New York's Woes Are Good Box Office," *New York Times*, November 10, 1974; quoted in Sanders, *Celluloid Skyline*, 367.
18. Martin Gottlieb, "Rail Fan Finds Rusting Dream of West Side," *New York Times*, January 16, 1984. While conducting an ethnography of the High Line in 2011, I noted that this detail was mentioned on every official tour of the park that I attended, for whatever reason taking a persistent place in the Friends of the High Line's redevelopment narrative.
19. The High Line represented the southern portion of this stage of the project: north of West Thirty-Fifth Street, the tracks were moved underground. "Mayor Dedicates West Side Project: 'Death to Death Av.,'" *New York Times*, June 29, 1934.
20. In addition to the High Line, these included Riverside Park, the West Side Highway, the Henry Hudson Parkway, the Henry Hudson Bridge, St. John's Park Terminal, and the Seventy-Ninth Street Boat Basin. See Robert Caro, *The Power Broker: Robert Moses and the Fall of New York* (New York: Vintage, 1974), 526–40.
21. Caro, *The Power Broker*, 525.
22. Harris, "Industry and Residence."
23. William W. Buzbee, *Fighting Westway: Environmental Law, Citizen Activism, and the Regulatory War That Transformed New York City* (Ithaca, NY: Cornell University Press, 2014).
24. Sugrue, *The Origins of the Urban Crisis*; Heather Ann Thompson, *Whose Detroit? Politics, Labor, and Race in a Modern American City* (Ithaca, NY: Cornell University Press, 2001); Colin Gordon, *Mapping Decline: St. Louis and the Fate of the American City* (Philadelphia: University of Pennsylvania Press, 2009).
25. Daniel Bluestone, *Constructing Chicago* (New Haven, CT: Yale University Press, 1991); Dominic A. Pacyga, *Chicago: A Biography* (Chicago: University of Chicago Press, 2009).
26. Population totals in 1900: (1) New York, 3.4 million; (2) Chicago, 1.7 million; (3) Philadelphia, 1.3 million; (4) St. Louis, 575,000; . . . (85) Houston, 45,000.
27. Carl Sandburg, "Chicago"; William Cronon, *Nature's Metropolis: Chicago and the Great West* (New York: Norton, 1991), 9.
28. Cronon, *Nature's Metropolis*, 23–54.
29. Dominic A. Pacyga, *Slaughterhouse: Chicago's Union Stock Yard and the World It Made* (Chicago: University of Chicago Press, 2015).

30. Hirsch, *Making the Second Ghetto*; Thomas J. Sugrue, *Sweet Land of Liberty: The Forgotten Struggle for Civil Rights in the North* (New York: Random House, 2008).

31. James R. Grossman, *Land of Hope: Chicago, Black Southerners, and the Great Migration* (Chicago: University of Chicago Press, 1989).

32. Amanda Seligman, *Block by Block: Neighborhoods and Public Policy on Chicago's West Side* (Chicago: University of Chicago Press, 2005).

33. Lilia Fernández, *Brown in the Windy City: Mexicans and Puerto Ricans in Postwar Chicago* (Chicago: University of Chicago Press, 2012).

34. U.S. Census of Population, https://www.socialexplorer.com.

35. There were dozens of exceptions to this pattern: Whites remained on the South Side in Bridgeport (historically Irish), Hyde Park (home to the University of Chicago), and elsewhere; Black communities formed in the North Side neighborhoods of Uptown and Old Town; Latinos lived in the South Side's South Chicago and the North Side's Rogers Park. But social or symbolic links between racial groups and Chicago's "sides," based in large part on demographic realities, have lasted for more than half a century and counting.

36. Pacyga, *Chicago*.

37. Thomas J. Gradel and Dick Simpson, *Corrupt Illinois: Patronage, Cronyism, and Criminality* (Champaign: University of Illinois Press, 2015).

38. Andrew J. Diamond, *Mean Streets: Chicago Youths and the Everyday Struggle for Empowerment in the Multiracial City, 1908–1969* (Berkeley: University of California Press, 2009).

39. Mike Royko, *Boss: Richard J. Daley of Chicago* (New York: Penguin, 1971).

40. Hirsch, *Making the Second Ghetto*.

41. Roger Biles, *Richard J. Daley: Politics, Race, and the Governing of Chicago* (DeKalb: Northern Illinois University Press, 1995).

42. Hirsch, *Making the Second Ghetto*, 100–34.

43. D. Bradford Hunt, *Blueprint for Disaster: The Unraveling of Chicago Public Housing* (Chicago: University of Chicago Press, 2009), 67–98.

44. Rashad Shabazz, *Spatializing Blackness: Architectures of Confinement and Black Masculinity in Chicago* (Chicago: University of Illinois Press, 2015); Eric Avila, *The Folklore of the Freeway: Race and Revolt in the Modernist City* (Minneapolis: University of Minnesota Press, 2014). Urban-renewal efforts to bulwark White areas against minority groups also included the

displacement of a Puerto Rican enclave in the Lincoln Park neighborhood through the use of eminent domain to create new housing. See Gina M. Pérez, *The Near Northwest Side Story: Migration, Displacement, and Puerto Rican Families* (Berkeley: University of California Press, 2004).

45. Hirsch, *Making the Second Ghetto*; Beryl Satter, *Family Properties: How the Struggle Over Race and Real Estate Transformed Chicago and Urban America* (New York: Metropolitan, 2009); Alan B. Anderson and George W. Pickering, *Confronting the Color Line: The Broken Promise of the Civil Rights Movement in Chicago* (Athens: University of Georgia Press, 1986); Jakobi Williams, *From the Bullet to the Ballot: The Illinois Chapter of the Black Panther Party and Racial Coalition Politics in Chicago* (Chapel Hill: University of North Carolina Press, 2013). This activism also included the Chicago Freedom Movement of 1965–1967, which featured Martin Luther King taking up residence in a West Side tenement in 1966 to draw attention to the issue while lobbying Mayor Daley for fair housing. See James R. Ralph, Jr., *Northern Protest: Martin Luther King, Jr., Chicago, and the Civil Rights Movement* (Cambridge, MA: Harvard University Press, 1993).

46. Royko, *Boss*. I use the term "Latino" here for rhetorical simplicity, even though it is not historically accurate for the time period in question. See G. Cristina Mora, *Making Hispanics: How Activists, Bureaucrats, and Media Constructed a New American* (Chicago: University of Chicago Press, 2014); Clara E. Rodríguez, *Changing Race: Latinos, the Census and the History of Ethnicity in the United States* (New York: New York University Press, 2000).

47. Williams, *From the Bullet to the Ballot*; Royko, *Boss*.

48. Pérez, *The Near Northwest Side Story*.

49. Ralph, *Northern Protest*.

50. Janice L. Reiff, Ann Durkin Keating, and James R. Grossman, eds., "West Madison Street, 1968," *Encyclopedia of Chicago*, http://www.encyclopedia.chicagohistory.org/pages/6354.html. See also Janet L. Abu-Lughod, *Race, Space, and Riots in Chicago, New York, and Los Angeles* (New York: Oxford University Press, 2007).

51. Frank Kusch, *Battleground Chicago: The Police and the 1968 Democratic National Convention* (Chicago: University of Chicago Press, 2004).

52. Larry Bennett, Roberta Garner, and Euan Hague, eds., *Neoliberal Chicago* (Champaign: University of Illinois Press, 2017).

53. Hirsch, *Making the Second Ghetto*; Catherine Fennell, *Last Project Standing: Civics and Sympathy in Post-Welfare Chicago* (Minneapolis: University of Minnesota Press, 2015).

54. Richard M. Bernard and Bradley R. Rice, eds., *Sunbelt Cities: Politics and Growth Since World War II* (Austin: University of Texas Press, 1983).

55. Thomas A. Lyson, *Two Sides to the Sunbelt* (New York: Praeger, 1989).

56. David G. McComb, *Houston, a History* (Austin: University of Texas Press, 1981).

57. Augustus Allen and John Kirby Allen, "The Town of Houston," *Telegraph and Texas Register*, August 30, 1836; cited in Kyle Shelton, *Power Moves: Transportation, Politics, and Development in Houston* (Austin: University of Texas Press, 2017), 10.

58. Quintard Taylor, *In Search of the Racial Frontier: African Americans in the American West 1528–1990* (New York: Norton, 1998), 59.

59. McComb, *Houston, a History*.

60. Martin V. Melosi and Joseph A. Pratt, eds., *Energy Metropolis: An Environmental History of Houston and the Gulf Coast* (Pittsburgh, PA: University of Pittsburgh Press, 2007).

61. Marilyn McAdams Sibley, *The Port of Houston: A History* (Austin: University of Texas Press, 1968).

62. Joseph A. Pratt, "A Mixed Blessing: Energy, Economic Growth, and Houston's Environment," in *Energy Metropolis: An Environmental History of Houston and the Gulf Coast*, ed. Martin V. Melosi and Joseph A. Pratt (Pittsburgh, PA: University of Pittsburgh Press, 2007).

63. Sean P. Cunningham, *Cowboy Conservatism: Texas and the Rise of the Modern Right* (Lexington: University of Kentucky Press, 2010); see also Bethany Moreton, *To Serve God and Wal-Mart* (Cambridge, MA: Harvard University Press, 2009); Darren Dochuk, *From Bible Belt to Sunbelt: Plain-Folk Religion, Grassroots Politics, and the Rise of Evangelical Conservatism* (New York: Norton, 2011).

64. Roger Biles, "The Urban South in the Great Depression," *Journal of Southern History* 56, no. 1 (1990): 71–100.

65. Cunningham, *Cowboy Conservatism*.

66. Joe R. Feagin, *Free Enterprise City: Houston in Political and Economic Perspective* (New Brunswick, NJ: Rutgers University Press, 1988).

67. Shelton, *Power Moves*.

68. Joseph Pratt, "8F and Many More: Business and Civic Leadership in Modern Houston," *Houston Review* 1, no. 2 (2004): 2–7, 31–44.

69. Shelton, *Power Moves*, 12–13.

70. Houston's red scare reached its zenith in 1953, when Dr. George Ebey, the recently appointed deputy superintendent of the Houston schools, was run out of town after allegations were made about his ties to communism. Ebey, who had been hired away from the public school system in Portland, Oregon, returned to the west coast to work at the Stanford Research Institute after the episode, which he referred to as "being lynched professionally by savages in a community where I was relatively a stranger." Note that the most politically moderate 8F member, Oveta Culp Hobby, would also become a target of this local red scare after joining Dwight Eisenhower's cabinet as the first secretary of the U.S. Department of Health, Education and Welfare (now the Department of Health & Human Services). See Don E. Carleton, *Red Scare: Right-Wing Hysteria, Fifties Fanaticism, and Their Legacy in Texas* (Austin: University of Texas Press, 1985), chap. 7-8, quote from p. 223.

71. Margaret Nunnelley Olsen, "Teaching Americanism: Ray K. Daily and the Persistence of Conservatism in Houston School Politics, 1943–1952," *Southwestern Historical Quarterly* 110, no. 2 (2006): 240–69.

72. Feagin, *Free Enterprise City*.

73. Pratt, "A Mixed Blessing."

74. Barry J. Kaplan, "Urban Development, Economic Growth, and Personal Liberty: The Rhetoric of the Houston Anti-Zoning Movements, 1947–1962," *Southwestern Historical Quarterly* 84, no. 2 (1980): 133–68.

75. U.S. Census of Population, Social Explorer.

76. Chandler Davidson, *Biracial Politics: Conflict and Coalition in the Metropolitan South* (Baton Rouge: Louisiana State University Press, 1972).

77. Robert E. Parker and Joe R. Feagin, "Houston: Administration by Economic Elites," in *Big City Politics in Transition*, ed. H. V. Savitch and John Clayton Thomas (Newbury Park: Sage, 1991).

78. Tyina L. Steptoe, *Houston Bound: Culture and Color in a Jim Crow City* (Oakland: University of California Press, 2016).

79. Barry J. Kaplan, "Race, Income, and Ethnicity: Residential Change in a Houston Community, 1920–1970," *Houston History* (Winter 1981): 178–202.

80. U.S. Census of Population, 1970. Demographic calculations are precarious for this period, as Hispanics/Latinos were not yet organized and recognized as a separate ethnoracial group. "Persons of Spanish language or Spanish surname," a commonly accepted proxy for Latino population prior to changes in Census categories, was only captured at the county level in 1970. Harris County, the principal county of Houston, contained more than 185,000 persons in this category, about 10 percent of the population. The official 1970 Census tally, "79 percent White," may be a slight overstatement given the murky data, but the real number is likely not far off. See also Mora, *Making Hispanics*; Rodríguez, *Changing Race*.

81. Shelton, *Power Moves*, 44; Bernard Brown, "Municipal Finances and Annexation: A Case Study of Post-War Houston," *Southwestern Social Science Quarterly* 48, no. 3 (1967): 339–51.

82. Like many places in the South, Dowling Street was named for a Confederate soldier. Shelton, *Power Moves*, 59–87.

83. Shelton, *Power Moves*, 91–119; Guadalupe San Miguel, Jr., *Brown, Not White: School Integration and the Chicano Movement in Houston* (College Station: Texas A&M University Press, 2001).

84. Martin V. Melosi, "Houston's Public Sinks: Sanitary Services from Local Concerns to Regional Challenges," in *Energy Metropolis: An Environmental History of Houston and the Gulf Coast*, ed. Martin V. Melosi and Joseph A. Pratt (Pittsburgh, PA: University of Pittsburgh Press, 2007).

85. Teresa Tomkins-Walsh, " 'A Concrete River Had to Be Wrong': Environmental Action on Houston's Bayous, 1935–1980" (Ph.D. diss, University of Houston, 2009).

86. Arthur Coleman Comey, *Houston: Tentative Plans for Its Development: A Report to the Houston Parks Commission* (Boston: Geo H. Ellis, 1913).

3. "THE YUPPIE EXPRESS"

1. "Obituary 1—No Title," *New York Times*, June 18, 1996, D23; Louis Calta, "Performers at Space Get Notice to Quit: A Nominal Rental Call for Investigation," *New York Times*, May 24, 1974, 22.

2. Georgia Dullea, "Nowadays, Man's (Yes, Man's) Best Friend Is Likely to Be a Cat (or a Houseful of Cats)," *New York Times*, September 9,

1990, 52; David W. Dunlap, "New Dimensions for a Low-Density Neighborhood: The Javits Center Draws a Plethora of Proposals," *New York Times*, April 1, 1990, R19.

3. "Calendar of Events: West Side Rail Line," *New York Times*, March 1, 1984, C7.

4. Christopher Gray, "On the Lower West Side, Fate of Old Rail Line Is Undecided," *New York Times*, January 3, 1988, R5.

5. David Halle and Elizabeth Tiso, *New York's New Edge: Contemporary Art, the High Line, and Urban Megaprojects on the Far West Side* (Chicago: University of Chicago Press, 2014).

6. "Tear Down the Tracks," Letter to the Editor, *New York Times*, January 30, 1984, 16.

7. Martin Gottlieb, "West Siders May Get a Reprieve from the IRT," *New York Times*, March 23, 1986, A7.

8. Gottlieb, "West Siders May Get a Reprieve."

9. David W. Dunlap, "Conrail Looking to a Revival of Its Freight Traffic: Property Owners Lose on Razing Elevated Tracks," *New York Times*, January 20, 1991, R13.

10. Bruce F. Berg, *New York City Politics: Governing Gotham* (New Brunswick, NJ: Rutgers University Press, 2007), 24–31.

11. Figures are drawn from the blocks between Eighth Avenue and Tenth Avenue, from West Fourteenth Street to West Thirty-Fourth Street.

12. All figures are from the U.S. Census of Population, 1980. Proxy for the core brownstone area of Chelsea is Census Tract 89, New York County, New York, which is bounded by Eighth and Tenth avenues and West Eighteenth and West Twenty-Second streets. "Persons of Spanish Origin" is used as a proxy for people identifying as Hispanic in 1980.

13. George Chauncey, *Gay New York: Gender, Urban Culture, and the Making of the Gay Male World, 1890–1940* (New York: Basic Books, 1994); Amin Ghaziani, *There Goes the Gayborhood?* (Princeton, NJ: Princeton University Press, 2014), 143–50; see also David Wilson, "Institutions and Urban Revitalization: The Case of Chelsea in New York City," *Urban Geography* 8, no. 2 (1987): 129–45.

14. Heeyeun Yoon and Elizabeth Currid-Halkett, "Industrial Gentrification in West Chelsea, New York: Who Survived and Who Did Not? Empirical Evidence from Discrete-Time Survival Analysis," *Urban Studies* 52, no. 1 (2015) 20–49; Harvey Molotch and Mark Treskon,

"Changing Art: SoHo, Chelsea, and the Dynamic Geography of Galleries in New York City," *International Journal of Urban and Regional Research* 33, no. 2 (2009): 517–41.

15. John Hull Mollenkopf, *Phoenix in the Ashes: The Rise and Fall of the Koch Coalition in New York City Politics* (Princeton, NJ: Princeton University Press, 1994).

16. Berg, *New York City Politics*.

17. Sam Roberts, "The 1989 Elections: The New York Vote; Almost Lost at the Wire," *New York Times*, November 9, 1989, 1.

18. David W. Dunlap, "Elevated Freight Line Being Razed Amid Protests," *New York Times*, January 15, 1991, B3.

19. Dunlap, "Elevated Freight Line Being Razed"; David W. Dunlap, "Planners Allow Rezoning of Site of Meat Market: Permit Residential Use, but Protect 2 Dealers," *New York Times*, April 17, 1984, B3; New York City Planning Commission, "Commercial Districts: C6," retrieved May 16, 2018, https://www1.nyc.gov/site/planning/zoning /districts-tools/c6.page; New York City Planning Commission, "Historical Zoning Map 8b," retrieved May 16, 2018, http://www1.nyc.gov /assets/planning/download/pdf/zoning/zoning-maps/historical-zoning -maps/maps08b.pdf.

20. Dunlap, "Conrail Looking to a Revival."

21. Dunlap, "Conrail Looking to a Revival."

22. Berg, *New York City Politics*, 163–89.

23. Raphael J. Sonenshein and Tom Hogen-Esch, "Bringing the State (Government) Back In: Home Rule and the Politics of Secession in Los Angeles and New York City," *Urban Affairs Review* 41, no. 4 (2006): 467–91.

24. Neil Smith, *The New Urban Frontier: Gentrification and the Revanchist City* (New York: Routledge, 1996); Alex S. Vitale, *City of Disorder: How the Quality of Life Campaign Transformed New York Politics* (New York: New York University Press, 2009).

25. Corey Kilgannon, "Neighborhood Report: West Side; Fight Over Unused Rail Line," *New York Times*, May 16, 1999, CY:8.

26. Regional Plan Association, "What to Do with the High Line? A Final Draft Report," prepared for CSX Transportation, Inc., June 21, 1999.

27. Regional Plan Association, "What to Do with the High Line?," 12.

28. Regional Plan Association, "What to Do with the High Line?," 20.

29. Thomas J. Lueck, "Up, but Not Running, on the West Side," *New York Times*, July 25, 1999, 23.

30. Lueck, "Up, but Not Running."

31. U.S. Census of Population, 2000.

32. Motoko Rich, "Turf: Edged Out by the Stroller Set," *New York Times*, May 27, 2004, F1; cited in Ghaziani, *There Goes the Gayborhood?*, 146.

33. Halle and Tiso, *New York's New Edge*, 22.

34. Graeme Evans, "Hard-Branding the Cultural City—from Prado to Prada," *International Journal of Urban and Regional Research* 27, no. 2 (2003): 417–40.

35. Sharon Zukin, *Loft Living: Culture and Capital in Urban Change* (Baltimore: Johns Hopkins University Press, 1982).

36. Joshua David and Robert Hammond, *High Line: The Inside Story of New York City's Park in the Sky* (New York: Farrar, Straus and Giroux, 2011), 20.

37. David and Hammond, *High Line*, 11.

38. David and Hammond, *High Line*, 9.

39. David and Hammond, *High Line*, 9–11.

40. Surface Transportation Board, *Chelsea Property Owners—Abandonment—Portion of the Consolidated Rail Corporation's West 30th Street Secondary Track in New York, NY*, Docket No. AB-167 (Sub-No. 1094)A, July 14, 1999.

41. Michael Sorkin and Sharon Zukin, eds., *After the World Trade Center: Rethinking New York City* (New York: Routledge, 2002).

42. David and Hammond, *High Line*, 39.

43. For an extended look at how the post-9/11 moment (and the aftermath of disasters in general) created opportunities to circumvent the normal channels of governance, see Kevin Fox Gotham and Miriam Greenberg, *Crisis Cities: Disaster and Redevelopment in New York and New Orleans* (New York: Oxford University Press, 2014).

44. Richard Pérez-Peña, "Giuliani's Quest for a Term Extension Hits a Wall in Albany," *New York Times*, October 2, 2001, D1.

45. Kelly Crow, "Chelsea: Fight Heats Up Again Over Grassy Bed of Rails," *New York Times*, January 27, 2002, CY6.

46. Crow, "Chelsea."

47. David and Hammond, *High Line*, 41.

48. David and Hammond, *High Line*, 45.

49. New York City Planning Commission, "Special West Chelsea District Rezoning and High Line Open Space EIS, Chapter 27: Response to Comments," 2005, http://www1.nyc.gov/assets/planning/download/pdf /plans/west-chelsea/wc_chap27_responses_feis.pdf.

50. Robin Pogrebin, "An Aesthetic Watchdog in the City Planning Office," *New York Times*, December 29, 2004, E1.

51. Charles V. Bagli, "Olympic Bid, Though Unsuccessful, Brought Benefits to the City, Its Champion Says," *New York Times*, August 4, 2012, A14. On the use of zoning deregulation as a principle of neoliberal urbanism, see also Rachel Weber, "Extracting Value from the City: Neoliberalism and Urban Redevelopment," *Antipode* 34, no. 3 (2002): 519–40.

52. City of New York, "PlaNYC: A Greener, Greater New York," 2007, http://www.nyc.gov/html/planyc/downloads/pdf/publications/full _report_2007.pdf, 31.

53. Julian Brash, *Bloomberg's New York: Class and Governance in the Luxury City* (Athens: University of Georgia Press, 2011), 123.

54. City of New York, "Mayor Michael R. Bloomberg Hosts Summit on New York City Economic Development for Top CEOs and City Leaders," 2003; cited in Brash, *Bloomberg's New York*, 123.

55. City of New York, "PlaNYC: A Greener, Greater New York," 33–36.

56. Gregory Smithsimon, "Dispersing the Crowd: Bonus Plazas and the Creation of Public Space," *Urban Affairs Review* 43, no. 3 (2008): 325–51.

57. Benjamin Shepard and Gregory Smithsimon, *The Beach Beneath the Streets: Contesting New York City's Public Spaces* (New York: State University of New York Press, 2011).

58. John Krinsky and Maud Simonet, *Who Cleans the Park?: Public Work and Urban Governance in New York City* (Chicago: University of Chicago Press, 2017); Sharon Zukin, *Naked City: The Death and Life of Authentic Urban Places* (New York: Oxford University Press, 2010).

59. David and Hammond, *High Line*, 36.

60. Field notes, November 16, 2011.

61. Linda Lee, "Glamour Rides the Rail," *New York Times*, July 18, 2004, ST4.

62. Karen E. Steen, "Friends in High Places," *Metropolis*, December 1, 2005, http://www.metropolismag.com/uncategorized/friends-in-high-places/.

63. Thomas De Monchaux, "How Everyone Jumped Aboard a Railroad to Nowhere," *New York Times*, May 8, 2005, A6.

64. Steen, "Friends in High Places," 9.

65. Andy Humm, "Crowds, Development and Concerns," *Villager*, July 4, 2012, https://www.amny.com/news/the-high-line-spurs-crowds-development -and-concerns/, 2.

66. Charles Bagli, "Biggest Building Site in Manhattan Up for Auction: Project Aims to Create High-Rise District on Far West Side," *New York Times*, May 17, 2007, A1.

67. Nicolai Ouroussoff, "Gardens in the Air Where the Rail Once Ran: Architects Selected to Make Over the High Line," *New York Times*, August 12, 2004, E1.

68. New York City Planning Commission, "Commercial Districts," 13.

69. Adam Sternbergh, "The High Line: It Brings Good Things to Life," *New York Magazine*, April 27, 2007, http://nymag.com/news /features/31273/.

70. Carol Vogel and Kate Taylor, "Rift in Family as Whitney Plans a Second Home," *New York Times*, April 12, 2010, A1.

71. Cost includes Section 1 (the part initially opened) and Section 2 (the stretch from Twentieth Street to Thirtieth Street); Section 3, not included in that figure, was the part of the High Line that wrapped around the rail yards. Robin Pogrebin, "First Phase of High Line Is Ready for Strolling," *New York Times*, June 8, 2009, https://artsbeat.blogs.nytimes .com/2009/06/08/first-phase-of-high-line-is-ready-for-strolling/.

72. Field Notes, October 3, 2011.

73. Nicolai Ouroussoff, "On High, A Fresh Outlook," *New York Times*, June 10, 2009, C1.

74. Paul Goldberger, "Miracle Above Manhattan," *National Geographic*, April 2011, https://www.nationalgeographic.com/magazine/2011/04/new -york-highline/, 5.

75. Diane Cardwell, "For High Line Visitors, Park Is a Railway Out of Manhattan," *New York Times*, July 22, 2009, A17; Kate Taylor, "The High Line, a Pioneer Aloft, Inspires Other Cities to Look Up," *New York Times*, July 15, 2010, A1; Daniel Geiger and Emily Laermer, "High Line's High Returns," *Crain's New York Business*, September 21, 2014, http://www .crainsnewyork.com/article/20140921/REAL_ESTATE/140919813 /high-lines-high-returns.

76. Kevin Loughran, "Urban Parks and Urban Problems: An Historical Perspective on Green Space Development as a Cultural Fix," *Urban Studies* 57, no. 11 (2020): 2321–38.

77. Josh Barbanel, "Developer to Pay Over $800 Million for Site Near High Line," *Wall Street Journal*, November 27, 2014, https://www.wsj .com/articles/new-york-city-developer-acquires-prime-site-near -high-line-1417042890.

4. "NO MORE BAKE SALES, MAN"

1. City of Chicago, "Logan Square Open Space Plan: Increasing and Improving Parks in the Logan Square Community Area," 2004, http:// www.cct.org/wp-content/uploads/2015/05/LoganSquareOpenSpace Plan2004.pdf.
2. Largest in terms of acres under management. According to the Chicago Park District, it "owns more than 8,800 acres of green space, making it the largest municipal park manager in the nation." Chicago Park District, "About Us," accessed April 5, 2018, https://www.chicagoparkdistrict .com/about-us.
3. Kevin Loughran, "Race and the Construction of City and Nature: A Study of Three Periods of Park Development in Chicago, 1870, 1945, 2010" (PhD diss., Northwestern University, 2017).
4. The Federal Bureau of Investigation conducted two probes into the Park District and its employees in the 1980s, Operation Phocus and Operation Lantern, both of which revealed that Park District employees were taking kickbacks in the hundreds of thousands of dollars in exchange for Park District contracts and other forms of influence. See Thomas J. Gradel and Dick Simpson, "Patronage, Cronyism and Criminality in Chicago Government Agencies: Anti-Corruption Report Number 4," University of Illinois at Chicago, 2011, http://tigger.uic.edu/depts /pols/ChicagoPolitics/AntiCorruptionReport_4.pdf; R. J. Nelson, *Dirty Waters: Confessions of Chicago's Last Harbor Boss* (Chicago: University of Chicago Press, 2016); William Crawford Jr., "Phony Invoices Seen as Key to Kickback Scheme," *Chicago Tribune*, November 11, 1987, 1.
5. David Axelrod, "Mayor Says Park Chief Mismanaging District," *Chicago Tribune*, September 16, 1983, A1; see also Gary Rivlin, *Fire on the Prairie: Harold Washington, Chicago Politics, and the Roots of the Obama Presidency* (Philadelphia: Temple University Press, 2013).
6. Brian McCammack, "Recovering Green in Bronzeville" (PhD diss., Harvard University, 2012), 136–39.

7. The two that were built in Black communities were Addams Park, on the Near West Side in the major site of Black settlement outside of the South Side's Black Belt, and Durso Playlot, adjacent to the Cabrini-Green Homes on the Near North Side.

8. Author calculation, Chicago Park District Annual Reports. For full data, see Loughran, "Race and the Construction of City and Nature," 93–95.

9. "Mayor Urges Fast Action on Park Nominees," *Chicago Tribune*, March 15, 1984, B16; James Strong and Robert Davis, "Mayor Captures Committees: Council Foes Stripped of their Power," *Chicago Tribune*, June 7, 1986, 1.

10. Michael Wright and Caroline Rand Herron, "In Chicago, City Hall Is for Fighting," *New York Times*, May 15, 1983, http://www.nytimes.com/1983/05/15/weekinreview/the-nation-in-chicago-city-hall-is-for-fighting.html; "U.S. Sues Chicago Park District, Charging Racial Bias in Programs," *New York Times*, December 1, 1982, http://www.nytimes.com/1982/12/01/us/us-sues-chicago-park-district-charging-racial-bias-in-programs.html, 1.

11. Larry Bennett, Roberta Garner, and Euan Hague, eds., *Neoliberal Chicago* (Champaign: University of Illinois Press, 2017.

12. William Sites, "God from the Machine? Urban Movements Meet Machine Politics in Neoliberal Chicago," *Environment and Planning A* 44, no. 11 (2012): 2579.

13. Evans, Graeme. "Hard-Branding the Cultural City—from Prado to Prada." *International Journal of Urban and Regional Research* 27, no. 2 (2003): 417–40.

14. Sorkin, Michael, ed., *Variations on a Theme Park: The New American City and the End of Public Space* (New York: Hill and Wang, 1992); Richard Lloyd and Terry Nichols Clark, "The City as an Entertainment Machine," *Research in Urban Sociology: Critical Perspectives on Urban Redevelopment* 6 (2001): 357–78.

15. Evans, "Hard-Branding the Cultural City."

16. Timothy J. Gilfoyle, *Millennium Park: Creating a Chicago Landmark* (Chicago: University of Chicago Press, 2006). Figures are in 2004 dollars.

17. Examples include "Chase (formerly BankOne) Promenade, the BP Bridge, the Exelon Pavilions, the Boeing Galleries, and the McCormick Tribune Plaza." Gilfoyle, *Millennium Park*, 345.

18. On neoliberal park management more generally, see John Krinsky and Maud Simonet, *Who Cleans the Park?: Public Work and Urban Governance in New York City* (Chicago: University of Chicago Press, 2017); Harold A. Perkins, "Out from the (Green) Shadow? Neoliberal Hegemony Through the Market Logic of Shared Urban Environmental Governance," *Political Geography* 28, no. 7 (2009): 395–405.

19. Chicago Park District, "CitySpace: An Open Space Plan for Chicago," January 1998, https://www.cityofchicago.org/city/en/depts/dcd/supp_info/cityspace_plan.html; City of Chicago, "Logan Square Open Space Plan."

20. City of Chicago, "Logan Square Open Space Plan," 21.

21. Gilfoyle, *Millennium Park*, 147.

22. Today there are seventy-seven community areas. The annexation of O'Hare Airport in the 1950s created #76, and the splitting off of Edgewater from Uptown on the North Side in 1980 created #77. See Sudhir Venkatesh, "Chicago's Pragmatic Planners: American Sociology and the Myth of Community," *Social Science History* 25, no. 2 (2001): 275–317.

23. The Trust for Public Land, "The 606 Is Chicago's Next Great Park," press release, June 17, 2013.

24. Making things somewhat confusing are the "official" designations: the Bloomingdale Trail is the linear park itself, and The 606 is the trail plus the street-level access parks that are scattered across the trail's 2.7 miles. However, the renaming has been successful in the sense that many people in Chicago refer to the trail as The 606, not the Bloomingdale Trail.

25. Richard Lloyd, *Neo-Bohemia: Art and Commerce in the Post-Industrial City* (New York: Routledge, 2006).

26. John J. Betancur, "The Politics of Gentrification: The Case of West Town in Chicago," *Urban Affairs Review* 37, no. 6 (2002), 780–814.

27. Lloyd, *Neo-Bohemia*.

28. U.S. Census of Population, 1980 and 2000; American Community Survey, 2016.

29. Jeffrey Nathaniel Parker, "Negotiating the Space Between Avant-Garde and 'Hip Enough': Businesses and Commercial Gentrification in Wicker Park," *City & Community* 17, no. 2 (2018): 442.

30. For example, the two census tracts that make up the core of Logan Square—2205 and 2206—were 53 and 63 percent Hispanic, respectively, at the 2000 Census. At the 2016 American Community Survey, those

tracts were down to 21 and 45 percent. (Tract 2206 was subsequently split into two, 2206.01 and 2206.02; the former was 40.4 and the latter 49.5 percent Hispanic in 2016.)

31. Gina M. Pérez, "An Upbeat West Side Story: Puerto Ricans and Postwar Racial Politics in Chicago," *Centro Journal* 13, no. 2 (2001): 47–71.

32. Nilda Flores-Gonzalez, "*Paseo Boriqua*: Claiming a Puerto Rican Space in Chicago," *Centro Journal* 13, no. 2 (2001): 8. Confusingly, the West Town *community area* includes about half of the Humboldt Park *neighborhood*, as locally understood in the past few decades; making matters more confusing, Humboldt Park is also a *separate community area*, encompassing the western half of the neighborhood. Thus, when Humboldt Park is discussed here, I am referring to contemporary social definitions of the neighborhood, not the 1920s definition of the community area.

33. David Wilson and Dennis Grammenos, "Gentrification, Discourse, and the Body: Chicago's Humboldt Park," *Environment and Planning D* 23 (2005): 300.

34. Maura Toro-Morn, Ivis García Zambrana, and Marixsa Alicea, "De Bandera a Bandera (From Flag to Flag): New Scholarship About the Puerto Rican Diaspora in Chicago," *Centro Journal* 28, no. 2 (2016): 4–35.

35. Flores-Gonzalez, "*Paseo Boriqua*."

36. Flores-Gonzalez, "*Paseo Boriqua*," 14.

37. For comparative cases, see Arlene Dávila, *Latinos, Inc.: The Marketing and Making of a People* (Berkeley: University of California Press, 2001); Frederick F. Wherry, *The Philadelphia Barrio: The Arts, Branding, and Neighborhood Transformation* (Chicago: University of Chicago Press, 2011).

38. Flores-Gonzalez, "*Paseo Boriqua*," 11.

39. Julia Thiel, "Is the Bloomingdale Trail a Path to Displacement?" *Chicago Reader*, June 4, 2015, https://www.chicagoreader.com/chicago /bloomingdale-trail-606-logan-square-humboldt-park-displacement /Content?oid=17899462; John Byrne, "Mayor Emanuel's 606 Affordable-Housing Plan Draws Doubts," *Chicago Tribune*, August 12, 2015, https://www.chicagotribune.com/politics/ct-emanuel-606-housing -met-20150811-story.html.

40. Elaine Coorens, "The 606: Streams Flowed Together Forming a River . . . The Bloomingdale Trail," *Our Urban Times*, June 4, 2015, http://www .oururbantimes.com/parks/606-streams-flowed-together-forming -riverthe-bloomingdale-trail.

41. Krinsky and Simonet, *Who Cleans the Park?*; Ryan Holifield and Kathleen C. Williams, "Urban Parks, Environmental Justice, and Voluntarism: The Distribution of Friends of the Parks Groups in Milwaukee County," *Environmental Justice* 7, no. 3 (2014): 70–76.

42. Friends of the Bloomingdale Trail, "2nd. Gen FBT Brochure," 2005, http://www.bloomingdaletrail.org/pdf/2nd_gen_FBT_brochure.pdf.

43. Friends of the Bloomingdale Trail, "Friends of the Bloomingdale Trail Board," 2017, https://www.bloomingdaletrail.org/board-of-directors, 1; Friends of the Bloomingdale Trail, "2nd. Gen FBT Brochure"; Friends of the Bloomingdale Trail, "Limpieza de Primavera y Picnic," 2005, http://www.bloomingdaletrail.org/pdf/fbt-spring-cleaning-2005-es .pdf.

44. Erica Gies, "Conservation: An Investment That Pays—The Economic Benefits of Parks and Open Space" (The Trust for Public Land, 2009), http://cloud.tpl.org/pubs/benefits_econbenefits_rpt_7_2009.pdf.

45. The Trust for Public Land, "$1M Commitment to Chicago's Haas Park Praised," November 23, 2004, https://www.tpl.org/media-room/1m -commitment-chicagos-haas-park-praised. Interestingly, in 2012 that same park would become the site of a new soccer field donated by the Embassy of the United Arab Emirates in the United States and Manchester City Football Club (majority owned by the Abu Dhabi royal family). Chicago Park District, "Haas Park," 2018, https://www.chicagoparkdistrict .com/parks-facilities/haas-park.

46. Friends of the Bloomingdale Trail, "City Moves to Acquire Parkland for New Elevated Trail," June 12, 2006, https://www.bloomingdaletrail .org/post/2006/06/12/city-moves-to-acquire-parkland-for-new-elevated -trail.

47. Alisa Hauser, "As a 606 Park Expands, Trailgoers Wonder Why Bathrooms Still Not Added," *DNAinfo*, January 11, 2016, https://www .dnainfo.com/chicago/20160111/humboldt-park/as-606-park-expands -trailgoers-wonder-why-bathrooms-still-not-added/.

48. Melissa Harris, "Chicago Confidential: City Makes Headway in Bloomingdale Trail Project," *Chicago Tribune*, January 24, 2013, http://articles .chicagotribune.com/2013-01-24/business/ct-biz-0124-confidential -bloomingdale-20130124_1_high-line-bloomingdale-trail-humboldt-park.

49. Friends of the Bloomingdale Trail, "Community Visioning Kick-Off a Great Success," March 27, 2007, https://www.bloomingdaletrail.org

/post/2007/03/27/community-visioning-kick-off-a-great-success; Friends of the Bloomingdale Trail, "New Gears Eve Fundraiser @ Handlebar," December 16, 2006, https://www.bloomingdaletrail.org/single-post/2006 /12/16/New-Gears-Eve-Fundraiser-Handlebar.

50. Friends of the Bloomingdale Trail, "Firm Selected for Initial Design and Engineering!," July 15, 2009, https://www.bloomingdaletrail.org /post/2009/07/15/firm-selected-for-initial-design-and-engineering . Note that this firm, ARUP, would later be replaced with Collins Engineers as the engineering contractor for the project.

51. Whet Moser, "What Emanuel Has in Mind for Chicago's Parks—and How to Pay for It," *Chicago Magazine*, July 22, 2015, http://www.chicagomag .com/city-life/July-2015/A-Friday-in-the-Park-With-Rahm/.

52. "Mayor Results, Ward-by-Ward," *Chicago Tribune*, March 16, 2011, http://municipal2011.elections.chicagotribune.com/results/mayor/index .html.

53. Bennett, Garner, and Hague, *Neoliberal Chicago*.

54. Jake Malooley, "Chicago's World-Class City Complex," *TimeOut Chicago*, March 23, 2012, https://www.timeout.com/chicago/things-to-do /chicagos-world-class-city-complex.

55. Whet Moser, "Why Rahm Emanuel Won," *Chicago Magazine*, February 23, 2011, http://www.chicagomag.com/Chicago-Magazine/The-312 /February-2011/Why-Rahm-Emanuel-Won/, 5.

56. City of Chicago, "Bloomingdale Trail Design Work Gets Under Way," June 8, 2011, https://www.cityofchicago.org/city/en/depts/cdot/provdrs /bike/news/2011/jun/bloomingdae_traildesignworkgetsunderway.html, 1.

57. Harris, "Chicago Confidential," 1.

58. Harris, "Chicago Confidential," 1; Kristen Mack and Blair Kamin, "Corporate Donations to Help Convert Old Rail Line Into Park: Emanuel Says Gifts Will Fund NW Side Park, Elevated Trail." *Chicago Tribune*, March 13, 2012, 1.7.

59. Alisa Hauser, "Atop Bloomingdale Trail, Emanuel Sees 'The 606' as Neighborhood Unifier," *DNAinfo*, June 2, 2015, https://www.dnainfo .com/chicago/20150602/humboldt-park/atop-trail-emanuel-sees-606 -as-neighborhood-unifier.

60. Friends of the Bloomingdale Trail, "Trail Recommended for $2.6M in Federal Funding," July 27, 2007, https://www.bloomingdaletrail.org /single-post/2007/07/27/Trail-recommended-for-26M-in-federal-funding.

61. David Lepeska, "A Chicago Park Learns from New York's High Line," *NextCity*, April 1, 2013, https://nextcity.org/features/view/A-Chicago-Park-Learns-From-New-Yorks-High-Line, 1. Officially, the three criteria for a project seeking funds from this program are "(1) be a transportation project, (2) generate a reduction in emissions, and (3) be located in or benefit a nonattainment or maintenance area for ozone, carbon monoxide, and particulate matter." National Park Service, "Congestion Mitigation and Air Quality Improvement (CMAQ) Program," https://www.nps.gov/transportation/pdfs/CMAQ_Fact_Sheet_Final.pdf.

62. Blair Kamin, "Chicago's New 606 Trail a Boon for Open Space, Neighborhoods It Links," *Chicago Tribune*, June 2, 2015, https://www.chicagotribune.com/columns/ct-606-trail-kamin-met-0531-20150529-column.html.

63. The Trust for Public Land, "The 606 Is Chicago's Next Great Park," June 17, 2013, https://www.tpl.org/media-room/606-chicagos-next-great-park.

64. The Trust for Public Land, "The 606 Is Chicago's Next Great Park."

65. Frances Whitehead, interview by the author, October 2016.

66. Frances Whitehead, interview.

67. Frances Whitehead, interview.

68. Alisa Hauser, "Elevated Bloomingdale Trail, Pulse of 'The 606,' Opens to Massive Crowds," *DNAinfo*, June 6, 2015, https://www.dnainfo.com/chicago/20150606/humboldt-park/elevated-bloomingdale-trail-pulse-of-606-opens-massive-crowds.

69. City of Chicago, "Mayor Emanuel Leads Groundbreaking on Bloomingdale Trail," August 27, 2013, https://www.cityofchicago.org/content/dam/city/depts/mayor/Press%20Room/Press%20Releases/2013/August/8.27.13Bloomingdaletrail.pdf, 1.

70. Thiel, "Is the Bloomingdale Trail a Path to Displacement?"

71. Edward Keegan, "The 606: Is That All There Is?" *Crain's Chicago Business*, June 2, 2015, https://www.chicagobusiness.com/article/20150602/NEWS07/150609969/the-606-is-that-all-there-is, 1, 4.

72. Blair Kamin, "The 606 Is a Gem but Still Needs Signs, Shade," *Chicago Tribune*, June 12, 2015, https://www.chicagotribune.com/columns/ct-606-trail-review-kamin-met-0612-20150612-column.html.

73. Kamin, "The 606 Is a Gem."

74. Alessandro Rigolon and Jeremy Németh, " 'We're Not in the Business of Housing': Environmental Gentrification and the Nonprofitization of Green Infrastructure Projects," *Cities* 81 (November 2018): 71–80.

75. A symbolic economy is understood as a city's network of cultural spaces that are centrally tied to economic capital. See Sharon Zukin, *The Cultures of Cities* (Cambridge: Blackwell, 1995).

5. "A PIECE OF CRUD"

1. Marti Lea Gottsch, "Cultural Inflations" (MArch thesis, Rice University, 2011).
2. Robert V. Haynes, *A Night of Violence: The Houston Riot of 1917* (Baton Rouge: Louisiana State University Press, 1976).
3. Sarah H. Emmott, *Memorial Park: A Priceless Legacy* (Houston: Herring, 1992).
4. James P. Sterba, "Plan to Drill for Oil in Park Creates Dispute in Houston," *New York Times*, January 22, 1976, 37, 44; see also Houston Public Library, "Terry Hershey," interviewed by Ann Hamilton, Houston Oral History Project, 2008.
5. Stephen Fox, "Big Park, Little Plans: A History of Hermann Park," http://www.georgekessler.org/index.php?option=com_content&view =article&id=113:big-park-little-plans-a-history-of-hermann-park-by -stephen-fox.
6. Fox, "Big Park, Little Plans," 4.
7. Kevin Loughran, "Race and the Construction of City and Nature," *Environment and Planning A* 49, no. 9 (2017): 1948–67; Stuart Wrede and William Howard Adams, eds., *Denatured Visions: Landscape and Culture in the Twentieth Century* (New York: Museum of Modern Art, 1991).
8. Arthur Coleman Comey, *Houston: Tentative Plans for Its Development: A Report to the Houston Parks Commission* (Boston: Geo H. Ellis, 1913), 9.
9. Comey, *Houston*, 22.
10. Emancipation Park had been donated to the city several decades after its purchase by a Black Baptist congregation, which had used the green space for Juneteenth celebrations. It should be noted that while Houston's system of racial exclusion and control in public space was extreme, it was not of an altogether different character than Black park access in Northern cities, where uneven development, institutional racism by park districts, and racial violence conspired to keep parks nearly as segregated as in the Jim Crow South. Robert D. Bullard, *Invisible Houston: The Black Experience in Boom and Bust* (College Station: Texas A&M

University Press, 2000); James R. Elliott, Elizabeth Korver-Glenn, and Daniel Bolger, "The Successive Nature of City Parks: Making and Remaking Unequal Access Over Time," *City & Community* 18, no. 1 (2019): 109–27. See also Loughran, "Race and the Construction of City and Nature."

11. Comey, *Houston*, 11.

12. Galen Cranz, *The Politics of Park Design: A History of Urban Parks in America* (Cambridge, MA: MIT Press, 1982).

13. Elliott et al., "The Successive Nature of City Parks."

14. Jonah Bea-Taylor, "Flood Control and Metropolitan Development in Houston, Miami and Tampa, 1935–1985" (PhD diss., Georgia Institute of Technology, 2018).

15. Harris County Flood Control District, "Riding the Waves of Change: 60 Years of Service," 1998, https://www.hcfcd.org.

16. Kyle Shelton, *Power Moves: Transportation, Politics, and Development in Houston* (Austin: University of Texas Press, 2017).

17. August O. Spain, "Politics of Recent Municipal Annexation in Texas," *Southwestern Social Science Quarterly* 30, no. 1 (1949): 18–28.

18. Teresa Tomkins-Walsh, " 'A Concrete River Had to Be Wrong': Environmental Action on Houston's Bayous, 1935–1980" (PhD diss., University of Houston, 2009), 14–18.

19. Buffalo Bayou Partnership, "Buffalo Bayou Park Vegetation Management Plan," 2004, 6.

20. Tomkins-Walsh, " 'A Concrete River Had to Be Wrong.' " Although this controversy was settled for a time, since 2013 there have been plans in the works, known as the Memorial Park Demonstration Project, to reengineer some of this "saved" waterway (though it would not involve concretization). See Harris County Flood Control District, "Fact Sheet: W100-00-00-X043 Memorial Park Demonstration Project," 2013, https://www.hcfcd.org.

21. Anne Olson and David Theis, *From Rendering to Reality: The Story of Buffalo Bayou Park* (Houston: Buffalo Bayou Partnership, 2017), 8; Charles Tapley, "Buffalo Bayou Master Plan Rendering," 1977, Rice Digital Scholarship Archive, https://scholarship.rice.edu/handle/1911/88623.

22. Olson and Theis, *From Rendering to Reality*, 11.

23. Louis B. Parks, "Where the Buffalo Roams: Cruise, Park Trails Are Drawing People Down on the Bayou," *Houston Chronicle*, June 10,

1988, 1; Geoff Winningham, *Along Forgotten River: Photographs of Buffalo Bayou and the Houston Ship Channel, 1997–2001; with Accounts of Early Travelers to Texas, 1767–1858* (Austin: Texas State Historical Association, 2003); Adam Doster, "The 'World's Smelliest Canoe Race' Celebrates Its 45th Anniversary," *Houstonia Magazine,* January 23, 2017, https://www.houstoniamag.com/articles/2017/1/23/the-buffalo-bayou-regatta-celebrates-its-45th-wet-year.

24. The park feels smaller than this official measurement, as the core open area of Sesquicentennial Park is only about ten acres.

25. Kyle Shelton, "Culture War in Downtown Houston: Jones Hall and the Postwar Battle Over Exclusive Space," *Southwestern Historical Quarterly* 116, no. 1 (2012): 1–24.

26. Jan Lin, "Ethnic Places, Postmodernism, and Urban Change in Houston," *Sociological Quarterly* 36, no. 4 (1995): 629–47.

27. Lin, "Ethnic Places."

28. Benjamin Shepard and Gregory Smithsimon, *The Beach Beneath the Streets: Contesting New York City's Public Spaces* (New York: State University of New York Press, 2011), 88.

29. Bob Tutt, "City Breaks Ground on Bayou Project," *Houston Chronicle,* October 28, 1987, 1:18.

30. Coordinated efforts to keep wealthy, White Houstonians downtown after nightfall have continued as recently as 2015. See Erin Mulvaney, "Proposal Would Put New Shine on Theater District Transformation: City Seeks to Create Urban Hub out of Uninviting Spaces," *Houston Chronicle,* August 14, 2015, A1; Clifford Pugh, "Redesigned Jones Plaza Stirs Discussion," *Houston Chronicle,* November 20, 2001, https://www.chron.com/entertainment/music/article/Redesigned-Jones-Plaza-stirs-discussion-2024334.php.

31. Igor Vojnovic, "Governance in Houston: Growth Theories and Urban Pressures," *Journal of Urban Affairs* 25, no. 5 (2003): 589–624.

32. Lettice Stuart, "Houston: Texas Medical Center Offers Builders $1.3 Billion Rx," *New York Times,* May 20, 1990, A10.

33. Michael Berryhill, "Prescription for Growth," *Cite* 47 (2000): 12–15.

34. I thank the great Caroline Graham for sharing this observation with me.

35. Joel Garreau, *Edge City: Life on the New Frontier* (New York: Anchor, 1991); Mike Davis, *City of Quartz: Excavating the Future in Los Angeles* (New York: Verso, 1990).

36. Judith K. De Jong, *New SubUrbanisms* (New York: Routledge, 2014), 152–60.

37. Alexander Garvin, *What Makes a Great City* (Washington, DC: Island, 2016), 255–66; Garreau, *Edge City*, 209–60.

38. Garvin, *What Makes a Great City*, 257.

39. Joseph A. Pratt, "8F and Many More: Business and Civic Leadership in Modern Houston," *Houston Review* 1, no. 2 (2004): 2–7, 31–44.

40. Alison Cook, "The Trial of Joe Russo," *HoustonPress*, December 1, 1994, http://www.houstonpress.com/news/the-trial-of-joe-russo-6572538.

41. Michael Oluf Emerson and Kevin T. Smiley, *Market Cities, People Cities: The Shape of Our Urban Future* (New York: New York University Press, 2018).

42. Dale Robertson, "New Year Leads to Creation of New Paths: Trail Projects Aim to Begin Construction Soon," *Houston Chronicle*, January 28, 2010, 9.

43. The complex was originally built as San Felipe Courts, providing housing for White defense-industry workers during World War II. In subsequent years it became public housing (renamed Allen Parkway Village) with a largely Black and Asian population. Like many public housing complexes in the United States, it was demolished and rebuilt in recent decades. See Lin, "Ethnic Places"; Tomiko Meeks, "Freedmen's Town, Texas: A Lesson in the Failure of Historic Preservation," *Houston History* 8, no. 2 (2011): 42–44; Scott Henson, "Allen Parkway Village: Politicians Plot to Raze Public Housing in Houston," *Texas Observer*, July 12, 1991, 1, 6–14. See also Lawrence J. Vale, *Purging the Poorest: Public Housing and the Design Politics of Twice-Cleared Communities* (Chicago: University of Chicago Press, 2013).

44. William H. Whyte, *The Social Life of Small Urban Spaces* (Washington, DC: Conservation Foundation, 1980).

45. U.S. Census of Population, 1990.

46. U.S. Census of Population, 1990.

47. U.S. Census of Population, 2000.

48. Buffalo Bayou Partnership, "Buffalo Bayou Park Fact Sheet," 2015, http://buffalobayou.org/bbpwordpress/wp-content/uploads/2015/11/BBPark-Fact-Sheet-FINAL-8.04.15.pdf.

49. It is difficult to fully discern the financial contributions of various public and private actors, especially if one considers that Buffalo Bayou Park

connects to other waterfront public spaces, built with other funding streams, complicating the drawing of clear spatial, organizational, and financial boundaries. Houston Parks and Recreation Department, "Big Idea Becomes Reality: Rosemont Bridge Grand Opening Scheduled," press release, March 21, 2011, http://www.houstontx.gov/parks/pdfs/2011/RosemontBridgeMarch26.pdf.

50. Urban Land Institute, "Rich Kinder on Business Resilience," Rich Kinder interviewed by William Fulton, May 18, 2015, https://www.youtube.com/watch?v=rfGUqV-yRoY.

51. Jenny Deam, "Deep-Pocketed Giving a Houston Mainstay Past and Present," *Houston Chronicle*, October 13, 2016, https://www.chron.com/local/history/economy-business/article/Deep-pocketed-giving-a-Houston-mainstay-past-and-9969588.php.

52. Urban Land Institute, "Rich Kinder on Business Resilience," 14:12-14:19.

53. Margaret Downing, "The HSPVA Fight Continues Even After Rich Kinder Offers to Take Back His Name," *Houston Press*, April 27, 2017, http://www.houstonpress.com/news/hspva-and-the-kinder-naming-rights-9389838.

54. Douglas Britt, "Invitation Only: Partnership Throws a Harvest-Inspired Gathering," *Houston Chronicle*, November 11, 2009, 3.

55. Thompson Design Group, Inc. and EcoPLAN, "Master Plan for Buffalo Bayou and Beyond," prepared for Buffalo Bayou Partnership, City of Houston, Harris County, and Harris County Flood Control District, 2002, 14; see also Winningham, *Along Forgotten River*.

56. Houston Parks Board, "IRS Form 990," 2016, http://houstonparksboard.org/about/2016_Form_990_for_Houston_Parks_Board.pdf.

57. Jayme Fraser, "$50 Million Donation, Maintenance Pact to Boost Greenways Project," *Houston Chronicle*, October 15, 2013, https://www.houstonchronicle.com/news/politics/houston/article/50-million-donation-maintenance-pact-to-boost-4899052.php.

58. "Meet Anne Olson of Buffalo Bayou Partnership," *VoyageHouston*, May 31, 2017, http://voyagehouston.com/interview/meet-anne-olson-buffalo-bayou-partnership-downtown-office/.

59. Houston Parks and Recreation Department, "2011 Annual Report," https://www.houstontx.gov/parks/pdfs/2011/2011AnnualReport.pdf, 3.

60. Mike Morris, "Park Project Beautifying Buffalo Bayou: Private Funding Would Be Used to Color the Waterway West of Downtown a More Attractive Shade of Green," *Houston Chronicle*, Febuary 14, 2011, B1.

61. Mimi Swartz, "Green Acres," *Texas Monthly*, October 2015, https://www.texasmonthly.com/the-culture/green-acres-2/.

62. Downtown Redevelopment Authority, "TIRZ #3 Map 2011 Annexation," 2011, http://www.mainstreettirz.com/images/TIRZ_3_As_Enlarged_Annexation.pdf.

63. Molly Glentzer, "Buffalo Bayou Reborn," *Houston Chronicle*, October 1, 2015, https://www.houstonchronicle.com/life/article/Buffalo-Bayou-Park-gives-Houstonians-a-new-6541659.php. Kinder made these comments just a month before Houston's 2015 mayoral election (incumbent Annise Parker, a supporter of the new park, was term-limited). Democrat Sylvester Turner would go on to narrowly defeat independent candidate Bill King in a runoff, becoming the city's second Black mayor.

64. Josh Pacewicz, "Tax Increment Financing, Economic Development Professionals and the Financialization of Urban Politics," *Socio-Economic Review* 11, no. 3 (2013): 413.

65. Dianna Wray, "Buffalo Bayou Park Is Getting Ready to Open," *Houston Press*, September 15, 2015, http://www.houstonpress.com/news/buffalo-bayou-park-is-getting-ready-to-open-7763987.

66. Buffalo Bayou Partnership, "News Release: 'Buffalo Bayou's Back'—Buffalo Bayou Park complete in Fall 2015," June 19, 2015, https://buffalobayou.org/news-release-buffalo-bayous-back-buffalo-bayou-park-complete-in-fall-2015/.

67. Swartz, "Green Acres," 2; Stephen Fox, "Foreword," in *From Rendering to Reality: The Story of Buffalo Bayou Park*, by Anne Olson and David Theis (Houston: Buffalo Bayou Partnership, 2017.

68. Fauzeya Rahman, "From Weedy to Wonderful: Buffalo Bayou Park Opens as a Prime Green Destination," *Houston Chronicle*, October 4, 2015, B1; Catherine Matusow, "The Tide Turns on Buffalo Bayou: Houston's Central Park Passes Its First Test," *Houstonia Magazine*, July 9, 2015, https://www.houstoniamag.com/news-and-city-life/2015/07/the-tide-turns-on-buffalo-bayou.

69. Houston Chronicle Editorial Board, "Houstonians of the Year: They Have a Passion for Transforming Houston," *Houston Chronicle*, December 22, 2013, B9.

70. Buffalo Bayou Partnership, "Buffalo Bayou Park Selected as a Winner of the Urban Land Institute's 2017–2018 Global Awards for Excellence," press release, November 14, 2017, https://buffalobayou.org/buffalo-bayou

-park-selected-as-a-winner-of-the-urban-land-institutes-2017
-2018-global-awards-for-excellence/.

71. Kyle Hagerty, "Huge Mixed-Use Coming Along Buffalo Bayou Park Houston," *Bisnow Houston*, June 23, 2016, https://www.bisnow.com /houston/news/mixed-use/buffalo-bayou-park-improvements-pay-off -attract-500m-mixed-use-development-61786;

72. "Two Pedestrian Accidents Highlight Dangers of Allen Parkway," KHOU11, March 19, 2014, https://www.khou.com/article/news/local /2-pedestrian-accidents-highlight-dangers-of-allen-parkway/285 -259050028.

73. Phaedra Cook, "A Look at the Dunlavy, the Breakfast and Lunch Hot Spot on Buffalo Bayou," *HoustonPress*, May 11, 2016, http://www .houstonpress.com/restaurants/a-look-at-the-dunlavy-the-breakfast-and -lunch-hot-spot-on-buffalo-bayou-8393488; Shelby Hodge, "Walk in the Park at Lost Lake Reserved for Donors and Partners at $58 Million Buffalo Bayou Park," *CultureMap Houston*, September 21, 2015, http://houston.culturemap.com/news/society/09-21-15-walk-in-the -park-reserved-for-donors-and-partners-at-58-million-lost-lake-project; Marcy de Luna, "Welcome to the Jungle: Partygoers Have a Wild Time at Glow-in-the-Dark Gala for Literacy," *CultureMap Houston*, September 25, 2017, http://houston.culturemap.com/news/society/09 -25-17-jungle-party-barbara-bush-houston-literacy-foundation-young -professionals.

74. Urban Land Institute, "Rich Kinder on Business Resilience," 26:50-27:04.

75. Author calculation, Houston Parks and Recreation Department annual reports, 2006–17. Available at https://www.houstontx.gov /parks/.

6. PARKS FOR PROFIT OR FOR PEOPLE?

1. Kevin Loughran, "Urban Parks and Urban Problems: An Historical Perspective on Green Space Development as a Cultural Fix," *Urban Studies* 57, no. 11 (2020): 2321–38; Roy Rosenzweig and Elizabeth Blackmar, *The Park and the People: A History of Central Park* (Ithaca, NY: Cornell University Press, 1992).

2. David J. Madden, "Revisiting the End of Public Space: Assembling the Public in an Urban Park," *City & Community* 9, no. 2 (2010): 187–207.

3. The High Line, for example, bans, among other activities, "throwing objects," "sitting on railings or climbing on any part of the High Line," along with "bicycles, skateboards, skates and scooters." Buffalo Bayou Park's bans include glass containers, "scooters, skateboards, rollerblading, and skating," and excessive noise levels. See Buffalo Bayou Partnership, "Rules & Regulations," retrieved June 22, 2018, https://buffalobayou.org/visit/destination/buffalo-bayou-park/; New York City Department of Parks and Recreation, "High Line Basics: Know Before You Go," retrieved June 22, 2018, https://www.nycgovparks.org/parks/the-high-line/highlights.

4. Alex S. Vitale, *City of Disorder: How the Quality of Life Campaign Transformed New York Politics* (New York: New York University Press, 2008).

5. Geoff Winningham, *Along Forgotten River: Photographs of Buffalo Bayou and the Houston Ship Channel, 1997–2001; with Accounts of Early Travelers to Texas, 1767–1858* (Austin: Texas State Historical Association, 2003); Joshua David and Robert Hammond, *High Line: The Inside Story of New York City's Park in the Sky* (New York: Farrar, Straus and Giroux, 2011); Mitch Dudek, "The Paved-Over, Unofficial History of the 606 Trail," *Chicago Sun-Times*, May 19, 2015, https://chicago.suntimes.com/2015/5/19/18425867/the-paved-over-unofficial-history-of-the-606-trail.

6. Kevin Loughran, "Race and the Construction of City and Nature: A Study of Three Periods of Park Development in Chicago, 1870, 1945, 2010" (PhD diss., Northwestern University, 2017).

7. Friends of the QueensWay, "Connections + Neighborhoods," retrieved June 22, 2018, https://thequeensway.org/the-plan/connections-neighborhoods/.

8. Kinder Foundation, "Emancipation Park," retrieved June 22, 2018, https://kinderfoundation.org/major-gifts/urban-green-space/emancipation-park/.

9. Molly Glentzer, "Memorial Park Restoration Gets a $70 Million Boost: City Council Must Still Approve the Largest Greenspace Gift in Houston's History," *Houston Chronicle*, April 25, 2018, https://www.chron.com/neighborhood/memorial-news/article/Memorial-Park-restoration-gets-a-70-million-boost-12863707.php.

10. Dug Begley, "Improvements: World Cup Runneth Over? If Houston Lands Some Games, a Parklike Space Atop I-45 Is Possible," *Houston Chronicle*, June 14, 2018, B1.

11. Charles V. Bagli, "'Diller Island' Is Back from the Dead," *New York Times*, October 25, 2017, https://www.nytimes.com/2017/10/25/nyregion /diller-island-revived-cuomo.html.

12. Robert Caro, *The Power Broker: Robert Moses and the Fall of New York* (New York: Vintage, 1974), 193.

7. DEFECTIVE LANDSCAPES

1. Lynda V. Mapes, "'Like Standing Rock': Trans Mountain Pipeline-Expansion Opponents Plan B.C. Protest," *Seattle Times*, March 8, 2018, https://www.seattletimes.com/seattle-news/environment/like-standing -rock-trans-mountain-pipeline-expansion-opponents-plan-b-c-protest/.

2. Kinder himself prefers "urban green space." See Kinder Foundation, "Urban Green Space," retrieved September 16, 2019, https://kinderfoundation .org/major-gifts/urban-green-space/.

3. Drawing on Bourdieu, I offer the following definition of cultural power: the ability to enact and enforce norms, values, aesthetic styles, tastes, and other cultural expressions; usually (but not always) tied to other dominant forces in society, such as cultural and political institutions. See Pierre Bourdieu, *The Rules of Art: Genesis and Structure of the Literary Field* (Stanford, CA: Stanford University Press, 1996). Social control is understood here in broader but related terms as the production of order by institutions of power in society: "the capacity of a society to regulate itself according to desired principles and values." Morris Janowitz, "Sociological Theory and Social Control," *American Journal of Sociology* 81, no. 1 (1975): 82. See also Michel Foucault, *Security, Territory, Population: Lectures at the Collège de France 1977–1978*, ed. Michel Senellart, trans. Graham Burchell (New York: Picador, 2009).

4. Frederick Law Olmsted, "Report Accompanying Plan for Laying Out the South Park" (Chicago: South Park Commission, 1871), 9.

5. See the two most influential early philosophical treatises on the picturesque: William Gilpin, *Three Essays: On Picturesque Beauty; On Picturesque Travel; and On Sketching Landscape: to Which Is Added a Poem, On Landscape Painting* (London: Strand, 1792); Edmund Burke, *A Philosophical Enquiry Into the Origin of Our Ideas of the Sublime and Beautiful* (New York: Oxford University Press, 2015).

6. Donna Landry, "The Geopolitical Picturesque," *Spatial Practices* 13, no. 1 (2012): 91–114; William Cronon, "The Trouble with Wilderness: Or, Getting Back to the Wrong Nature," *Environmental History* 1, no. 1 (1996): 7–28.

7. Stephen Copley and Peter Garside, eds., *The Politics of the Picturesque: Literature, Landscape and Aesthetics Since 1770* (New York: Cambridge University Press, 1994); Malcolm Andrews, *The Search for the Picturesque: Landscape Aesthetics and Tourism in Britain, 1760–1800* (Stanford, CA: Stanford University Press, 1989).

8. Olmsted, "Report Accompanying Plan for Laying Out the South Park," 10.

9. Dorceta E. Taylor, *The Environment and the People in American Cities, 1600s–1900s* (Durham, NC: Duke University Press, 2009); Robert Topinka, *Racing the Street: Race, Rhetoric, and Technology in Metropolitan London, 1840–1900* (Oakland: University of California Press, 2020).

10. Hillary Angelo, *How Green Became Good: Urbanized Nature and the Making of Cities and Citizens* (Chicago: University of Chicago Press, 2020).

11. Nicole M. Evans and William P. Stewart, "The Role of Naturalness in Ecological Restoration: A Case Study from the Cook County Forest Preserves," *Nature and Culture* 13, no. 2 (2018): 232–52.

8. IMBRICATED SPACES

1. David Wachsmuth, "Three Ecologies: Urban Metabolism and the Society-Nature Opposition," *Sociological Quarterly* 53, no. 4 (2012): 506–23.

2. Gary Alan Fine, *Morel Tales: The Culture of Mushrooming* (Cambridge, MA: Harvard University Press, 1998), 2.

3. Rob J. F. Burton, "Understanding Farmers' Aesthetic Preference for Tidy Agricultural Landscapes: A Bourdieusian Perspective," *Landscape Research*, 37, no. 1 (2012): 51–71; Daanish Mustafa, Thomas A. Smucker, Franklin Ginn, Rebecca Johns, and Shanon Connely, "Xeriscape People and the Cultural Politics of Turfgrass Transformation," *Environment and Planning D: Society and Space* 28, no. 4 (2010): 600–17.

4. Catherine McNeur, *Taming Manhattan: Environmental Battles in the Antebellum City* (Cambridge, MA: Harvard University Press, 2014).

5. Arguably the marker of the quality of picturesque landscape architecture (in the opinion of critics) is how well the landscape convincingly

conveys this fiction. See, for example, the praise along these lines heaped upon Olmsted and Vaux's Prospect Park (Brooklyn, New York), usually considered their best urban park. See, for example, Alan Tate, *Great City Parks* (London: Taylor & Francis, 2001).

6. David P. Jordan, *Transforming Paris: The Life and Labors of Baron Hauss-mann* (New York: Free Press, 1995); Peter Marcuse, "The Grid as City Plan: New York City and Laissez-Faire Planning in the Nineteenth Century," *Planning Perspectives* 2, no. 3 (1987): 287–310.

7. William Cronon, *Nature's Metropolis: Chicago and the Great West* (New York: Norton, 1991).

8. Roy Rosenzweig and Elizabeth Blackmar, *The Park and the People: A History of Central Park* (Ithaca, NY: Cornell University Press, 1992).

9. Cronon, *Nature's Metropolis*.

10. Frederick Law Olmsted, "Public Parks and the Enlargement of Towns," in *Frederick Law Olmsted: Essential Texts*, ed. Robert Twombly (New York: Norton, 2010).

11. David Schuyler, *The New Urban Landscape: The Redefinition of City Form in Nineteenth-Century America* (Baltimore: Johns Hopkins University Press, 1986).

12. Note that this was not universally true; many Sunbelt cities that were only coming of age in the twentieth century often started their park building with picturesque spaces as a means of playing cultural catch-up—see, for example, Houston's Hermann Park (1916).

13. Galen Cranz, *The Politics of Park Design: A History of Urban Parks in America* (Cambridge, MA: MIT Press, 1982).

14. Small parks were built with a moral agenda, as reformers believed they would increase socially desired behaviors among the industrial working classes, as indicated in the following assessment by Jane Addams: "In Chicago a map has recently been made demonstrating that juvenile crime is decreasing in the territory surrounding the finely equipped playgrounds and athletic fields which the South Park Board three years ago placed in thirteen small parks. We know in Chicago, from ten years' experience in a juvenile court, that many boys are arrested from sheer excess of animal spirits. . . . The women of Chicago are study-ing the effect of these recreational centers provided by the South Park Committee upon the social life of the older people who use them. One thing they have done is enormously to decrease the patronage of the

neighboring saloons. Before we had these park houses, the saloon hall was hired for weddings and christenings, or any sort of event which in the foreign mind is associated with general feasting. . . . As you know, the saloon hall is rented free, with the understanding that a certain amount of money be paid across the bar. . . . The park hall, of course, is under no such temptation and, therefore, drinking has almost ceased at the parties held in the parks." Jane Addams, "Women's Conscience and Social Amelioration," in *The Jane Addams Reader*, ed. Jean Bethke Elshtain (New York: Basic Books, 2002), 258–59. See also Marta Gutman, *A City for Children: Women, Architecture, and the Charitable Landscapes of Oakland, 1850–1950* (Chicago: University of Chicago Press, 2014).

15. Joan E. Draper, "The Art and Science of Park Planning in the United States: Chicago's Small Parks, 1902–1905," in *Planning the Twentieth-Century American City*, ed. Mary Corbin Sies and Christopher Silver (Baltimore: Johns Hopkins University Press, 1996).

16. In picturesque parks, such activities took place by temporarily appropriating open fields or ponds, respectively. See Cranz, *The Politics of Park Design*. See also Shepard and Smithsimon's discussion of "temporary autonomous zones." Benjamin Shepard and Gregory Smithsimon, *The Beach Beneath the Streets: Contesting New York City's Public Spaces* (New York: State University of New York Press, 2011), 44–49.

17. Dorceta E. Taylor, *The Environment and the People in American Cities, 1600s–1900s* (Durham, NC: Duke University Press, 2009); Rosenzweig and Blackmar, *The Park and the People*.

18. Frederick Law Olmsted, "Report Accompanying Plan for Laying Out the South Park" (Chicago: South Park Commission, 1871), 5. See also Phil Birge-Liberman, "(Re)greening the City: Urban Park Restoration as a Spatial Fix," *Geography Compass* 4, no. 9 (2010): 1392–1407; Kevin Loughran, "Urban Parks and Urban Problems: An Historical Perspective on Green Space Development as a Cultural Fix," *Urban Studies* 57, no. 11 (2020): 2321–38.

19. Alastair Bonnett, "The Metropolis and White Modernity," *Ethnicities* 2, no. 3 (2002): 354.

20. Marian L. Osborn, "The Development of Recreation in the South Park System of Chicago" (master's thesis, University of Chicago, 1928); Noel Ignatiev, *How the Irish Became White* (New York: Routledge, 1995);

David R. Roedinger, *Wages of Whiteness: Race and the Making of the American Working Class* (New York: Verso, 1991).

21. Tyina L. Steptoe, *Houston Bound: Culture and Color in a Jim Crow City* (Oakland: University of California Press, 2016); Brian McCammack, *Landscapes of Hope: Nature and the Great Migration in Chicago* (Cambridge, MA: Harvard University Press, 2017).

22. Stuart Wrede and William Howard Adams, eds., *Denatured Visions: Landscape and Culture in the Twentieth Century* (New York: Museum of Modern Art, 1991).

23. James Wright Steely, *Parks for Texas: Enduring Landscapes of the New Deal* (Austin: University of Texas Press, 2010); Albert D. Wittman, *Architecture of Minneapolis Parks* (Chicago: Arcadia, 2010).

24. D. Bradford Hunt, *Blueprint for Disaster: The Unraveling of Chicago Public Housing.* (Chicago: University of Chicago Press, 2009); Kyle Shelton, *Power Moves: Transportation, Politics, and Development in Houston* (Austin: University of Texas Press, 2017); A. Dan Tarlock, "United States Flood Control Policy: The Incomplete Transition from the Illusion of Total Protection to Risk Management," *Duke Environmental Law & Policy Forum* 23 (2012), 151–83.

25. Cranz, *The Politics of Park Design.*

26. To take Chicago as a key example: As noted by the Park District in its 1947 "Police and Minority Groups" report, "the pressure of the Negro community for unrestricted uses of beaches, pools, and parks is one area in which friction is continuous." Black political organizations like the Urban League encouraged supporters to cease "bunch[ing] up in Washington Park or at the Jackson Park or 31st Street beaches. . . . With all the parks and beaches there are, we ought to spread ourselves all over the city. . . . Let's go everywhere we want to—to the Oak St. Beach, to Lincoln Park, to the Brookfield Zoo—all over town." These three sites—significant because of their social location, the first two on the White North Side and the third in the White western suburb of Brookfield—spoke to a socio-spatial strategy that confronted the uneven development of Chicago parkland. The corollary to the push for park development in the Black Belt was this: if the Park District would not adequately develop or maintain park space in Black areas, Black people would assert their rights to use parks "all over town." Other political efforts included a series of "wade-ins" at South Side beaches in the early

1960s. The most notable of these incidents occurred in 1961 at Rainbow Beach, a Park District site in the South Shore neighborhood. Here, civil rights groups, including the NAACP and the Congress of Racial Equality (CORE), led integration efforts in the face of prolonged anti-Black mob violence. Joseph D. Lohman and Roger F. Shanahan, *The Police and Minority Groups* (Chicago Park District archives, 1947), 71; Chicago Urban League, "Summer Time" (UIC, Chicago Urban League records, Series I, Box 268, Folder 2738, n.d.), 4–5, 11; "Kennedy Jabbed on Chicago," *Chicago Defender*, national edition, July 15, 1961. See Kevin Loughran, "Race and the Construction of City and Nature: A Study of Three Periods of Park Development in Chicago, 1870, 1945, 2010" (PhD diss., Northwestern University, 2017), 95–124. See also Arnold R. Hirsch, "Massive Resistance in the Urban North: Trumbull Park, Chicago, 1953–1966," *Journal of American History* 82, no. 2 (1995): 522–50.

27. Andrew J. Diamond, *Mean Streets: Chicago Youths and the Everyday Struggle for Empowerment in the Multiracial City, 1908–1969* (Berkeley: University of California Press, 2009); Kevin M. Kruse, "The Politics of Race and Public Space: Desegregation, Privatization, and the Tax Revolt in Atlanta," *Journal of Urban History* 31, no. 5 (2005), 610–33.

28. Other notable examples include the Mercer Arboretum and Botanic Gardens (opened in 1974 in a suburb of Houston) and the Getty Villa (opened in 1974 at the boundary of Los Angeles and Malibu).

Note that mid-century landscape architects were being commissioned for suburban corporate campuses rather than updates to older urban parks; that is, cultural producers' talents were moving to the suburbs as well (see Wrede and Adams, *Denatured Visions*). Even farther from city limits, the postwar period was also an era of rediscovery of the national parks, as tourists embraced rustic, rural sites of nature. See Richard West Sellers, *Preserving Nature in the National Parks: A History* (New Haven, CT: Yale University Press, 1997).

29. Lynnell Hancock, "Wolf Pack: The Press and the Central Park Jogger," *Columbia Journalism Review* 41, no. 5 (2003): 38–42; Cindi Katz and Andrew Kirby, "In the Nature of Things: The Environment and Everyday Life," *Transactions of the Institute of British Geographers* 16, no. 3 (1991): 259–71.

30. T. Le'roy, "Fort Turns Over Baby Killing Suspect to Cops," *Chicago Defender*, June 25, 1970, 1.

31. Jane Jacobs, *The Death and Life of Great American Cities* (New York: Random House, 1961).

32. Miriam Greenberg, *Branding New York: How a City in Crisis Was Sold to the World* (New York: Routledge, 2008), 3; Alex S. Vitale, *City of Disorder: How the Quality of Life Campaign Transformed New York Politics* (New York: New York University Press, 2008).

33. Cranz, *The Politics of Park Design*; Elliott, Korver-Glenn, and Bolger, "The Successive Nature of City Parks." In Chicago, the U.S. Department of Justice obtained a consent decree against the Park District in 1983 in an effort to counteract racially unequal park policies, arguing that "parks in Black and Hispanic neighborhoods have fewer indoor facilities, . . . fewer outdoor facilities, . . . fewer instructional programs, . . . and spend less money on recreational personnel, maintenance and capital improvement." See "U.S. Sues Chicago Park District, Charging Racial Bias in Programs," *New York Times*, December 1, 1982, http://www.nytimes.com/1982/12/01/us/us-sues-chicago-park-district-charging-racial-bias-in-programs.html, 1.

34. Amanda I. Seligman, *Chicago's Block Clubs: How Neighbors Shape the City* (Chicago: University of Chicago Press, 2016), 117–40; Jeffrey Nathaniel Parker, "Broken Windows as Growth Machines: Who Benefits from Urban Disorder and Crime?" *City & Community* 17, no. 4 (2018): 945–71.

35. Richard Lloyd, *Neo-Bohemia: Art and Commerce in the Post-Industrial City* (New York: Routledge, 2006), 138. This acceptance of weedy disorder followed from the aesthetic and economic transformation of manufacturing lofts, a process that itself relied on the accumulation of cultural cachet associated with artists working and residing in such spaces. See Sharon Zukin, *Loft Living: Culture and Capital in Urban Change* (Baltimore: Johns Hopkins University Press, 1982).

36. Zukin, *Loft Living*.

37. Kevin Loughran, "Imbricated Spaces: The High Line, Urban Parks, and the Cultural Meaning of City and Nature," *Sociological Theory* 34, no. 4 (2016): 311–34.

38. The movement of postindustrial aesthetics from avant-garde to mainstream maps onto Pierre Bourdieu's understanding of the temporality of cultural production—specifically, the process of "consecration," whereby the existing avant-garde is slowly enshrined by various cultural institutions (and often co-opted by the bourgeoisie as well). Thus, the

contemporary avant-garde is continually positioning itself again the past. See Pierre Bourdieu, *The Rules of Art: Genesis and Structure of the Literary Field* (Stanford, CA: Stanford University Press, 1996), 121–25; see p. 159 for a visual representation.

9. CONSTRUCTING ENVIRONMENTAL AUTHENTICITY

1. "Sacred" here in the Durkheimian sense: belonging to a category of cultural objects and practices that are "protected and isolated by prohibitions" and stand in contrast to profane ones, "those things to which prohibitions apply and which must keep their distance from what is sacred." Émile Durkheim, *The Elementary Forms of Religious Life*, ed. Mark S. Cladis, trans. Carol Cosman (New York: Oxford University Press, 2008), 40.

2. Joshua David and Robert Hammond, *High Line: The Inside Story of New York City's Park in the Sky* (New York: Farrar, Straus and Giroux, 2011), 6.

3. David and Hammond, *High Line*, 75.

4. Mitch Dudek, "The Paved-Over, Unofficial History of the 606 Trail," *Chicago Sun-Times*, May 19, 2015, https://chicago.suntimes.com /2015/5/19/18425867/the-paved-over-unofficial-history-of-the-606 -trail, 2.

5. Dudek, "The Paved-Over, Unofficial History of the 606 Trail," 3.

6. On collective memory and urban space, see Kevin Loughran, Gary Alan Fine, and Marcus Anthony Hunter, "Urban Spaces, City Cultures, and Collective Memories," in *Routledge International Handbook of Memory Studies*, ed. Anna Lisa Tota and Trever Hagen (New York: Routledge, 2015), 193–204.

7. James Robinson, "14-Year Homeless Encampment Broken Up: Complaints Prompt Action by Police," *Houston Chronicle*, January 26, 1996, A22.

8. Lisa Gray, "Where the Wild Things Were," *Houston Chronicle*, March 23, 2008, ZEST 11. See also Geoff Winningham, *Along Forgotten River: Photographs of Buffalo Bayou and the Houston Ship Channel, 1997–2001; with Accounts of Early Travelers to Texas, 1767–1858* (Austin: Texas State Historical Association, 2003).

9. Urban Land Institute, "Rich Kinder on Business Resilience," interviewed by William Fulton, May 18, 2015, https://www.youtube.com /watch?v=rfGUqV-yRoY&t=990s, 29:10–20.

10. Sharon Zukin, *Loft Living: Culture and Capital in Urban Change* (Baltimore: Johns Hopkins University Press, 1982), 58–81.

11. Indeed, we might wonder whether such value judgments would be attached to the spaces by the people who more often frequented or lived in these spaces—that is, by the homeless people whose narratives are absent from the collective memories that have been produced around the three parks.

12. See Gastón R. Gordillo, *Rubble: The Afterlife of Destruction* (Durham, NC: Duke University Press, 2014).

13. See, for example, Benjamin Shepard and Gregory Smithsimon, *The Beach Beneath the Streets: Contesting New York City's Public Spaces* (New York: State University of New York Press, 2011), chap. 4, "Fences and Piers: An Investigation of a Disappearing Queer Public Space."

14. David and Hammond, *High Line*.

15. David and Hammond, *High Line*, 12.

16. David and Hammond, *High Line*, 12, emphasis added.

17. Dating to the brownfield and vacant-lot park conversions of earlier decades, imbricated spaces have a history of being made into parks. This process was often initiated by community groups seeking to turn empty spaces into recreational amenities and embraced by city governments for their low cost. Community gardens are products of a similar process. See Galen Cranz, *The Politics of Park Design: A History of Urban Parks in America* (Cambridge, MA: MIT Press, 1982), 144–46; Miranda J. Martinez, *Power at the Roots: Gentrification, Community Gardens, and the Puerto Ricans of the Lower East Side* (Lanham, MD: Lexington, 2010).

18. Muffie Dunn and Tom Piper, *Diller Scofidio + Renfro: Reimagining Lincoln Center and the High Line*, DVD (New York: Checkerboard Films, 2012), 6:48–7:14.

19. Quoted in Sally McGrane, "A Landscape in Winter, Dying Heroically," *New York Times*, January 31, 2008, http://www.nytimes.com/2008/01/31 /garden/31piet.html, 1.

20. Matt Wolf, *High Line Stories: Joshua David and Robert Hammond*, DVD (New York: Sundance Channel, 2009), 1:28–1:59.

21. Coco McPherson, "Public Sex and the Standard Hotel," *New York Magazine*, June 11, 2009, http://nymag.com/intelligencer/2009/06 /standard_hotel.html.

22. Dunn and Piper, *Diller Scofidio + Renfro*, 11:19–11:41.

23. Margaret Rhodes, "James Corner Field Operations: For Creating Intimate Green Spaces out of Industrial Urban Blight," *Fast Company*, February 7, 2012, https://www.fastcompany.com/3017475/35james-corner-field-operations, 1–2.

24. Nicolai Ouroussoff, "On High, a Fresh Outlook," *New York Times*, June 10, 2009, C1.

25. Paul Goldberger, "Miracle Above Manhattan," *National Geographic*, April 2011, https://www.nationalgeographic.com/magazine/2011/04/new-york-highline/, 1.

26. Kevin Loughran, Gary Alan Fine, and Marcus Anthony Hunter, "Architectures of Memory: When Growth Machines Embrace Preservationists," *Sociological Forum* 33, no. 4 (2018): 855–76.

27. Eric Klinenberg, "Climate Change: Adaptation, Mitigation, and Critical Infrastructures," *Public Culture* 28, no. 2 (2016): 187–92.

28. Zukin, *Loft Living*; Richard Lloyd, *Neo-Bohemia: Art and Commerce in the Post-Industrial City* (New York: Routledge, 2006); Susan Herrington, "Framed Again: The Picturesque Aesthetics of Contemporary Landscapes," *Landscape Journal* 25, no. 1 (2006): 22–37; Gastón R. Gordillo, *Rubble: The Afterlife of Destruction* (Durham, NC: Duke University Press, 2014).

29. David Lepeska, "A Chicago Park Learns from New York's High Line," *NextCity*, April 1, 2013, https://nextcity.org/features/view/A-Chicago-Park-Learns-From-New-Yorks-High-Line, 1.

30. Melissa Harris, "Chicago Confidential: City Makes Headway in Bloomingdale Trail Project," *Chicago Tribune*, January 24, 2013, http://articles.chicagotribune.com/2013-01-24/business/ct-biz-0124-confidential-bloomingdale-20130124_1_high-line-bloomingdale-trail-humboldt-park, 1.

31. Whet Moser, "What Emanuel Has in Mind for Chicago's Parks—and How to Pay for It," *Chicago Magazine*, July 22, 2015, http://www.chicagomag.com/city-life/July-2015/A-Friday-in-the-Park-With-Rahm/, 1.

32. Frances Whitehead, interview by the author, October 2016.

33. Patrick McGeehan, "The High Line Isn't Just a Sight to See; It's Also an Economic Dynamo," *New York Times*, June 5, 2011, https://www.nytimes.com/2011/06/06/nyregion/with-next-phase-ready-area-around-high-line-is-flourishing.html; Goldberger, "Miracle Above Manhattan."

34. Pierre Bourdieu, *Distinction: A Social Critique of the Judgment of Taste*, trans. Richard Nice (Cambridge, MA: Harvard University Press, 1984).

35. Herrington, "Framed Again."

36. Collins Engineers, Inc., "Chicago DOT Project Coordination Office," retrieved April 2019, https://www.collinsengr.com/project/chicago-dot -project-coordination-office/; Frances Whitehead, interview by the author, October 2016.

37. Julie V. Iovine, "Elevated Visions," *New York Times*, July 11, 2004, http:// www.nytimes.com/2004/07/11/arts/architecture-elevated-visions.html, 4. Josh David averred, "The Van Valkenburgh team showed a real affec-tion for the self-seeded landscapes. They treated the wilderness on the High Line like a big green animal, a rare creature that lived up there, nesting in the gravel, and that had to be kept alive no matter what." David and Hammond, *High Line*, 74.

38. Frances Whitehead, interview by the author, October 2016.

39. Frances Whitehead, "Site Narratives: Art + Design Integration," June 23, 2014 (personal communication, October 2016), 23.

40. Whitehead, "Site Narratives," 23.

41. Whitehead, "Site Narratives," 20.

42. Whitehead, "Site Narratives," 20.

43. Whet Moser, "The 606 Shows How to Design a Park in the 21st Century (and Beyond)," *Chicago Magazine*, June 5, 2015, https://www.chicagomag .com/city-life/June-2015/The-606-Park-Design/, 6.

44. Frances Whitehead, interview by the author, October 2016.

45. Moser, "The 606 Shows How to Design a Park," 6.

46. City of Chicago, "Bloomingdale Trail and Park: Framework Plan," 18.

47. Shepard and Smithsimon, *The Beach Beneath the Streets*, 88. This is a broader point about the High Line's long-term prospects argued by Shepard and Smithsimon, following William H. Whyte, in 2011: "As an elevated walk-way, [the High Line] joined the ranks of the sky-bridges of Atlanta's Peachtree Center and San Francisco's Embarcadero. Such passages are attractive, but soon become dated, under-used white elephants. If anything, the High Line at present has even less utility as a passageway. The hubris of the city's latest public space is reflected in the assumption that the High Line couldn't fail to be a popular success." See also William H. Whyte, *City: Rediscovering the Center* (New York: Doubleday, 1988); *The Social Life of Small Urban Spaces* (Washington, DC: Conservation Foundation, 1980).

48. Whitehead, "Site Narratives: Art + Design Integration," 9.

49. Matthew Urbanski, "New Parks for the Livable City" (presentation, Kansas State University, Manhattan, KS, January 29, 2015), https://www.youtube.com/watch?v=Sf8VCo21aZs, 1:15:30–1:18:10.

50. Frederic Jameson, *Postmodernism, Or, The Cultural Logic of Late Capitalism* (Durham, NC: Duke University Press, 1991), 98.

51. As documented by Osman, this kind of gentrifier narrative long predates the twenty-first century. See Suleiman Osman, *The Invention of Brownstone Brooklyn: Gentrification and the Search for Authenticity in Postwar New York* (New York: Oxford University Press, 2011).

52. David Wachsmuth and Hillary Angelo, "Green and Gray: New Ideologies of Nature in Urban Sustainability Policy," *Annals of the American Association of Geographers* 108, no. 4 (2018): 1038–56.

53. Karl Marx, "The German Ideology," in *The Marx-Engels Reader*, ed. Robert C. Tucker, 2nd ed. (New York: Norton, 1978), 174.

54. Karl Marx, "Manifesto of the Communist Party," in *The Marx-Engels Reader*, ed. Robert C. Tucker, 2nd ed. (New York: Norton, 1978), 476.

55. Larry Speck, "Creativity Born from Constraints," TEDxUTAustin, May 23, 2019, https://www.youtube.com/watch?v=6jUzFcqAH50, 9:20–10:59.

56. Roxanna Asgarian, "How Do You Plan a Park That's Meant to Flood?" *Houstonia*, January 23, 2017, https://www.houstoniamag.com/articles/2017/1/23/flooding-buffalo-bayou-park, 1.

57. Asgarian, "How Do You Plan a Park That's Meant to Flood?"

58. Speck, "Creativity Born from Constraints," 11:30–12:06.

59. Kinder Baumgardner and Scott McCready, "Leading with Landscape II: The Houston Transformation," Houston Transformation Conference, April 25, 2016, https://www.youtube.com/watch?v=dXltxhSYEsc, 5:32–45, 11:45–12:26.

60. Baumgardner and McCready, "Leading with Landscape II," 9:20–31.

61. Baumgardner and McCready, "Leading with Landscape II," 14:17–42.

62. Baumgardner and McCready, "Leading with Landscape II," 8:57–9:04.

63. Buffalo Bayou Partnership, "'Monumental Moments'—New Public Art Installed," retrieved June 14, 2019, https://buffalobayou.org/monumental-moments-new-public-art-installed/.

64. Baumgardner and McCready, "Leading with Landscape II," 13:33–45.

65. Edmund Burke, *A Philosophical Enquiry Into the Origin of Our Ideas of the Sublime and Beautiful* (New York: Oxford University Press, 2015), 60.

66. Some readers might wince at this claim; to clarify, I mean "picturesque" in terms of its philosophical definition, as an aesthetic form that offers a distinct, prescribed perspective on a landscape. It is not used here as a synonym for "beautiful"—indeed, that is a category of aesthetic judgment that thinkers like Burke and Gilpin sought to set the picturesque apart from. See Burke, *A Philosophical Enquiry*; William Gilpin, *Three Essays: On Picturesque Beauty; On Picturesque Travel; and On Sketching Landscape: To Which Is Added a Poem, On Landscape Painting* (London: Strand, 1792).

67. Landscape architects in the twenty-first century tend to celebrate Olmsted's vision and accomplishments; given the "denatured visions" of urban parks in the twentieth century, they too harken back to the nineteenth century's pastoral visions for inspiration, often intentionally repurposing concepts from the picturesque in contemporary landscape projects. James Corner, codesigner of New York's High Line, is particularly influential in this regard. See James Corner, ed., *Recovering Landscape: Essays in Contemporary Landscape Theory* (Princeton, NJ: Princeton Architectural Press, 1999); see also Herrington, "Framed Again"; Kevin Loughran, "Imbricated Spaces: The High Line, Urban Parks, and the Cultural Meaning of City and Nature," *Sociological Theory* 34, no. 4 (2016): 311–34; Stuart Wrede and William Howard Adams, eds., *Denatured Visions: Landscape and Culture in the Twentieth Century* (New York: Museum of Modern Art, 1991).

68. Herrington, "Framed Again."

10. SPATIAL PRACTICES AND SOCIAL CONTROL

1. Joshua David and Robert Hammond, *High Line: The Inside Story of New York City's Park in the Sky* (New York: Farrar, Straus and Giroux, 2011), 126.

2. Frederick Law Olmsted, "Address to the Prospect Park Scientific Association," in *Frederick Law Olmsted: Essential Texts*, ed. Robert Twombly (New York: Norton, 2010), 194.

3. Don Mitchell, "The End of Public Space? People's Park, Definitions of the Public, and Democracy," *Annals of the Association of American Geographers* 85, no. 1 (1995): 108–33.

4. See Brian McCammack, *Landscapes of Hope: Nature and the Great Migration in Chicago* (Cambridge, MA: Harvard University Press,

2017); Robinson Block, "Moody Park: From the Riots to the Future for the Northside Community," *Houston History* 9, no. 3 (2012): 20–24; Neil Smith, "Class Struggle on Avenue B: The Lower East Side as Wild Wild West," in *The People, Place, and Space Reader*, ed. Jen Jack Gieseking, William Mangold, Cindi Katz, Setha Low, and Susan Saegert (London: Routledge, 2014), 3–29.

5. Ronald Shiffman, Rick Bell, Lance Jay Brown, and Lynne Elizabeth, eds., *Beyond Zuccotti Park: Freedom of Assembly and the Occupation of Public Space* (Oakland, CA: New Village Press, 2012).

6. As Olmsted wrote, "The objection, then, to monumental and architectural objects in works of landscape gardening is this, that, as a rule, they are not adapted to contribute to any concerted effect, but are likely to demand attention to themselves in particular, distracting the mind from the contemplation of the landscape as such, and disturbing its suggestions to the imagination." Frederick Law Olmsted, "On Landscape Gardening," in *Frederick Law Olmsted: Essential Texts*, ed. Robert Twombly (New York: Norton, 2010), 141.

7. See Shamus Khan, *Privilege: The Making of an Adolescent Elite at St. Paul's School* (Princeton, NJ: Princeton University Press, 2011), chap. 3.

8. Steven Flusty, *Building Paranoia: The Proliferation of Interdictory Space and the Erosion of Spatial Justice* (Los Angeles: Los Angeles Forum for Architecture and Urban Design, 1994), 17. See also Ryan Centner, "Places of Privileged Consumption Practices: Spatial Capital, the Dot-Com Habitus, and San Francisco's Internet Boom," *City & Community* 7, no. 3 (2008): 193–223.

9. Matthew Gandy, *Concrete and Clay: Reworking Nature in New York City* (Cambridge, MA: MIT Press, 2002); Dorceta E. Taylor, *The Environment and the People in American Cities, 1600s—1900s* (Durham, NC: Duke University Press, 2009).

10. This is not to say that people of color do not also experience anxieties and fears in parks and public spaces; rather, it is that parks have long sought to provide spatial protections for Whiteness and White privileges and therefore, given White-dominated urban power structures and the weight of history, park designs and policing strategies cater first and foremost to Whites' racialized anxieties about being in public.

11. Frederick Law Olmsted, "Report Accompanying Plan for Laying out the South Park" (Chicago: South Park Commission, 1871), 17.

228 10. Spatial Practices and Social Control

12. Olmsted, "Report Accompanying Plan for Laying out the South Park," 23.

13. Olmsted, "Report Accompanying Plan for Laying out the South Park," 17.

14. Taylor, *The Environment and the People in American Cities*; Roy Rosenzweig and Elizabeth Blackmar, *The Park and the People: A History of Central Park* (Ithaca, NY: Cornell University Press, 1992).

15. Frederick Law Olmsted, *Mount Royal, Montreal* (New York: G. P. Putnam's Sons, 1881), 53.

16. Stuart Wrede and William Howard Adams, eds., *Denatured Visions: Landscape and Culture in the Twentieth Century* (New York: Museum of Modern Art, 1991); Galen Cranz, *The Politics of Park Design: A History of Urban Parks in America* (Cambridge, MA: MIT Press, 1982).

17. See Jane Jacobs, *The Death and Life of Great American Cities* (New York: Random House, 1961), 35.

18. Joseph D. Lohman and Roger F. Shanahan, *The Police and Minority Groups* (Chicago Park District archives, 1947), 43.

19. Lohman and Shanahan, *The Police and Minority Groups*, 72. See also Cranz, *The Politics of Park Design*.

20. The Chicago Park District's *Police and Minority Groups*, for example, was written largely in response to the 1943 Detroit race riots, which ignited in the city's Belle Isle Park. For broader national context on these issues, see, for example, Marilynn S. Johnson, *Street Justice: A History of Police Violence in New York City* (Boston: Beacon Press, 2003); Victoria W. Wolcott, *Race, Riots, and Roller Coasters: The Struggle Over Segregated Recreation in America* (Philadelphia: University of Pennsylvania Press, 2012); Robin D. G. Kelley, " 'We Are Not What We Seem': Rethinking Black Working-Class Opposition in the Jim Crow South," *Journal of American History* 80, no. 1 (1993): 75–112; Alexander B. Elkins, "Battle of the Corner: Urban Policing and Rioting in the United States, 1943–1971" (PhD diss., Temple University, 2017).

21. Sharon Zukin, *The Cultures of Cities* (Malden, MA: Blackwell, 1995), 27–28.

22. Benjamin Shepard and Gregory Smithsimon, *The Beach Beneath the Streets: Contesting New York City's Public Spaces* (New York: State University of New York Press, 2011), 35.

23. David J. Madden, "Revisiting the End of Public Space: Assembling the Public in an Urban Park," *City & Community* 9, no. 2 (2010): 198. Madden notes that one of the leaders of the private park agency, the Bryant Park Restoration Corporation (later shortened to the Bryant Park Corporation), commented with regard to this effort: "All the hiding places have been eliminated."

24. Madden, "Revisiting the End of Public Space," 199.

25. Recall, for example, Rich Kinder's disdain for the syringes and beer bottles he would encounter in Buffalo Bayou Park prior to his $30 million donation for the park's redevelopment.

26. Madden, "Revisiting the End of Public Space," 201. Another factor, of course, is that revanchist policing takes place at larger geographic scales than the individual parks, forming violent barriers to entry. See Shepherd and Smithsimon, *The Beach Beneath the Streets*, 36–38.

27. Alex S. Vitale, *City of Disorder: How the Quality of Life Campaign Transformed New York Politics* (New York: New York University Press, 2008). On the topic of the High Line's trash, I wrote in 2014 about "Megan," a White food vendor in her twenties, who told me in an interview about how the Friends of the High Line regulated her immediate space: "[The Friends of the High Line] are OCD [obsessive-compulsive disorder] about it being clean up here. We aren't allowed to have any trash bags. We can't even give napkins to people unless they ask for them." She also noted how she was instructed to deposit her cart's trash, contained in a small black box hidden behind a plant at the High Line's edge: "It has to be hidden back there so that people can't see it. I have to empty it away from the park at the end of the night." Kevin Loughran, "Parks for Profit: The High Line, Growth Machines, and the Uneven Development of Urban Public Spaces," *City & Community* 13, no. 1 (2014): 49–68, 58–59.

28. Madden, "Revisiting the End of Public Space," 197. Madden terms this concept a "theory of social surveillance," which he argues was articulated by the actions of the Bryant Park Restoration Corporation.

29. Jeremy Bentham, *The Panopticon Writings* (New York: Verso, 1995).

30. See Foucault on governmentality: Michel Foucault, *Security, Territory, Population: Lectures at the Collège de France 1977–1978*, ed. Michel Senellart, trans. Graham Burchell (New York: Picador, 2009).

31. Although postindustrial parks, owing in large part to their private control and lack of open gathering space, seem unlikely to host large-scale political demonstrations, they nevertheless have been home to at least two protests since the High Line opened in 2009. Shortly after its opening, activists protested the use of rainforest wood in the park's construction; similarly, after the opening of the Bloomingdale Trail/606, activists from Humboldt Park and Logan Square protested the gentrification portended by the park's opening. See Shepard and Smithsimon, *The Beach Beneath the Streets*, 88; Paul Biasco, "Hundreds March on the 606 Over Gentrification," *DNAinfo*, May 18, 2016, https://www.dnainfo.com/chicago/20160518/humboldt-park/hundreds-march-on-606-over-gentrification.

32. Friends of the Bloomingdale Trail, "Community Visioning Update," July 2008, 1.

33. Frances Whitehead, "Site Narratives: Art + Design Integration," June 23, 2014, 1. Note that this concept of wandering over landscape in search of new vantage points mirrors the classical picturesque. See William Gilpin, *Three Essays: On Picturesque Beauty; On Picturesque Travel; and On Sketching Landscape: To Which Is Added a Poem, On Landscape Painting* (London: Strand, 1792); Malcolm Andrews, *The Search for the Picturesque: Landscape Aesthetics and Tourism in Britain, 1760–1800* (Stanford, CA: Stanford University Press, 1989).

34. *Bloomberg TV*, "Architect James Corner on Section 2 of the High Line," June 7, 2011 (http://www.bloomberg.com/video/70550814-architect-james-corner-on-section-2-of-high-line.html).

35. City of Chicago, "Bloomingdale Trail and Park: Framework Plan," 47.

36. Muffie Dunn and Tom Piper, *Diller Scofidio + Renfro: Reimagining Lincoln Center and the High Line* (DVD) (New York: Checkerboard Films, 2012), 11:44–12:06.

37. Dunn and Piper, *Diller Scofidio + Renfro*, 9:02–18. Codesigner Ric Scofidio, speaking to the kind of passive leisure structured by their design, added, "It's a bit like looking into a fireplace. You sit there and you watch the cars, and you watch the red taillights, after a while your mind escapes to some other place." 9:19–31.

38. Gregory Smithsimon, "Dispersing the Crowd: Bonus Plazas and the Creation of Public Space," *Urban Affairs Review* 43, no. 3 (2008): 325–51.

39. Jonathan Barnett, *An Introduction to Urban Design* (New York: Harper & Row, 1982), 179, cited in Shepard and Smithsimon, *The Beach Beneath the Streets*, 58.

40. Dorothy E. Roberts, "Race, Vagueness, and the Social Meaning of Order-Maintenance Policing," *Journal of Criminal Law and Criminology* 89, no. 3 (1999): 775–836; John Eligon, "City Is Held in Contempt on Loitering," *New York Times*, April 26, 2010, https://www.nytimes.com/2010/04/27/nyregion/27contempt.html; William Glaberson, "Long Fight Ends Over Arrests for Loitering," *New York Times*, February 7, 2012, https://www.nytimes.com/2012/02/08/nyregion/new-york-settles-suit-on-illegal-arrests-for-loitering.html.

41. Forrest Stuart, *Down, Out, and Under Arrest: Policing and Everyday Life in Skid Row* (Chicago: University of Chicago Press, 2016), 111.

42. Flusty, *Building Paranoia*, 16. This is an insight originally offered by Greg Smithsimon about the High Line in particular (personal communication, June 2011).

43. Julie V. Iovine, "Elevated Visions," *New York Times*, July 11, 2004, http://www.nytimes.com/2004/07/11/arts/architecture-elevated-visions.html, 4.

44. Carol Vogel and Kate Taylor, "Rift in Family as Whitney Plans a Second Home," *New York Times*, April 12, 2010, A1.

45. David and Hammond, *High Line*, 58.

46. David and Hammond, *High Line*, 58.

47. Note that both the Bloomingdale Trail/606 and Buffalo Bayou Park include other aspects beyond their linear walking paths. By virtue of connecting to a series of "access parks," the 606 (the city government's catchall for the trail and the street-level parks) includes features like a baseball field, a skate park, and playgrounds. Buffalo Bayou Park similarly contains a dog park, a skate park, a lawn, and other recreational areas. While much could be said about these other elements (and what they connote about access and exclusion—tellingly, with room for all of these extra amenities, Buffalo Bayou Park does not include a basketball court or a soccer field, which would be likely to draw athletes of color), the linear walking paths are nevertheless the central features of the parks and the elements that most clearly make use of their infrastructural heritage, distinguishing them from park designs of the past.

48. Writing of slippery spaces in 1990s Los Angeles, Flusty argued that "slippery space provides public relations benefits in that it may be blamed on pre-existent topographical constraints as a means of defraying criticism" about lack of accessibility. This argument holds true for postindustrial parks, where architects can quite reasonably blame site conditions for the lack of clear entrances. See Flusty, *Building Paranoia*, 16.

49. Kinder Baumgardner and Scott McCready, "Leading with Landscape II: The Houston Transformation," Houston Transformation Conference, April 25, 2016, https://www.youtube.com/watch?v=dXltxhSYEsc," 9:41–48.

50. Frances Whitehead, interview by the author, October 2016.

51. It would seem that the most inclusive versions of these parks would have entrances at every street with which they intersect, but whether that would or could fully redress their "slipperiness" is an open question. See also Jack Byers, "The Privatization of Downtown Public Space: The Emerging Grade-Separated City in North America," *Journal of Planning Education and Research* 17, no. 3 (1998): 189–205.

52. For a much broader argument about how places influence identity formation, see Japonica Brown-Saracino, *How Places Make Us: Novel LBQ Identities in Four Small Cities* (Chicago: University of Chicago Press, 2018).

53. Walter Benjamin, *The Arcades Project*, trans. Howard Eiland and Kevin McLaughlin (Cambridge, MA: Belknap Press, 2002); Mike Featherstone, "The Flâneur, the City and Virtual Public Life," *Urban Studies* 35, no. 5–6 (1998): 909–25; Dong-Hoo Lee, "Digital Cameras, Personal Photography and the Reconfiguration of Spatial Experiences," *Information Society* 26, no. 4 (2010): 266–75.

54. David and Hammond, *High Line*, 96.

55. David and Hammond, *High Line*, 97.

56. On contemporary privileged food tastes, see Josée Johnston and Shyon Baumann, *Foodies: Democracy and Distinction in the Gourmet Foodscape* (New York: Routledge, 2009).

57. Friends of the High Line, "Eat & Drink," retrieved September 2019, https://www.thehighline.org/eat-drink/, 4.

58. New York City Department of Parks and Recreation, "Rules & Regulations," retrieved September 2019, https://www.nycgovparks.org/about/faq.

59. Buffalo Bayou Partnership, "Bike & Boat Rentals," https://buffalobayou
.org/visit/destination/buffalo-bayou-park/, retrieved Sept. 2019.

60. Ibid; The Dunlavy, "The Kitchen at the Dunlavy," retrieved September
2019, https://www.thedunlavy.com/team/, 1.

61. The website advertises: "The Water Works in Buffalo Bayou Park is
the perfect venue for a cocktail reception, birthday party, wedding
or large-scale event. Available for rental are: The Brown Foundation
Lawn[,] Hobby Family Pavilion[,] Wortham Insurance Terrace[, and]
The Water Works." Buffalo Bayou Partnership, "The Water Works in
Buffalo Bayou Park," retrieved September 2019, https://buffalobayou
.org/facility-rentals/the-water-works-in-buffalo-bayou-park/,1; Buffalo
Bayou Partnership, "Venue Rental Fees & Guidelines 2019: The Water
Works in Buffalo Bayou Park," https://buffalobayou.org/bbpwordpress
/wp-content/uploads/2018/11/The-Water-Works-in-Buffalo-Bayou
-Park-Venue-Rental.pdf.

62. Park Concession Management, "Chicago Park District List of Available Concession Opportunities," retrieved September 2019, http://www
.parkconcessions.com/documents/2017-NOA-Location-Available.pdf.

63. John Greenfield, "Closing Trails for Fancy Events Sends the Wrong
Message: A Dinner for One Percenters on the 606 Will Feed Fears
About Trail-Related Displacement," *Streetsblog Chicago*, September
25, 2017, https://chi.streetsblog.org/2017/09/25/shutting-down-public
-trails-for-private-dinners-sends-the-wrong-message-to-residents/.

64. Author field notes, September 30, 2011.

65. Author field notes, September 30, 2011.

66. John Kalinski, "Liberation and the Naming of Paranoid Space," introduction to *Building Paranoia: The Proliferation of Interdictory Space and
the Erosion of Spatial Justice*, by Steven Flusty (Los Angeles: LA Forum
for Architecture and Urban Design, 2015), 7.

11. AFTER THE HIGH LINE

1. David Harvey, "The Geography of Capitalist Accumulation: A Reconstruction of the Marxian Theory," *Antipode* 7, no. 2 (1975): 9–21.

2. Robin Pogrebin, "First Phase of High Line Is Ready for Strolling," *New
York Times*, June 8, 2009, https://artsbeat.blogs.nytimes.com/2009/06/08
/first-phase-of-high-line-is-ready-for-strolling/, C3; Friends of the

High Line, "Major Federal Authorization for High Line Project," press release, June 13, 2005, http://files.thehighline.org/original_site /newsletters/061305_pr.html, 1, emphasis added.

3. "The 606 and Bloomingdale Trail Opening Ceremony," LoganSquare. TV, June 14, 2015, https://www.youtube.com/watch?v=_DYpW7gwG -Q, 7:33–8:06.

4. The area remains so largely because of the persistence of a large public housing complex that borders the High Line. For a study of the park's demographics, see Alexander J. Reichl, "The High Line and the Ideal of Democratic Public Space," *Urban Geography* 37, no. 6 (2016): 904–25.

5. Laura Bliss, "The High Line's Next Balancing Act," *CityLab*, February 7, 2017, https://www.citylab.com/solutions/2017/02/the-high-lines -next-balancing-act-fair-and-affordable-development/515391/, 2. See also David Halle and Elizabeth Tiso, *New York's New Edge: Contemporary Art, the High Line, and Urban Megaprojects on the Far West Side* (Chicago: University of Chicago Press, 2014), 168–69.

6. Brian Perea, interview by the author, January 2017.

7. See, for example, an early press release by the Friends of the QueensWay that extolled their own virtues on these fronts: "The QueensWay builds on the Mayor's Vision Zero plan to reduce automobile-pedestrian fatalities—as well as addresses parks equity issues that will provide a new linear park to underserved neighborhoods." Friends of the QueensWay, "QueensWay Honored by Association for a Better New York," press release, April 30, 2015, https://www.thequeensway.org /press-release-queensway-honored-by-association-for-a-better-new -york/, 4.

8. Brian McCammack, "Recovering Green in Bronzeville" (PhD diss., Harvard University, 2012); Kevin Loughran, "Race and the Construction of City and Nature," *Environment and Planning A* 49, no. 9 (2017): 1948–67.

9. In the core of the Great Migration–era Black Belt, only one park served the tens of thousands of people pouring into this section of the city: Madden Park, constructed between 1927 and 1930 after years of advocacy by the *Chicago Defender*, alderman Robert Jackson, settlement workers, and local residents. This ten-acre mix of playgrounds, baseball fields, and a swimming pool "languished for years with few improvements" in its first decades of existence; it was demolished in the early

2000s along with the adjacent Madden Park public housing complex. See McCammack, "Recovering Green in Bronzeville," 136–39.

10. George Lipsitz, *The Possessive Investment in Whiteness: How White People Profit from Identity Politics* (Philadelphia: Temple University Press, 2006).

11. Author's field notes, November 16, 2011.

12. "A Green Gift from Rich and Nancy Kinder," *Houston Chronicle*, April 28, 2018, https://www.houstonchronicle.com/opinion/editorials /article/A-green-gift-Editorial-12870490.php, 3.

13. Julia Thiel, "Is the Bloomingdale Trail a Path to Displacement?," *Chicago Reader*, June 4, 2015, https://www.chicagoreader.com/chicago /bloomingdale-trail-606-logan-square-humboldt-park-displacement /Content?oid=178994627.

14. Probably the furthest I have seen this argument taken to date has been by Kinder Baumgardner, one of the architects of Buffalo Bayou Park, who suggested that the right-of-way under power lines seemed like a promising next phase of linear parks. See Kinder Baumgardner and Scott McCready, "Leading with Landscape II: The Houston Transformation," Houston Transformation Conference, April 25, 2016, https:// www.youtube.com/watch?v=dXltxhSYEsc, 5:28–6:02.

15. This scenario is currently playing out in Kashmere Gardens, a predominantly Black neighborhood in Houston, which in 2018 became home to a small part of the Bayou Greenways 2020 project. Traversing the neighborhood's Hunting Bayou, the Hunting Bayou Greenway (also known as the Hunting Bayou Hike & Bike Trail) is starkly unadorned compared to its sibling along Buffalo Bayou. That public and private park builders would invest considerably less in architectural and landscape interventions in Kashmere Gardens compared to the flagship, tourist-oriented site downtown is of course unsurprising. What is interesting is that not only has the one-mile stretch of trail raised questions about potential gentrification in the area, but the park has become a locus of concern about crime because of a lack of lighting. As local Super Neighborhood council president Keith Downey put it, "You don't want law abiding citizens to be able to use this during the day and the criminals at night." "Kashmere Gardens Neighbors Fight for Lights Along Hunting Bayou Trail," *ABC News*, August 10, 2018, https://abc13.com/bayou -greenways-2020-project-lights-lighting-kashmere-gardens/3926213/, 2.

16. Benjamin Shepard and Gregory Smithsimon, *The Beach Beneath the Streets: Contesting New York City's Public Spaces* (New York: State University of New York Press, 2011), 88.

12. ABOLISH, DECOLONIZE, ROT

1. Patrick Radden Keefe, "Anthony Bourdain's Moveable Feast," *New Yorker*, February 5, 2017, https://www.newyorker.com/magazine/2017/02/13/anthony-bourdains-moveable-feast, 19.
2. Robert Caro, *The Power Broker: Robert Moses and the Fall of New York* (New York: Vintage, 1974), 218.
3. Additionally, these were groups with broad social-justice agendas—they did not coalesce for the sole purpose of park improvements.
4. See also Matthew Gandy and Sandra Jasper, eds., *The Botanical City* (Berlin: Jovis, 2020).
5. See also Kevin Loughran, Gary Alan Fine, and Marcus Anthony Hunter, "Architectures of Memory: When Growth Machines Embrace Preservationists," *Sociological Forum* 33, no. 4 (2018): 855–76.
6. Permaculture is defined as "the harmonious integration of design with ecology." See Ross Mars, *The Basics of Permaculture Design* (White River Junction, VT: Chelsea Green, 2005), 2.

REFERENCES

Aalbers, Manuel B. "Do Maps Make Geography? Part 1: Redlining, Planned Shrinkage, and the Places of Decline." *ACME: An International E-Journal for Critical Geographies* 13, no. 4 (2014): 525–56.

Abu-Lughod, Janet L. *Race, Space, and Riots in Chicago, New York, and Los Angeles.* New York: Oxford University Press, 2007.

Addams, Jane. "Women's Conscience and Social Amelioration." In *The Jane Addams Reader,* ed. Jean Bethke Elshtain. New York: Basic Books, 2002.

Allen, Augustus, and John Kirby Allen. "The Town of Houston." *Telegraph and Texas Register,* August 30, 1836.

Anderson, Alan B., and George W. Pickering. *Confronting the Color Line: The Broken Promise of the Civil Rights Movement in Chicago.* Athens: University of Georgia Press, 1986.

Andrews, Malcolm. *The Search for the Picturesque: Landscape Aesthetics and Tourism in Britain, 1760–1800.* Stanford, CA: Stanford University Press, 1989.

Angelo, Hillary. *How Green Became Good: Urbanized Nature and the Making of Cities and Citizens.* Chicago: University of Chicago Press, 2020.

Asgarian, Roxanna. "How Do You Plan a Park That's Meant to Flood?" *Houstonia,* January 23, 2017. https://www.houstoniamag.com/articles/2017/1/23/flooding-buffalo-bayou-park.

Avila, Eric. *The Folklore of the Freeway: Race and Revolt in the Modernist City.* Minneapolis: University of Minnesota Press, 2014.

Axelrod, David. "Mayor Says Park Chief Mismanaging District." *Chicago Tribune,* September 16, 1983, A1.

Bagli, Charles V. "Biggest Building Site in Manhattan Up for Auction: Project Aims to Create High-Rise District on Far West Side." *New York Times,* May 17, 2007, A1.

Bagli, Charles V. "'Diller Island' Is Back from the Dead." *New York Times,* October 25, 2017. https://www.nytimes.com/2017/10/25/nyregion/diller -island-revived-cuomo.html.

Bagli, Charles V. "Olympic Bid, Though Unsuccessful, Brought Benefits to the City, Its Champion Says." *New York Times,* August 4, 2012, A14.

Barbanel, Josh. "Developer to Pay Over $800 Million for Site Near High Line." *Wall Street Journal,* November 27, 2014. https://www.wsj.com/articles /new-york-city-developer-acquires-prime-site-near-high-line-1417042890.

Barnett, Jonathan. *An Introduction to Urban Design.* New York: Harper & Row, 1982.

Baumgardner, Kinder, and Scott McCready. "Leading with Landscape II: The Houston Transformation." Houston Transformation Conference, April 25, 2016. https://www.youtube.com/watch?v=dXltxhSYEsc.

Bea-Taylor, Jonah. "Flood Control and Metropolitan Development in Houston, Miami and Tampa, 1935–1985." PhD diss., Georgia Institute of Technology, 2018.

Beauregard, Robert A. *When America Became Suburban.* Minneapolis: University of Minnesota Press, 2006.

Begley, Dug. "Improvements: World Cup Runneth Over? If Houston Lands Some Games, a Parklike Space Atop I-45 Is Possible." *Houston Chronicle,* June 14, 2018, B1.

Benjamin, Walter. *The Arcades Project,* trans. Howard Eiland and Kevin McLaughlin. Cambridge, MA: Belknap Press, 2002.

Bennett, Larry, Roberta Garner, and Euan Hague, eds. *Neoliberal Chicago.* Champaign: University of Illinois Press, 2017.

Bentham, Jeremy. *The Panopticon Writings.* New York: Verso, 1995.

Berg, Bruce F. *New York City Politics: Governing Gotham.* New Brunswick, NJ: Rutgers University Press, 2007.

Bernard, Richard M., and Bradley R. Rice, eds. *Sunbelt Cities: Politics and Growth Since World War II.* Austin: University of Texas Press, 1983.

Berryhill, Michael. "Prescription for Growth." *Cite* 47 (2000): 12–15.

Betancur, John J. "The Politics of Gentrification: The Case of West Town in Chicago." *Urban Affairs Review* 37, no. 6 (2002): 780–814.

Biasco, Paul. "Hundreds March on the 606 Over Gentrification." *DNAinfo*, May 18, 2016. https://www.dnainfo.com/chicago/20160518/humboldt-park /hundreds-march-on-606-over-gentrification.

Biles, Roger. *Richard J. Daley: Politics, Race, and the Governing of Chicago.* DeKalb: Northern Illinois University Press, 1995.

Biles, Roger. "The Urban South in the Great Depression." *Journal of Southern History* 56, no. 1 (1990): 71–100.

Birge-Liberman, Phil. "(Re)greening the City: Urban Park Restoration as a Spatial Fix." *Geography Compass* 4, no. 9 (2010): 1392–1407.

Bliss, Laura. "The High Line's Next Balancing Act." *CityLab*, February 7, 2017. https://www.citylab.com/solutions/2017/02/the-high-lines-next-balancing -act-fair-and-affordable-development/515391/.

Block, Robinson. "Moody Park: From the Riots to the Future for the North-side Community." *Houston History* 9, no. 3 (2012): 20–24.

Bloomberg TV. "Architect James Corner on Section 2 of the High Line." June 7, 2011. http://www.bloomberg.com/video/70550814-architect-james-corner -on-section-2-of-high-line.html), last accessed March 2014.

Bluestone, Daniel. *Constructing Chicago.* New Haven, CT: Yale University Press, 1991.

Bonnett, Alastair. "The Metropolis and White Modernity." *Ethnicities* 2, no. 3 (2002): 349–66.

Bourdieu, Pierre. *Distinction: A Social Critique of the Judgment of Taste*, trans. Richard Nice. Cambridge, MA: Harvard University Press, 1984.

Bourdieu, Pierre. *The Rules of Art: Genesis and Structure of the Literary Field.* Stanford, CA: Stanford University Press, 1996.

Brash, Julian. *Bloomberg's New York: Class and Governance in the Luxury City.* Athens: University of Georgia Press, 2011.

Britt, Douglas. "Invitation Only: Partnership Throws a Harvest-Inspired Gathering." *Houston Chronicle*, November 11, 2009, 3.

Brown, Bernard. "Municipal Finances and Annexation: A Case Study of Post-War Houston." *Southwestern Social Science Quarterly* 48, no. 3 (1967): 339–51.

Brown-Saracino, Japonica. *How Places Make Us: Novel LBQ Identities in Four Small Cities.* Chicago: University of Chicago Press, 2018.

Buffalo Bayou Partnership. "Bike & Boat Rentals." Retrieved September 2019. https://buffalobayou.org/visit/destination/buffalo-bayou-park/.

Buffalo Bayou Partnership. "Buffalo Bayou Park Fact Sheet." 2015. http://buffalobayou.org/bbpwordpress/wp-content/uploads/2015/11/BBPark-Fact-Sheet-FINAL-8.04.15.pdf.

Buffalo Bayou Partnership. "Buffalo Bayou Park Selected as a Winner of the Urban Land Institute's 2017–2018 Global Awards for Excellence." Press release, November 14, 2017. https://buffalobayou.org/buffalo-bayou-park-selected-as-a-winner-of-the-urban-land-institutes-2017-2018-global-awards-for-excellence/.

Buffalo Bayou Partnership. "Buffalo Bayou Park Vegetation Management Plan," 2004. https://www.houstontx.gov/planhouston/sites/default/files/plans/BuffaloBayouParkVegetationManagementPlanJW.pdf.

Buffalo Bayou Partnership. "'Monumental Moments'—New Public Art Installed." Retrieved June 14, 2019. https://buffalobayou.org/monumental-moments-new-public-art-installed/.

Buffalo Bayou Partnership. "News Release: 'Buffalo Bayou's Back'—Buffalo Bayou Park Complete in Fall 2015." June 19, 2015. https://buffalobayou.org/news-release-buffalo-bayous-back-buffalo-bayou-park-complete-in-fall-2015/.

Buffalo Bayou Partnership. "Rules & Regulations." Retrieved June 22, 2018. https://buffalobayou.org/visit/destination/buffalo-bayou-park/.

Buffalo Bayou Partnership. "Venue Rental Fees & Guidelines 2019: The Water Works in Buffalo Bayou Park." https://buffalobayou.org/bbpwordpress/wp-content/uploads/2018/11/The-Water-Works-in-Buffalo-Bayou-Park-Venue-Rental.pdf.

Buffalo Bayou Partnership. "The Water Works in Buffalo Bayou Park." Retrieved September 2019. https://buffalobayou.org/facility-rentals/the-water-works-in-buffalo-bayou-park/.

Bullard, Robert D. *Invisible Houston: The Black Experience in Boom and Bust.* College Station: Texas A&M University Press, 2000.

Burke, Edmund. *A Philosophical Enquiry Into the Origin of Our Ideas of the Sublime and Beautiful.* New York: Oxford University Press, 2015.

Burton, Rob J. F. "Understanding Farmers' Aesthetic Preference for Tidy Agricultural Landscapes: A Bourdieusian Perspective." *Landscape Research*, 37, no. 1 (2012): 51–71.

Buzbee, William W. *Fighting Westway: Environmental Law, Citizen Activism, and the Regulatory War That Transformed New York City.* Ithaca, NY: Cornell University Press, 2014.

Byers, Jack. "The Privatization of Downtown Public Space: The Emerging Grade-Separated City in North America." *Journal of Planning Education and Research* 17, no. 3 (1998): 189–205.

Byrne, John. "Mayor Emanuel's 606 Affordable-Housing Plan Draws Doubts." *Chicago Tribune*, August 12, 2015. https://www.chicagotribune.com/politics/ct-emanuel-606-housing-met-20150811-story.html.

"Calendar of Events: West Side Rail Line." *New York Times*, March 1, 1984, C7.

Calta, Louis. "Performers at Space Get Notice to Quit: A Nominal Rental Call for Investigation." *New York Times*, May 24, 1974, 22.

Canby, Vincent. "New York's Woes Are Good Box Office." *New York Times*, November 10, 1974, 141.

Cardwell, Diane. "For High Line Visitors, Park Is a Railway Out of Manhattan." *New York Times*, July 22, 2009, A17.

Carleton, Don E. *Red Scare: Right-Wing Hysteria, Fifties Fanaticism, and Their Legacy in Texas*. Austin: University of Texas Press, 1985.

Caro, Robert. *The Power Broker: Robert Moses and the Fall of New York*. New York: Vintage, 1974.

Centner, Ryan. "Places of Privileged Consumption Practices: Spatial Capital, the Dot-Com Habitus, and San Francisco's Internet Boom." *City & Community* 7, no. 3 (2008): 193–223.

Chauncey, George. *Gay New York: Gender, Urban Culture, and the Making of the Gay Male World, 1890–1940*. New York: Basic Books, 1994.

Chicago Park District. "About Us." Accessed April 5, 2018. https://www.chicago parkdistrict.com/about-us.

Chicago Park District. "CitySpace: An Open Space Plan for Chicago." January 1998. https://www.cityofchicago.org/city/en/depts/dcd/supp_info/cityspace _plan.html.

Chicago Park District. "Haas Park." 2018. https://www.chicagoparkdistrict .com/parks-facilities/haas-park.

Chicago Urban League. "Summer Time." Chicago Urban League records, University of Illinois at Chicago. Series I, Box 268, Folder 2738, n.d.

City of Chicago. "Bloomingdale Trail Design Work Gets Under Way." June 8, 2011. https://www.cityofchicago.org/city/en/depts/cdot/provdrs/bike /news/2011/jun/bloomingdae_traildesignworkgetsunderway.html.

City of Chicago. "Bloomingdale Trail and Park: Framework Plan." 2012. https:// www.chicago.gov/content/dam/city/depts/cdot/BloomingdaleTrail /Bloomingdale_Framework_Plan.pdf

City of Chicago. "Logan Square Open Space Plan: Increasing and Improving Parks in the Logan Square Community Area." 2004. http://www.cct
.org/wp-content/uploads/2015/05/LoganSquareOpenSpacePlan2004.pdf.

City of Chicago. "Mayor Emanuel Leads Groundbreaking on Bloomingdale Trail." August 27, 2013. https://www.cityofchicago.org/content/dam/city
/depts/mayor/Press%20Room/Press%20Releases/2013/August/8.27
.13Bloomingdaletrail.pdf.

City of New York. "PlaNYC: A Greener, Greater New York." 2007. http://
www.nyc.gov/html/planyc/downloads/pdf/publications/full_report_2007
.pdf.

City of New York. "Mayor Michael R. Bloomberg Hosts Summit on New York City Economic Development for Top CEOs and City Leaders." 2003.

Comey, Arthur Coleman. *Houston: Tentative Plans for Its Development: A Report to the Houston Parks Commission.* Boston: Geo H. Ellis, 1913.

Cook, Alison. "The Trial of Joe Russo." *HoustonPress*, December 1, 1994, http://www.houstonpress.com/news/the-trial-of-joe-russo-6572538.

Cook, Phaedra. "A Look at the Dunlavy, the Breakfast and Lunch Hot Spot on Buffalo Bayou." *HoustonPress*, May 11, 2016. http://www.houstonpress
.com/restaurants/a-look-at-the-dunlavy-the-breakfast-and-lunch-hot
-spot-on-buffalo-bayou-8393488.

Coorens, Elaine. "The 606: Streams Flowed Together Forming a River . . . The Bloomingdale Trail." *Our Urban Times*, June 4, 2015. http://www
.oururbantimes.com/parks/606-streams-flowed-together-forming-riverthe
-bloomingdale-trail.

Copley, Stephen, and Peter Garside, eds. *The Politics of the Picturesque: Literature, Landscape and Aesthetics Since 1770.* New York: Cambridge University Press, 1994.

Corner, James, ed. *Recovering Landscape: Essays in Contemporary Landscape Theory.* Princeton, NJ: Princeton Architectural Press, 1999.

Cranz, Galen. *The Politics of Park Design: A History of Urban Parks in America.* Cambridge, MA: MIT Press, 1982.

Crawford, William, Jr. "Phony Invoices Seen as Key to Kickback Scheme." *Chicago Tribune*, November 11, 1987.

Cronon, William. *Nature's Metropolis: Chicago and the Great West.* New York: Norton, 1991.

Cronon, William. "The Trouble with Wilderness: Or, Getting Back to the Wrong Nature." *Environmental History* 1, no. 1 (1996): 7–28.

Crow, Kelly. "Chelsea: Fight Heats Up Again Over Grassy Bed of Rails." *New York Times*, January 27, 2002, CY6.

Cunningham, Sean P. *Cowboy Conservatism: Texas and the Rise of the Modern Right*. Lexington: University of Kentucky Press, 2010.

David, Joshua, and Robert Hammond. *High Line: The Inside Story of New York City's Park in the Sky*. New York: Farrar, Straus and Giroux, 2011.

Davidson, Chandler. *Biracial Politics: Conflict and Coalition in the Metropolitan South*. Baton Rouge: Louisiana State University Press, 1972.

Dávila, Arlene. *Latinos, Inc.: The Marketing and Making of a People*. Berkeley: University of California Press, 2001.

Davis, Mike. *City of Quartz: Excavating the Future in Los Angeles*. New York: Verso, 1990.

Deam, Jenny. "Deep-Pocketed Giving a Houston Mainstay Past and Present." *Houston Chronicle*, October 13, 2016. https://www.chron.com/local/history/economy-business/article/Deep-pocketed-giving-a-Houston-mainstay-past-and-9969588.php.

De Jong, Judith K. *New SubUrbanisms*. New York: Routledge, 2014.

Delany, Samuel R. *Times Square Red, Times Square Blue*. New York: New York University Press, 1999.

de Luna, Marcy. "Welcome to the Jungle: Partygoers Have a Wild Time at Glow-in-the-Dark Gala for Literacy." *CultureMap Houston*, September 25, 2017. http://houston.culturemap.com/news/society/09-25-17-jungle-party-barbara-bush-houston-literacy-foundation-young-professionals.

De Monchaux, Thomas. "How Everyone Jumped Aboard a Railroad to Nowhere." *New York Times*, May 8, 2005, A6.

Diamond, Andrew J. *Mean Streets: Chicago Youths and the Everyday Struggle for Empowerment in the Multiracial City, 1908–1969*. Berkeley: University of California Press, 2009.

Dochuk, Darren. *From Bible Belt to Sunbelt: Plain-Folk Religion, Grassroots Politics, and the Rise of Evangelical Conservatism*. New York: Norton, 2011.

Doster, Adam. "The 'World's Smelliest Canoe Race' Celebrates Its 45th Anniversary." *Houstonia Magazine*, January 23, 2017. https://www.houstoniamag.com/articles/2017/1/23/the-buffalo-bayou-regatta-celebrates-its-45th-wet-year.

Downing, Margaret. "The HSPVA Fight Continues Even After Rich Kinder Offers to Take Back His Name." *Houston Press*, April 27, 2017. http://www.houstonpress.com/news/hspva-and-the-kinder-naming-rights-9389838.

Downtown Redevelopment Authority. "TIRZ #3 Map 2011 Annexation." 2011. http://www.mainstreettirz.com/images/TIRZ_3_As_Enlarged _Annexation.pdf.

Draper, Joan E. "The Art and Science of Park Planning in the United States: Chicago's Small Parks, 1902–1905." In *Planning the Twentieth-Century American City*, ed. Mary Corbin Sies and Christopher Silver. Baltimore: Johns Hopkins University Press, 1996.

Dudek, Mitch. "The Paved-Over, Unofficial History of the 606 Trail." *Chicago Sun-Times*, May 19, 2015. https://chicago.suntimes.com/2015/5/19/18425867 /the-paved-over-unofficial-history-of-the-606-trail.

Dullea, Georgia. "Nowadays, Man's (Yes, Man's) Best Friend Is Likely to Be a Cat (or a Houseful of Cats)." *New York Times*, September 9, 1990, 52.

Dunlap, David W. "Conrail Looking to a Revival of Its Freight Traffic: Property Owners Lose on Razing Elevated Tracks." *New York Times*, January 20, 1991, R13.

Dunlap, David W. "Elevated Freight Line Being Razed Amid Protests." *New York Times*, January 15, 1991, B3.

Dunlap, David W. "New Dimensions for a Low-Density Neighborhood: The Javits Center Draws a Plethora of Proposals." *New York Times*, April 1, 1990, R19.

Dunlap, David W. "Planners Allow Rezoning of Site of Meat Market: Permit Residential Use, but Protect 2 Dealers." *New York Times*, April 17, 1984, B3.

Dunn, Muffie, and Tom Piper. *Diller Scofidio + Renfro: Reimagining Lincoln Center and the High Line*. DVD. New York: Checkerboard Films, 2012.

Durkheim, Émile. *The Elementary Forms of Religious Life*, ed. Mark S. Cladis, trans. Carol Cosman. New York: Oxford University Press, 2008.

Eligon, John. "City Is Held in Contempt on Loitering." *New York Times*, April 26, 2010, https://www.nytimes.com/2010/04/27/nyregion/27contempt .html.

Elkins, Alexander B. *Battle of the Corner: Urban Policing and Rioting in the United States, 1943–1971*. PhD diss., Temple University, 2017.

Elliott, James R., Elizabeth Korver-Glenn, and Daniel Bolger. "The Successive Nature of City Parks: Making and Remaking Unequal Access Over Time." *City & Community* 18, no. 1 (2019): 109–27.

Emerson, Michael Oluf, and Kevin T. Smiley. *Market Cities, People Cities: The Shape of Our Urban Future*. New York: New York University Press, 2018.

Emmott, Sarah H. *Memorial Park: A Priceless Legacy*. Houston: Herring, 1992.

Evans, Graeme. "Hard-Branding the Cultural City—from Prado to Prada." *International Journal of Urban and Regional Research* 27, no. 2 (2003): 417–40.

Evans, Nicole M., and William P. Stewart. "The Role of Naturalness in Ecological Restoration: A Case Study from the Cook County Forest Preserves." *Nature and Culture* 13, no. 2 (2018): 232–52.

Feagin, Joe R. *Free Enterprise City: Houston in Political and Economic Perspective.* New Brunswick, NJ: Rutgers University Press, 1988.

Featherstone, Mike. "The Flâneur, the City and Virtual Public Life." *Urban Studies* 35, no. 5–6 (1998): 909–25.

Fennell, Catherine. *Last Project Standing: Civics and Sympathy in Post-Welfare Chicago.* Minneapolis: University of Minnesota Press, 2015.

Fernández, Lilia. *Brown in the Windy City: Mexicans and Puerto Ricans in Postwar Chicago.* Chicago: University of Chicago Press, 2012.

Fine, Gary Alan. *Morel Tales: The Culture of Mushrooming.* Cambridge, MA: Harvard University Press, 1998.

Flores-Gonzalez, Nilda. "*Paseo Boriqua*: Claiming a Puerto Rican Space in Chicago." *Centro Journal* 13, no. 2 (2001): 7–23.

Florida, Richard. *Cities and the Creative Class.* New York: Routledge, 2004.

Flusty, Steven. *Building Paranoia: The Proliferation of Interdictory Space and the Erosion of Spatial Justice.* Los Angeles: Los Angeles Forum for Architecture and Urban Design, 1994.

Foucault, Michel. *Security, Territory, Population: Lectures at the Collège de France 1977–1978*, ed. Michel Senellart, trans. Graham Burchell. New York: Picador, 2009.

Fox, Stephen. "Big Park, Little Plans: A History of Hermann Park." http://www.georgekessler.org/index.php?option=com_content&view=article&id=113:big-park-little-plans-a-history-of-hermann-park-by-stephen-fox.

Fox, Stephen. "Foreword." In *From Rendering to Reality: The Story of Buffalo Bayou Park*, by Anne Olson and David Theis. Houston: Buffalo Bayou Partnership, 2017.

Fraser, Jayme. "$50 Million Donation, Maintenance Pact to Boost Greenways Project." *Houston Chronicle*, October 15, 2013. https://www.houstonchronicle.com/news/politics/houston/article/50-million-donation-maintenance-pact-to-boost-4899052.php.

Fried, Joseph P. "There Are Many Motives, but Chief Among Them Is Profit." *New York Times*, August 14, 1977.

Friends of the Bloomingdale Trail. "2nd. Gen FBT Brochure." 2005. http://www.bloomingdaletrail.org/pdf/2nd_gen_FBT_brochure.pdf.

Friends of the Bloomingdale Trail. "City Moves to Acquire Parkland for New Elevated Trail." June 12, 2006. https://www.bloomingdaletrail.org/post/2006/06/12/city-moves-to-acquire-parkland-for-new-elevated-trail.

Friends of the Bloomingdale Trail. "Community Visioning Kick-Off a Great Success." March 27, 2007. https://www.bloomingdaletrail.org/post/2007/03/27/community-visioning-kick-off-a-great-success.

Friends of the Bloomingdale Trail. "Community Visioning Update." July 2008.

Friends of the Bloomingdale Trail. "Firm Selected for Initial Design and Engineering!" July 15, 2009. https://www.bloomingdaletrail.org/post/2009/07/15/firm-selected-for-initial-design-and-engineering.

Friends of the Bloomingdale Trail. "Friends of the Bloomingdale Trail Board." 2017. https://www.bloomingdaletrail.org/board-of-directors.

Friends of the Bloomingdale Trail. "Limpieza de Primavera y Picnic." 2005. http://www.bloomingdaletrail.org/pdf/fbt-spring-cleaning-2005-es.pdf.

Friends of the Bloomingdale Trail. "New Gears Eve Fundraiser @ Handlebar." December 16, 2006. https://www.bloomingdaletrail.org/single-post/2006/12/16/New-Gears-Eve-Fundraiser-Handlebar.

Friends of the Bloomingdale Trail. "Trail Recommended for $2.6M in Federal Funding." July 27, 2007. https://www.bloomingdaletrail.org/single-post/2007/07/27/Trail-recommended-for-26M-in-federal-funding.

Friends of the High Line. "Eat & Drink." Retrieved September 2019. https://www.thehighline.org/eat-drink/.

Friends of the High Line. "Major Federal Authorization for High Line Project." Press release, June 13, 2005. http://files.thehighline.org/original_site/newsletters/061305_pr.html.

Friends of the QueensWay. "Connections + Neighborhoods." Retrieved June 22, 2018. https://thequeensway.org/the-plan/connections-neighborhoods/.

Friends of the QueensWay. "QueensWay Honored by Association for a Better New York." Press release, April 30, 2015. https://www.thequeensway.org/press-release-queensway-honored-by-association-for-a-better-new-york/.

Gandy, Matthew. *Concrete and Clay: Reworking Nature in New York City.* Cambridge, MA: MIT Press, 2002.

Gandy, Matthew, and Sandra Jasper, eds. *The Botanical City*. Berlin: Jovis, 2020.

Gans, Herbert J. *The Levittowners: Ways of Life and Politics in a New Suburban Community*. New York: Columbia University Press, 1982.

Garreau, Joel. *Edge City: Life on the New Frontier*. New York: Anchor, 1991.

Garvin, Alexander. *What Makes a Great City*. Washington, DC: Island, 2016.

Geiger, Daniel, and Emily Laermer. "High Line's High Returns." *Crain's New York Business*, September 21, 2014. http://www.crainsnewyork.com /article/20140921/REAL_ESTATE/140919813/high-lines-high-returns.

Ghaziani, Amin. *There Goes the Gayborhood?* Princeton, NJ: Princeton University Press, 2014.

Gies, Erica. "Conservation: An Investment That Pays—The Economic Benefits of Parks and Open Space." The Trust for Public Land, 2009. http:// cloud.tpl.org/pubs/benefits_econbenefits_rpt_7_2009.pdf.

Gilfoyle, Timothy J. *Millennium Park: Creating a Chicago Landmark*. Chicago: University of Chicago Press, 2006.

Gilpin, William. *Three Essays: On Picturesque Beauty; On Picturesque Travel; and On Sketching Landscape: To Which Is Added a Poem, On Landscape Painting*. London: Strand, 1792.

Glaberson, William. "Long Fight Ends Over Arrests for Loitering." *New York Times*, February 7, 2012. https://www.nytimes.com/2012/02/08/nyregion /new-york-settles-suit-on-illegal-arrests-for-loitering.html.

Glentzer, Molly. "Buffalo Bayou Reborn." *Houston Chronicle*, October 1, 2015. https://www.houstonchronicle.com/life/article/Buffalo-Bayou-Park-gives -Houstonians-a-new-6541659.php.

Glentzer, Molly. "Memorial Park Restoration Gets a $70 Million Boost: City Council Must Still Approve the Largest Greenspace Gift in Houston's History." *Houston Chronicle*, April 25, 2018. https://www.chron.com /neighborhood/memorial-news/article/Memorial-Park-restoration-gets -a-70-million-boost-12863707.php.

Goldberger, Paul. "Miracle Above Manhattan." *National Geographic*, April 2011. https://www.nationalgeographic.com/magazine/2011/04/new-york -highline/.

Gordillo, Gastón R. *Rubble: The Afterlife of Destruction*. Durham, NC: Duke University Press, 2014.

Gordon, Colin. *Mapping Decline: St. Louis and the Fate of the American City*. Philadelphia: University of Pennsylvania Press, 2009.

Gotham, Kevin Fox, and Miriam Greenberg. *Crisis Cities: Disaster and Redevelopment in New York and New Orleans*. New York: Oxford University Press, 2014.

Gottlieb, Martin. "Rail Fan Finds Rusting Dream of West Side," *New York Times*, January 16, 1984, B1.

Gottlieb, Martin. "West Siders May Get a Reprieve from the IRT." *New York Times*, March 23, 1986, A7.

Gottsch, Marti Lea. "Cultural Inflations." MArch thesis, Rice University, 2011.

Gould, Kenneth A., and Tammy L. Lewis. *Green Gentrification: Urban Sustainability and the Struggle for Environmental Justice*. New York: Routledge, 2017.

Gradel, Thomas J., and Dick Simpson. *Corrupt Illinois: Patronage, Cronyism, and Criminality*. Champaign: University of Illinois Press, 2015.

Gradel, Thomas J., and Dick Simpson. "Patronage, Cronyism and Criminality in Chicago Government Agencies: Anti-Corruption Report Number 4." University of Illinois at Chicago, 2011. http://tigger.uic.edu/depts/pols /ChicagoPolitics/AntiCorruptionReport_4.pdf.

Grant, Jill. "The Ironies of New Urbanism." *Canadian Journal of Urban Research* 15, no. 2 (2006): 158–74.

Gray, Christopher. "On the Lower West Side, Fate of Old Rail Line Is Undecided." *New York Times*, January 3, 1988, R5.

Gray, Lisa. "Where the Wild Things Were." *Houston Chronicle*, March 23, 2008, ZEST 11.

"A Green Gift from Rich and Nancy Kinder." *Houston Chronicle*, April 28, 2018. https://www.houstonchronicle.com/opinion/editorials/article/A-green -gift-Editorial-12870490.php.

Greenberg, Miriam. *Branding New York: How a City in Crisis Was Sold to the World*. New York: Routledge, 2008.

Greenfield, John. "Closing Trails for Fancy Events Sends the Wrong Message: A Dinner for One Percenters on the 606 Will Feed Fears About Trail-Related Displacement." *Streetsblog Chicago*, September 25, 2017. https://chi.streetsblog.org/2017/09/25/shutting-down-public-trails-for -private-dinners-sends-the-wrong-message-to-residents/.

Grossman, James R. *Land of Hope: Chicago, Black Southerners, and the Great Migration*. Chicago: University of Chicago Press, 1989.

Gutman, Marta. *A City for Children: Women, Architecture, and the Charitable Landscapes of Oakland, 1850–1950*. Chicago: University of Chicago Press, 2014.

Hagerty, Kyle. "Huge Mixed-Use Coming Along Buffalo Bayou Park Houston." *Bisnow Houston*, June 23, 2016. https://www.bisnow.com /houston/news/mixed-use/buffalo-bayou-park-improvements-pay-off -attract-500m-mixed-use-development-61786.

Halle, David, and Elizabeth Tiso. *New York's New Edge: Contemporary Art, the High Line, and Urban Megaprojects on the Far West Side*. Chicago: University of Chicago Press, 2014.

Hancock, Lynnell. "Wolf Pack: The Press and the Central Park Jogger." *Columbia Journalism Review* 41, no. 5 (2003): 38–42.

Harris, Melissa. "Chicago Confidential: City Makes Headway in Bloomingdale Trail Project." *Chicago Tribune*, January 24, 2013. http://articles .chicagotribune.com/2013-01-24/business/ct-biz-0124-confidential -bloomingdale-20130124_1_high-line-bloomingdale-trail-humboldt-park.

Harris, Richard. "Industry and Residence: The Decentralization of New York City, 1900–1940." *Journal of Historical Geography* 19, no. 2 (1993): 169–90.

Harris County Flood Control District. "Fact Sheet: W100-00-00-X043 Memorial Park Demonstration Project." 2013. https://www.hcfcd.org.

Harris County Flood Control District. "Riding the Waves of Change: 60 Years of Service." 1998. https://www.hcfcd.org.

Harvey, David. "Flexible Accumulation Through Urbanization: Reflections on 'Post-Modernism' in the American City." *Perspecta* 26 (1990): 251–72.

Harvey, David. "The Geography of Capitalist Accumulation: A Reconstruction of the Marxian Theory." *Antipode* 7, no. 2 (1975): 9–21.

Hauser, Alisa. "As a 606 Park Expands, Trailgoers Wonder Why Bathrooms Still Not Added." *DNAinfo*, January 11, 2016. https://www.dnainfo.com /chicago/20160111/humboldt-park/as-606-park-expands-trailgoers-wonder -why-bathrooms-still-not-added/.

Hauser, Alisa. "Atop Bloomingdale Trail, Emanuel Sees 'The 606' as Neighborhood Unifier." *DNAinfo*, June 2, 2015. https://www.dnainfo.com /chicago/20150602/humboldt-park/atop-trail-emanuel-sees-606-as -neighborhood-unifier.

Hauser, Alisa. "Elevated Bloomingdale Trail, Pulse of 'The 606,' Opens to Massive Crowds." *DNAinfo*, June 6, 2015, https://www.dnainfo.com /chicago/20150606/humboldt-park/elevated-bloomingdale-trail-pulse -of-606-opens-massive-crowds.

Haynes, Robert V. *A Night of Violence: The Houston Riot of 1917*. Baton Rouge: Louisiana State University Press, 1976.

Henson, Scott. "Allen Parkway Village: Politicians Plot to Raze Public Housing in Houston." *Texas Observer*, July 12, 1991, 1, 6–14.

Herrington, Susan. "Framed Again: The Picturesque Aesthetics of Contemporary Landscapes." *Landscape Journal* 25, no. 1 (2006): 22–37.

Hirsch, Arnold R. *Making the Second Ghetto: Race and Housing in Chicago, 1940–1960*. Chicago: University of Chicago Press, 1983.

Hirsch, Arnold R. "Massive Resistance in the Urban North: Trumbull Park, Chicago, 1953–1966." *Journal of American History* 82, no. 2 (1995): 522–50.

Hodge, Shelby. "Walk in the Park at Lost Lake Reserved for Donors and Partners at $58 Million Buffalo Bayou Park." *CultureMap Houston*, September 21, 2015. http://houston.culturemap.com/news/society/09-21-15-walk-in-the-park-reserved-for-donors-and-partners-at-58-million-lost-lake-project.

Holifield, Ryan, and Kathleen C. Williams. "Urban Parks, Environmental Justice, and Voluntarism: The Distribution of Friends of the Parks Groups in Milwaukee County." *Environmental Justice* 7, no. 3 (2014): 70–76.

Houston Chronicle Editorial Board. "Houstonians of the Year: They Have a Passion for Transforming Houston." *Houston Chronicle*, December 22, 2013, B9.

Houston Parks Board. "IRS Form 990." 2016. https://houston-parks-board.cdn.prismic.io/houston-parks-board%2Ff15e7140-8f57-4923-880b-1c359a20eb33_2016_form_990_for_houston_parks_board_-_public_copy.pdf.

Houston Parks and Recreation Department. "2011 Annual Report." 2011. https://www.houstontx.gov/parks/pdfs/2011/2011AnnualReport.pdf

Houston Parks and Recreation Department. "Big Idea Becomes Reality: Rosemont Bridge Grand Opening Scheduled." Press release, March 21, 2011. http://www.houstontx.gov/parks/pdfs/2011/RosemontBridgeMarch26.pdf.

Houston Public Library. "Terry Hershey," interviewed by Ann Hamilton, Houston Oral History Project, 2008.

Humm, Andy. "Crowds, Development and Concerns." *Villager*, July 4, 2012. https://www.amny.com/news/the-high-line-spurs-crowds-development-and-concerns/.

Hunt, D. Bradford. *Blueprint for Disaster: The Unraveling of Chicago Public Housing*. Chicago: University of Chicago Press, 2009.

Ignatiev, Noel. *How the Irish Became White*. New York: Routledge, 1995.

Iovine, Julie V. "Elevated Visions." *New York Times*, July 11, 2004, http://www
.nytimes.com/2004/07/11/arts/architecture-elevated-visions.html.

Jackson, Kenneth T. *Crabgrass Frontier: The Suburbanization of the United States*. New York: Oxford University Press, 1985.

Jacobs, Jane. *The Death and Life of Great American Cities*. New York: Random House, 1961.

Jameson, Frederic. *Postmodernism, Or, The Cultural Logic of Late Capitalism*. Durham, NC: Duke University Press, 1991.

Janowitz, Morris. "Sociological Theory and Social Control." *American Journal of Sociology* 81, no. 1 (1975): 82–108.

Johnson, Marilynn S. *Street Justice: A History of Police Violence in New York City*. Boston: Beacon Press, 2003.

Johnston, Josée, and Shyon Baumann. *Foodies: Democracy and Distinction in the Gourmet Foodscape*. New York: Routledge, 2009.

Jordan, David P. *Transforming Paris: The Life and Labors of Baron Haussmann*. New York: Free Press, 1995.

Kalinski, John. "Liberation and the Naming of Paranoid Space." Introduction to *Building Paranoia: The Proliferation of Interdictory Space and the Erosion of Spatial Justice*, by Steven Flusty. Los Angeles: LA Forum for Architecture and Urban Design, 2015.

Kamin, Blair. "The 606 Is a Gem but Still Needs Signs, Shade." *Chicago Tribune*, June 12, 2015. https://www.chicagotribune.com/columns/ct-606-trail-review-kamin-met-0612-20150612-column.html.

Kamin, Blair. "Chicago's New 606 Trail a Boon for Open Space, Neighborhoods It Links." *Chicago Tribune*, June 2, 2015. https://www.chicagotribune.com/columns/ct-606-trail-kamin-met-0531-20150529-column.html.

Kaplan, Barry J. "Race, Income, and Ethnicity: Residential Change in a Houston Community, 1920–1970." *Houston History*, Winter 1981, 178–202.

Kaplan, Barry J. "Urban Development, Economic Growth, and Personal Liberty: The Rhetoric of the Houston Anti-Zoning Movements, 1947–1962." *Southwestern Historical Quarterly* 84, no. 2 (1980): 133–68.

"Kashmere Gardens Neighbors Fight for Lights Along Hunting Bayou Trail." *ABC News*. August 10, 2018. https://abc13.com/bayou-greenways-2020-project-lights-lighting-kashmere-gardens/3926213/.

Katz, Cindi, and Andrew Kirby. "In the Nature of Things: The Environment and Everyday Life." *Transactions of the Institute of British Geographers* 16, no. 3 (1991): 259–71.

Keefe, Patrick Radden. "Anthony Bourdain's Moveable Feast." *New Yorker*, February 5, 2017. https://www.newyorker.com/magazine/2017/02/13/anthony -bourdains-moveable-feast.

Keegan, Edward. "The 606: Is That All There Is?" *Crain's Chicago Business*, June 2, 2015. https://www.chicagobusiness.com/article/20150602/NEWS07 /150609969/the-606-is-that-all-there-is.

Keil, Roger. "The Urban Politics of Roll-with-It Neoliberalization." *City* 13, nos. 2–3 (2009): 231–45.

Kelley, Robin D. G. " 'We Are Not What We Seem': Rethinking Black Working-Class Opposition in the Jim Crow South." *Journal of American History* 80, no. 1 (1993): 75–112.

"Kennedy Jabbed on Chicago." *Chicago Defender*, national edition, July 15, 1961.

Khan, Shamus. *Privilege: The Making of an Adolescent Elite at St. Paul's School.* Princeton, NJ: Princeton University Press, 2011.

Kilgannon, Corey. "Neighborhood Report: West Side; Fight Over Unused Rail Line." *New York Times*, May 16, 1999, CY8.

Kinder Foundation. "Emancipation Park." Retrieved June 22, 2018. https:// kinderfoundation.org/major-gifts/urban-green-space/emancipation -park/.

Kinder Foundation. "Urban Green Space." Retrieved September 16, 2019. https://kinderfoundation.org/major-gifts/urban-green-space/.

Klinenberg, Eric. "Climate Change: Adaptation, Mitigation, and Critical Infrastructures." *Public Culture* 28, no. 2 (2016): 187–92.

Krinsky, John, and Maud Simonet. *Who Cleans the Park?: Public Work and Urban Governance in New York City.* Chicago: University of Chicago Press, 2017.

Kruse, Kevin M. "The Politics of Race and Public Space: Desegregation, Privatization, and the Tax Revolt in Atlanta." *Journal of Urban History* 31, no. 5 (2005), 610–33.

Kruse, Kevin M. *White Flight: Atlanta and the Making of Modern Conservatism.* Princeton, NJ: Princeton University Press, 2005).

Landry, Donna. "The Geopolitical Picturesque." *Spatial Practices* 13, no. 1 (2012): 91–114.

Lee, Dong-Hoo. "Digital Cameras, Personal Photography and the Reconfiguration of Spatial Experiences." *Information Society* 26, no. 4 (2010): 266–75.

Lee, Linda. "Glamour Rides the Rail." *New York Times*, July 18, 2004, ST4.

Lepeska, David. "A Chicago Park Learns from New York's High Line." *NextCity*, April 1, 2013. https://nextcity.org/features/view/A-Chicago-Park-Learns-From-New-Yorks-High-Line.

Le'roy, T. "Fort Turns Over Baby Killing Suspect to Cops." *Chicago Defender*, June 25, 1970.

Lin, Jan. "Ethnic Places, Postmodernism, and Urban Change in Houston." *Sociological Quarterly* 36, no. 4 (1995): 629–47.

Lipsitz, George. *The Possessive Investment in Whiteness: How White People Profit from Identity Politics*. Philadelphia: Temple University Press, 2006.

Lloyd, Richard. *Neo-Bohemia: Art and Commerce in the Post-Industrial City*. New York: Routledge, 2006.

Lloyd, Richard, and Terry Nichols Clark. "The City as an Entertainment Machine." *Research in Urban Sociology: Critical Perspectives on Urban Redevelopment* 6 (2001): 357–78.

Lohman, Joseph D., and Roger F. Shanahan. *The Police and Minority Groups*. Chicago Park District archives, 1947.

Loughran, Kevin. "Imbricated Spaces: The High Line, Urban Parks, and the Cultural Meaning of City and Nature." *Sociological Theory* 34, no. 4 (2016): 311–34.

Loughran, Kevin. "Parks for Profit: The High Line, Growth Machines, and the Uneven Development of Urban Public Spaces." *City & Community* 13, no. 1 (2014): 49–68.

Loughran, Kevin. "Race and the Construction of City and Nature." *Environment and Planning A* 49, no. 9 (2017): 1948–67.

Loughran, Kevin. "Race and the Construction of City and Nature: A Study of Three Periods of Park Development in Chicago, 1870, 1945, 2010." PhD diss., Northwestern University, 2017.

Loughran, Kevin. "Urban Parks and Urban Problems: An Historical Perspective on Green Space Development as a Cultural Fix." *Urban Studies* 57, no. 11 (2020): 2321–38.

Loughran, Kevin, Gary Alan Fine, and Marcus Anthony Hunter. "Architectures of Memory: When Growth Machines Embrace Preservationists." *Sociological Forum* 33, no. 4 (2018): 855–76.

Loughran, Kevin, Gary Alan Fine, and Marcus Anthony Hunter. "Urban Spaces, City Cultures, and Collective Memories." In *Routledge International Handbook of Memory Studies*, ed. Anna Lisa Tota and Trever Hagen. New York: Routledge, 2015.

Lueck, Thomas J. "Up, but Not Running, on the West Side." *New York Times*, July 25, 1999, 23.

Lyson, Thomas A. *Two Sides to the Sunbelt*. New York: Praeger, 1989.

Mack, Kristen, and Blair Kamin. "Corporate Donations to Help Convert Old Rail Line Into Park: Emanuel Says Gifts Will Fund NW Side Park, Elevated Trail." *Chicago Tribune*, March 13, 2012, 1.7.

Madden, David J. "Revisiting the End of Public Space: Assembling the Public in an Urban Park." *City & Community* 9, no. 2 (2010): 187–207.

Malooley, Jake. "Chicago's World-Class City Complex." *TimeOut Chicago*, March 23 2012. https://www.timeout.com/chicago/things-to-do/chicagos-world-class-city-complex.

Mapes, Lynda V. "'Like Standing Rock': Trans Mountain Pipeline-Expansion Opponents Plan B.C. Protest." *Seattle Times*, March 8, 2018. https://www.seattletimes.com/seattle-news/environment/like-standing-rock-trans-mountain-pipeline-expansion-opponents-plan-b-c-protest/.

Marcuse, Peter. "The Grid as City Plan: New York City and Laissez-Faire Planning in the Nineteenth Century." *Planning Perspectives* 2, no. 3 (1987): 287–310.

Mars, Ross. *The Basics of Permaculture Design*. White River Junction, VT: Chelsea Green, 2005.

Martinez, Miranda J. *Power at the Roots: Gentrification, Community Gardens, and the Puerto Ricans of the Lower East Side*. Lanham, MD: Lexington, 2010.

Marx, Karl. "The German Ideology." In *The Marx–Engels Reader*, 2nd ed., ed. Robert C. Tucker. New York: Norton, 1978.

Marx, Karl. "Manifesto of the Communist Party." In *The Marx–Engels Reader*, 2nd ed., ed. Robert C. Tucker. New York: Norton, 1978.

Matusow, Catherine. "The Tide Turns on Buffalo Bayou: Houston's Central Park Passes Its First Test." *Houstonia Magazine*, July 9, 2015. https://www.houstoniamag.com/news-and-city-life/2015/07/the-tide-turns-on-buffalo-bayou.

"Mayor Dedicates West Side Project: 'Death to Death Av.'" *New York Times*, June 29, 1934, 10.

"Mayor Results, Ward-by-Ward." *Chicago Tribune*, March 16, 2011. http://municipal2011.elections.chicagotribune.com/results/mayor/index.html.

"Mayor Urges Fast Action on Park Nominees." *Chicago Tribune*, March 15, 1984, B16.

McCammack, Brian. *Landscapes of Hope: Nature and the Great Migration in Chicago*. Cambridge, MA: Harvard University Press, 2017.

McCammack, Brian. "Recovering Green in Bronzeville." PhD diss., Harvard University, 2012.

McComb, David G. *Houston, a History*. Austin: University of Texas Press, 1981.

McGeehan, Patrick. "The High Line Isn't Just a Sight to See; It's Also an Economic Dynamo." *New York Times*, June 5, 2011. https://www.nytimes.com/2011/06/06/nyregion/with-next-phase-ready-area-around-high-line-is-flourishing.html.

McGrane, Sally. "A Landscape in Winter, Dying Heroically." *New York Times*, January 31, 2008. http://www.nytimes.com/2008/01/31/garden/31piet.html.

McNeur, Catherine. *Taming Manhattan: Environmental Battles in the Antebellum City*. Cambridge, MA: Harvard University Press, 2014.

McPherson, Coco. "Public Sex and the Standard Hotel." *New York Magazine*, June 11, 2009. http://nymag.com/intelligencer/2009/06/standard_hotel.html.

Meeks, Tomiko. "Freedmen's Town, Texas: A Lesson in the Failure of Historic Preservation." *Houston History* 8, no. 2 (2011): 42–44.

"Meet Anne Olson of Buffalo Bayou Partnership." *VoyageHouston*, May 31, 2017. http://voyagehouston.com/interview/meet-anne-olson-buffalo-bayou-partnership-downtown-office/.

Melosi, Martin V. "Houston's Public Sinks: Sanitary Services from Local Concerns to Regional Challenges." In *Energy Metropolis: An Environmental History of Houston and the Gulf Coast*, ed. Martin V. Melosi and Joseph A. Pratt. Pittsburgh, PA: University of Pittsburgh Press, 2007.

Melosi, Martin V., and Joseph A. Pratt, eds. *Energy Metropolis: An Environmental History of Houston and the Gulf Coast*. Pittsburgh, PA: University of Pittsburgh Press, 2007.

Mitchell, Chris. "The Killing of Murder." *New York Magazine*, January 7, 2008. http://nymag.com/news/features/crime/2008/42603/.

Mitchell, Don. "The End of Public Space? People's Park, Definitions of the Public, and Democracy." *Annals of the Association of American Geographers* 85, no. 1 (1995): 108–33.

Mollenkopf, John Hull. *Phoenix in the Ashes: The Rise and Fall of the Koch Coalition in New York City Politics*. Princeton, NJ: Princeton University Press, 1994.

Molotch, Harvey, and Mark Treskon. "Changing Art: SoHo, Chelsea, and the Dynamic Geography of Galleries in New York City." *International Journal of Urban and Regional Research* 33, no. 2 (2009): 517–41.

Mora, G. Cristina. *Making Hispanics: How Activists, Bureaucrats, and Media Constructed a New American.* Chicago: University of Chicago Press, 2014.

Moreton, Bethany. *To Serve God and Wal-Mart.* Cambridge, MA: Harvard University Press, 2009.

Morris, Mike. "Park Project Beautifying Buffalo Bayou: Private Funding Would Be Used to Color the Waterway West of Downtown a More Attractive Shade of Green." *Houston Chronicle,* February 14, 2011, B1.

Moser, Whet. "The 606 Shows How to Design a Park in the 21st Century (and Beyond)." *Chicago Magazine,* June 5, 2015. https://www.chicagomag .com/city-life/June-2015/The-606-Park-Design/.

Moser, Whet. "What Emanuel Has in Mind for Chicago's Parks—and How to Pay for It." *Chicago Magazine,* July 22, 2015. http://www.chicagomag .com/city-life/July-2015/A-Friday-in-the-Park-With-Rahm/.

Moser, Whet. "Why Rahm Emanuel Won." *Chicago Magazine,* February 23, 2011. http://www.chicagomag.com/Chicago-Magazine/The-312/February -2011/Why-Rahm-Emanuel-Won/.

Mulvaney, Erin. "Proposal Would Put New Shine on Theater District Transformation: City Seeks to Create Urban Hub out of Uninviting Spaces." *Houston Chronicle,* August 14, 2015, A1.

Mustafa, Daanish, Thomas A. Smucker, Franklin Ginn, Rebecca Johns, and Shanon Connely. "Xeriscape People and the Cultural Politics of Turfgrass Transformation." *Environment and Planning D: Society and Space* 28, no. 4 (2010): 600–17.

National Park Service. "Congestion Mitigation and Air Quality Improvement (CMAQ) Program." https://www.nps.gov/transportation/pdfs /CMAQ_Fact_Sheet_Final.pdf.

Nelson, R. J. *Dirty Waters: Confessions of Chicago's Last Harbor Boss.* Chicago: University of Chicago Press, 2016.

New York City Department of Parks & Recreation. "High Line Basics: Know Before You Go." Retrieved June 22, 2018. https://www.nycgovparks .org/parks/the-high-line/highlights.

New York City Department of Parks & Recreation. "Rules & Regulations." Retrieved September 2019. https://www.nycgovparks.org/about/faq.

New York City Planning Commission. "Commercial Districts: C6." Retrieved May 16, 2018, https://www1.nyc.gov/site/planning/zoning/districts-tools /c6.page;

New York City Planning Commission. "Historical Zoning Map 8b." Retrieved May 16, 2018. http://www1.nyc.gov/assets/planning/download /pdf/zoning/zoning-maps/historical-zoning-maps/maps08b.pdf.

New York City Planning Commission. "Special West Chelsea District Rezoning and High Line Open Space EIS, Chapter 27: Response to Comments." 2005. http://www1.nyc.gov/assets/planning/download/pdf/plans /west-chelsea/wc_chap27_responses_feis.pdf.

"Obituary 1—No Title." *New York Times*, June 18, 1996, D23.

Olmsted, Frederick Law. "Address to the Prospect Park Scientific Association." In *Frederick Law Olmsted: Essential Texts*, ed. Robert Twombly. New York: Norton, 2010.

Olmsted, Frederick Law. *Mount Royal, Montreal*. New York: G. P. Putnam's Sons, 1881.

Olmsted, Frederick Law. "On Landscape Gardening." In *Frederick Law Olmsted: Essential Texts*, ed. Robert Twombly. New York: Norton, 2010.

Olmsted, Frederick Law. "Public Parks and the Enlargement of Towns." In *Frederick Law Olmsted: Essential Texts*, ed. Robert Twombly. New York: Norton, 2010.

Olmsted, Frederick Law. "Report Accompanying Plan for Laying Out the South Park." Chicago: South Park Commission, 1871.

Olsen, Margaret Nunnelley. "Teaching Americanism: Ray K. Daily and the Persistence of Conservatism in Houston School Politics, 1943–1952." *Southwestern Historical Quarterly* 110, no. 2 (2006): 240–69.

Olson, Anne, and David Theis, *From Rendering to Reality: The Story of Buffalo Bayou Park*. Houston: Buffalo Bayou Partnership, 2017.

Osborn, Marian L. "The Development of Recreation in the South Park System of Chicago." Master's thesis, University of Chicago, 1928.

Osman, Suleiman. *The Invention of Brownstone Brooklyn: Gentrification and the Search for Authenticity in Postwar New York*. New York: Oxford University Press, 2011.

Ouroussoff, Nicolai. "Gardens in the Air Where the Rail Once Ran: Architects Selected to Make Over the High Line." *New York Times*, August 12, 2004, E1.

Ouroussoff, Nicolai. "On High, A Fresh Outlook." *New York Times*, June 10, 2009, C1.

Pacewicz, Josh. "Tax Increment Financing, Economic Development Professionals and the Financialization of Urban Politics." *Socio-Economic Review* 11, no. 3 (2013): 413–40.

Pacyga, Dominic A. *Chicago: A Biography*. Chicago: University of Chicago Press, 2009.

Pacyga, Dominic A. *Slaughterhouse: Chicago's Union Stock Yard and the World It Made*. Chicago: University of Chicago Press, 2015.

Parker, Jeffrey Nathaniel. "Broken Windows as Growth Machines: Who Benefits from Urban Disorder and Crime?" *City & Community* 17, no. 4 (2018): 945–71.

Parker, Jeffrey Nathaniel. "Negotiating the Space Between Avant-Garde and 'Hip Enough': Businesses and Commercial Gentrification in Wicker Park." *City & Community* 17, no. 2 (2018): 438–60.

Parker, Robert E., and Joe R. Feagin. "Houston: Administration by Economic Elites," in *Big City Politics in Transition*, ed. H. V. Savitch and John Clayton Thomas. Newbury Park, CA: SAGE, 1991.

Parks, Louis B. "Where the Buffalo Roams: Cruise, Park Trails Are Drawing People Down on the Bayou." *Houston Chronicle*, June 10, 1988, 1.

Peck, Jamie. "Struggling with the Creative Class." *International Journal of Urban and Regional Research* 29, no. 4 (2005): 740–70.

Pérez, Gina M. *The Near Northwest Side Story: Migration, Displacement, and Puerto Rican Families*. Berkeley: University of California Press, 2004.

Pérez, Gina M. "An Upbeat West Side Story: Puerto Ricans and Postwar Racial Politics in Chicago." *Centro Journal* 13, no. 2 (2001): 47–71.

Pérez-Peña, Richard. "Giuliani's Quest for a Term Extension Hits a Wall in Albany." *New York Times*, October 2, 2001, D1.

Perkins, Harold A. "Out from the (Green) Shadow? Neoliberal Hegemony Through the Market Logic of Shared Urban Environmental Governance." *Political Geography* 28, no. 7 (2009): 395–405.

Phillips-Fein, Kim. *Fear City: New York's Fiscal Crisis and the Rise of Austerity Politics*. New York: Metropolitan, 2017.

Pogrebin, Robin. "An Aesthetic Watchdog in the City Planning Office." *New York Times*, December 29, 2004, E1.

Pogrebin, Robin. "First Phase of High Line Is Ready for Strolling." *New York Times*, June 8, 2009. https://artsbeat.blogs.nytimes.com/2009/06/08/first-phase-of-high-line-is-ready-for-strolling/.

Pratt, Joseph A. "8F and Many More: Business and Civic Leadership in Modern Houston." *Houston Review* 1, no. 2 (2004): 2–7, 31–44.

Pratt, Joseph A. "A Mixed Blessing: Energy, Economic Growth, and Houston's Environment." In *Energy Metropolis: An Environmental History of Houston and the Gulf Coast*, ed. Martin V. Melosi and Joseph A. Pratt. Pittsburgh, PA: University of Pittsburgh Press, 2007.

Pugh, Clifford. "Redesigned Jones Plaza Stirs Discussion." *Houston Chronicle*, November 20, 2001. https://www.chron.com/entertainment/music/article /Redesigned-Jones-Plaza-stirs-discussion-2024334.php.

Rahman, Fauzeya. "From Weedy to Wonderful: Buffalo Bayou Park Opens as a Prime Green Destination." *Houston Chronicle*, October 4, 2015, B1.

Ralph, James R., Jr. *Northern Protest: Martin Luther King, Jr., Chicago, and the Civil Rights Movement.* Cambridge, MA: Harvard University Press, 1993.

Regional Plan Association. "What to Do with the High Line? A Final Draft Report." Prepared for CSX Transportation, Inc., June 21, 1999.

Reichl, Alexander J. "The High Line and the Ideal of Democratic Public Space." *Urban Geography* 37, no. 6 (2016): 904–25.

Rhodes, Margaret. "James Corner Field Operations: For Creating Intimate Green Spaces out of Industrial Urban Blight." *Fast Company*, February 7, 2012. https://www.fastcompany.com/3017475/35james-corner-field-operations.

Rich, Motoko. "Turf: Edged Out by the Stroller Set." *New York Times*, May 27, 2004, F1.

Rigolon, Alessandro, and Jeremy Németh. " 'We're Not in the Business of Housing': Environmental Gentrification and the Nonprofitization of Green Infrastructure Projects." *Cities* 81 (November 2018): 71–80.

Rivlin, Gary. *Fire on the Prairie: Harold Washington, Chicago Politics, and the Roots of the Obama Presidency.* Philadelphia: Temple University Press, 2013.

Roberts, Dorothy E. "Race, Vagueness, and the Social Meaning of Order-Maintenance Policing." *Journal of Criminal Law and Criminology* 89, no. 3 (1999): 775–836.

Roberts, Sam. "The 1989 Elections: The New York Vote; Almost Lost at the Wire." *New York Times*, November 9, 1989, 1.

Robertson, Dale. "New Year Leads to Creation of New Paths: Trail Projects Aim to Begin Construction Soon." *Houston Chronicle*, January 28, 2010, 9.

Robinson, James. "14-Year Homeless Encampment Broken Up: Complaints Prompt Action by Police." *Houston Chronicle*, January 26, 1996, A22.

Rodríguez, Clara E. *Changing Race: Latinos, the Census and the History of Ethnicity in the United States.* New York: New York University Press, 2000.

Roedinger, David R. *Wages of Whiteness: Race and the Making of the American Working Class.* New York: Verso, 1991.

Rosenzweig, Roy, and Elizabeth Blackmar. *The Park and the People: A History of Central Park*. Ithaca, NY: Cornell University Press, 1992.

Royko, Mike. *Boss: Richard J. Daley of Chicago*. New York: Penguin, 1971.

Sandburg, Carl. "Chicago."

Sanders, James. *Celluloid Skyline: New York and the Movies*. New York: Knopf, 2001.

San Miguel, Guadalupe, Jr. *Brown, Not White: School Integration and the Chicano Movement in Houston*. College Station: Texas A&M University Press, 2001.

Satter, Beryl. *Family Properties: How the Struggle Over Race and Real Estate Transformed Chicago and Urban America*. New York: Metropolitan, 2009.

Schuyler, David. *The New Urban Landscape: The Redefinition of City Form in Nineteenth-Century America*. Baltimore: Johns Hopkins University Press, 1986.

Seligman, Amanda. *Block by Block: Neighborhoods and Public Policy on Chicago's West Side*. Chicago: University of Chicago Press, 2005.

Seligman, Amanda I. *Chicago's Block Clubs: How Neighbors Shape the City*. Chicago: University of Chicago Press, 2016.

Sellers, Richard West. *Preserving Nature in the National Parks: A History*. New Haven, CT: Yale University Press, 1997.

Shabazz, Rashad. *Spatializing Blackness: Architectures of Confinement and Black Masculinity in Chicago*. Chicago: University of Illinois Press, 2015.

Shelton, Kyle. "Culture War in Downtown Houston: Jones Hall and the Postwar Battle Over Exclusive Space." *Southwestern Historical Quarterly* 116, no. 1 (2012): 1–24.

Shelton, Kyle. *Power Moves: Transportation, Politics, and Development in Houston*. Austin: University of Texas Press, 2017.

Shepard, Benjamin, and Gregory Smithsimon. *The Beach Beneath the Streets: Contesting New York City's Public Spaces*. New York: State University of New York Press, 2011.

Shermer, Elizabeth Tandy. *Sunbelt Capitalism: Phoenix and the Transformation of American Politics*. Philadelphia: University of Pennsylvania Press, 2013.

Shiffman, Ronald, Rick Bell, Lance Jay Brown, and Lynne Elizabeth, eds. *Beyond Zuccotti Park: Freedom of Assembly and the Occupation of Public Space*. Oakland, CA: New Village, 2012.

Sibley, Marilyn McAdams. *The Port of Houston: A History*. Austin: University of Texas Press, 1968.

Sites, William. "God from the Machine?: Urban Movements Meet Machine Politics in Neoliberal Chicago." *Environment and Planning A* 44, no. 11 (2012): 2574–90.

Smith, Neil. " 'Class Struggle on Avenue B': The Lower East Side as Wild Wild West." In *The People, Place, and Space Reader*, ed. Jen Jack Gieseking, William Mangold, Cindi Katz, Setha Low, and Susan Saegert, 3–29. London: Routledge, 2014.

Smith, Neil. *The New Urban Frontier: Gentrification and the Revanchist City.* New York: Routledge, 1996.

Smithsimon, Gregory. "Dispersing the Crowd: Bonus Plazas and the Creation of Public Space." *Urban Affairs Review* 43, no. 3 (2008): 325–51.

Sonenshein, Raphael J., and Tom Hogen-Esch. "Bringing the State (Government) Back In: Home Rule and the Politics of Secession in Los Angeles and New York City." *Urban Affairs Review* 41, no. 4 (2006): 467–91.

Sorkin, Michael, ed. *Variations on a Theme Park: The New American City and the End of Public Space.* New York: Hill and Wang, 1992.

Sorkin, Michael, and Sharon Zukin, eds. *After the World Trade Center: Rethinking New York City.* New York: Routledge, 2002.

Spain, August O. "Politics of Recent Municipal Annexation in Texas." *Southwestern Social Science Quarterly* 30, no. 1 (1949): 18–28.

Speck, Larry. "Creativity Born from Constraints." TEDxUTAustin, May 23, 2019. https://www.youtube.com/watch?v=6jUzFcqAH50.

Steely, James Wright. *Parks for Texas: Enduring Landscapes of the New Deal.* Austin: University of Texas Press, 2010.

Steen, Karen E. "Friends in High Places." *Metropolis*, December 1, 2005. http://www.metropolismag.com/uncategorized/friends-in-high-places/.

Steptoe, Tyina L. *Houston Bound: Culture and Color in a Jim Crow City.* Oakland: University of California Press, 2016.

Sterba, James P. "Plan to Drill for Oil in Park Creates Dispute in Houston." *New York Times*, January 22, 1976, 37, 44.

Sternbergh, Adam. "The High Line: It Brings Good Things to Life." *New York Magazine*, April 27, 2007. http://nymag.com/news/features/31273/.

Strong, James, and Robert Davis. "Mayor Captures Committees: Council Foes Stripped of Their Power." *Chicago Tribune*, June 7, 1986, 1.

Stuart, Forrest. *Down, Out, and Under Arrest: Policing and Everyday Life in Skid Row.* Chicago: University of Chicago Press, 2016.

Stuart, Lettice. "Houston: Texas Medical Center Offers Builders $1.3 Billion Rx." *New York Times*, May 20, 1990, A10.

Sugrue, Thomas J. *The Origins of the Urban Crisis: Race and Inequality in Postwar Detroit*. Princeton, NJ: Princeton University Press, 1996.

Sugrue, Thomas J. *Sweet Land of Liberty: The Forgotten Struggle for Civil Rights in the North*. New York: Random House, 2008.

Surface Transportation Board. "Chelsea Property Owners—Abandonment—Portion of the Consolidated Rail Corporation's West 30th Street Secondary Track in New York, NY." Docket No. AB-167 (Sub-No. 1094)A, July 14, 1999.

Swartz, Mimi. "Blood in the Streets." *Texas Monthly*, November 1991. https://www.texasmonthly.com/articles/blood-in-the-streets/.

Swartz, Mimi. "Green Acres." *Texas Monthly*, October 2015. https://www.texasmonthly.com/the-culture/green-acres-2/.

Tapley, Charles. "Buffalo Bayou Master Plan Rendering." 1977. Rice Digital Scholarship Archive. https://scholarship.rice.edu/handle/1911/88623.

Tarlock, A. Dan. "United States Flood Control Policy: The Incomplete Transition from the Illusion of Total Protection to Risk Management." *Duke Environmental Law & Policy Forum* 23 (2012): 151–83.

Tate, Alan. *Great City Parks*. London: Taylor & Francis, 2001.

Taylor, Dorceta E. *The Environment and the People in American Cities, 1600s–1900s*. Durham, NC: Duke University Press, 2009.

Taylor, Kate. "The High Line, a Pioneer Aloft, Inspires Other Cities to Look Up." *New York Times*, July 15, 2010, A1.

Taylor, Quintard. *In Search of the Racial Frontier: African Americans in the American West 1528–1990*. New York: Norton, 1998.

"Tear Down the Tracks." Letter to the Editor. *New York Times*, January 30, 1984, 16.

"The 606 and Bloomingdale Trail Opening Ceremony." LoganSquare.TV. June 14, 2015. https://www.youtube.com/watch?v=_DYpW7gwG-Q, 7:33–8:06.

Thiel, Julia. "Is the Bloomingdale Trail a Path to Displacement?" *Chicago Reader*, June 4, 2015. https://www.chicagoreader.com/chicago/bloomingdale-trail-606-logan-square-humboldt-park-displacement/Content?oid=17899462.

Thompson, Heather Ann. *Whose Detroit? Politics, Labor, and Race in a Modern American City*. Ithaca, NY: Cornell University Press, 2001.

Thompson Design Group, Inc. and EcoPLAN. "Master Plan for Buffalo Bayou and Beyond." Prepared for Buffalo Bayou Partnership, City of Houston, Harris County, and Harris County Flood Control District, 2002.

Tomkins-Walsh,Teresa. "'A Concrete River Had to Be Wrong': Environmental Action on Houston's Bayous,1935–1980." PhD diss.,University of Houston, 2009.

Topinka, Robert. *Racing the Street: Race, Rhetoric, and Technology in Metropolitan London, 1840–1900*. Oakland: University of California Press, 2020.

Toro-Morn, Maura, Ivis García Zambrana, and Marixsa Alicea. "De Bandera a Bandera (From Flag to Flag): New Scholarship About the Puerto Rican Diaspora in Chicago." *Centro Journal* 28, no. 2 (2016): 4–35.

The Trust for Public Land. "$1M Commitment to Chicago's Haas Park Praised." November 23, 2004. https://www.tpl.org/media-room/1m-commitment -chicagos-haas-park-praised.

The Trust for Public Land. "The 606 Is Chicago's Next Great Park." June 17, 2013. https://www.tpl.org/media-room/606-chicagos-next-great-park.

Tutt, Bob. "City Breaks Ground on Bayou Project." *Houston Chronicle*, October 28, 1987, 1:18.

"Two Pedestrian Accidents Highlight Dangers of Allen Parkway." KHOU-11. March 19, 2014. https://www.khou.com/article/news/local/2-pedestrian -accidents-highlight-dangers-of-allen-parkway/285-259050028.

Urban Land Institute. "Rich Kinder on Business Resilience." Interviewed by William Fulton.May 18,2015.https://www.youtube.com/watch?v=rfGUqV -yRoY&t=990s.

Urbanski, Matthew. "New Parks for the Livable City." Presentation, Kansas State University, Manhattan, KS, January 29, 2015. https://www.youtube .com/watch?v=Sf8VCo21aZs.

"U.S. Sues Chicago Park District, Charging Racial Bias in Programs." *New York Times*, December 1, 1982. http://www.nytimes.com/1982/12/01/us/us -sues-chicago-park-district-charging-racial-bias-in-programs.html.

Vale, Lawrence J. *Purging the Poorest: Public Housing and the Design Politics of Twice-Cleared Communities*. Chicago: University of Chicago Press, 2013.

Venkatesh, Sudhir. "Chicago's Pragmatic Planners: American Sociology and the Myth of Community." *Social Science History* 25, no. 2 (2001): 275–317.

Vitale, Alex S. *City of Disorder: How the Quality of Life Campaign Transformed New York Politics*. New York: New York University Press, 2008.

Vogel, Carol, and Kate Taylor. "Rift in Family as Whitney Plans a Second Home." *New York Times*, April 12, 2010, A1.

Vojnovic, Igor. "Governance in Houston: Growth Theories and Urban Pressures." *Journal of Urban Affairs* 25, no. 5 (2003): 589–624.

Wachsmuth, David. "Three Ecologies: Urban Metabolism and the Society-Nature Opposition." *Sociological Quarterly* 53, no. 4 (2012): 506–23.

Wachsmuth, David, and Hillary Angelo. "Green and Gray: New Ideologies of Nature in Urban Sustainability Policy." *Annals of the American Association of Geographers* 108, no. 4 (2018): 1038–56.

Ward, Kevin. "Entrepreneurial Urbanism, State Restructuring and Civilizing 'New' East Manchester." *Area* 35, no. 2 (2003): 116–27.

Weber, Rachel. "Extracting Value from the City: Neoliberalism and Urban Redevelopment." *Antipode* 34, no. 3 (2002): 519–40.

Weiss, Marion. "Geographical Iconography and Signification: How Space Creates Meaning in the New York City Film." *Journal of Visual Verbal Languaging* 3, no. 2 (1983): 85–89.

"West Madison Street, 1968." In *Encyclopedia of Chicago*, ed. Janice L. Reiff, Ann Durkin Keating, and James R. Grossman. Chicago: University of Chicago Press, 2004. http://www.encyclopedia.chicagohistory.org/pages /6354.html.

Wherry, Frederick F. *The Philadelphia Barrio: The Arts, Branding, and Neighborhood Transformation*. Chicago: University of Chicago Press, 2011.

Whitehead, Frances. "Site Narratives: Art + Design Integration." June 23, 2014.

Whyte, William H. *City: Rediscovering the Center*. New York: Doubleday, 1988.

Whyte, William H. *The Social Life of Small Urban Spaces*. Washington, DC: Conservation Foundation, 1980.

Williams, Jakobi. *From the Bullet to the Ballot: The Illinois Chapter of the Black Panther Party and Racial Coalition Politics in Chicago*. Chapel Hill: University of North Carolina Press, 2013.

Wilson, David. "Institutions and Urban Revitalization: The Case of Chelsea in New York City." *Urban Geography* 8, no. 2 (1987): 129–45.

Wilson, David, and Dennis Grammenos. "Gentrification, Discourse, and the Body: Chicago's Humboldt Park." *Environment and Planning D* 23 (2005): 295–312.

Winningham, Geoff. *Along Forgotten River: Photographs of Buffalo Bayou and the Houston Ship Channel, 1997–2001; with Accounts of Early Travelers to Texas, 1767–1858*. Austin: Texas State Historical Association, 2003.

Wittman, Albert D. *Architecture of Minneapolis Parks*. Chicago: Arcadia, 2010.

Wolcott, Victoria W. *Race, Riots, and Roller Coasters: The Struggle Over Segregated Recreation in America*. Philadelphia: University of Pennsylvania Press, 2012.

Wolf, Matt. *High Line Stories: Joshua David and Robert Hammond*. DVD. New York: Sundance Channel, 2009.

Wray, Dianna. "Buffalo Bayou Park Is Getting Ready to Open." *Houston Press*, September 15, 2015. http://www.houstonpress.com/news/buffalo -bayou-park-is-getting-ready-to-open-7763987.

Wrede, Stuart, and William Howard Adams, eds. *Denatured Visions: Landscape and Culture in the Twentieth Century*. New York: Museum of Modern Art, 1991.

Wright, Michael, and Caroline Rand Herron. "In Chicago, City Hall Is for Fighting."*New York Times*, May 15, 1983. http://www.nytimes.com/1983/05/15 /weekinreview/the-nation-in-chicago-city-hall-is-for-fighting.html.

Yoon, Heeyeun, and Elizabeth Currid-Halkett. "Industrial Gentrification in West Chelsea, New York: Who Survived and Who Did Not? Empirical Evidence from Discrete-Time Survival Analysis." *Urban Studies* 52, no. 1 (2015): 20–49.

Zukin, Sharon. *The Cultures of Cities*. Malden, MA: Blackwell, 1995.

Zukin, Sharon. *Loft Living: Culture and Capital in Urban Change*. Baltimore: Johns Hopkins University Press, 1982.

Zukin, Sharon. *Naked City: The Death and Life of Authentic Urban Places*. New York: Oxford University Press, 2010.

INDEX

606, The. *See* Bloomingdale Trail
"8F," 22–23, 77–78, 192n70

accessibility, 89, 161–164, 182, 232n48
adaptive reuse, 57, 133–134, 161–162
aesthetic philosophy, 101–103,
    106–107, 109–110, 112–114, 115–117,
    125–126, 129–131, 134, 136–137,
    139–145, 181–182, 226n66
architectural critics, 47–48, 69,
    88–89, 124–125, 215n5
art worlds, 34, 38, 44–48, 53, 72–73,
    102
authenticity, 113, 121, 126, 133, 137,
    141–144, 162, 183

Bayou Greenways 2020, 86–87, 143,
    235n15
Black Belt (Chicago), 14–17, 24–25,
    110, 200n7, 218n26
Black park access, 75, 94, 152–153, 174,
    200n7, 206n10, 218n26, 234n9
Bloomberg, Michael, 40–46, 120, 172

Bloomingdale Trail: design of, 53–54,
    68–70, 100, 113–114, 116–118,
    126–137, 143–146, 148–150, 157–158,
    161–165; location of, 14–15, 50,
    56–60, 70, 172–173, 177; politics
    of, 53–57, 60–71, 92–95, 172–184,
    201n24, 230n31
Bloomingdale Trail, Friends of the,
    54, 59–63, 65, 67, 69, 117, 157, 180
bonus plazas, 43, 159–160
boosters. *See* growth machine/
    growth coalition
botanical gardens, 110–111, 121–122,
    219n28
branding, 10–11, 52–55, 58, 65–68, 70,
    72, 78, 83, 85, 127–128, 136, 179
Buffalo Bayou Park: design of,
    77–79, 82–83, 85–86, 88–90, 100,
    116, 118–119, 137–146, 156–157,
    161–163, 165–168, 182–184;
    eastward expansion of, 86,
    167–168, 174; location of, 76–78,
    82–83, 85–86, 89, 99, 116, 137–139,

CPSIA information can be obtained
at www.ICGtesting.com
Printed in the USA
BVHW031734100122
625900BV00001B/18